PROLOG AND NATURAL-LANGUAGE ANALYSIS

CSLI
Lecture Notes
Number 10

PROLOG AND NATURAL-LANGUAGE ANALYSIS

Fernando C.N. Pereira
and
Stuart M. Shieber

CENTER FOR THE STUDY
OF LANGUAGE
AND INFORMATION

CSLI was founded early in 1983 by researchers from Stanford University, SRI International, and Xerox PARC to further research and development of integrated theories of language, information, and computation. CSLI headquarters and the publication offices are located at the Stanford site.

CSLI/SRI International
333 Ravenswood Avenue
Menlo Park, CA 94025

CSLI/Stanford
Ventura Hall
Stanford, CA 94305

CSLI/Xerox PARC
3333 Coyote Hill Road
Palo Alto, CA 94304

Library of Congress Cataloging-in-Publication Data

Pereira, Fernando C. N.
    Prolog and natural-language analysis.

    (CSLI lecture notes ; no. 10)
Bibliography: p.
Includes index.

    1. Linguistics–Data processing. 2. Prolog
(Computer program language) I. Shieber, Stuart M.
II. Title. III. Series.
P98.T47   1987   410'.28'5   87–17861
ISBN 0–937073–18–0 (Paper)
ISBN 0–937073–17–2 (Cloth)

Library of Congress Catalog Card Number: 87–70774

Contents

Preface

Over the last few years, we have led a series of tutorials and classes introducing the programming language Prolog by way of example programs that apply it to the problem of natural-language analysis and processing. This volume began as the notes for a tutorial taught by one of the authors, Pereira, at the Twenty-Third Annual Meeting of the Association for Computational Linguistics in Chicago during July of 1985. During the fall of 1986, we organized a course at Stanford University on the same subject for which the original notes were extended. The impetus for organizing and expanding these various lecture notes into a more coherent text came from our colleagues at the Center for the Study of Language and Information (CSLI), and the project was made possible by a gift from the System Development Foundation.

Along the way, we were aided by a number of our colleagues. Ray Perrault was kind enough to allow us to pursue work on this project even when our other responsibilities at SRI International were now and then overlooked. David Israel was instrumental in procuring the occasional grant under which the book was written and without which it would not have been; we must also thank other members of the CSLI administration—in particular, Jon Barwise, John Perry, and Brian Smith—for their support and facilitation of this project.

The text was improved considerably by the efforts of several colleagues who volunteered to read drafts of the book. John Bear, Mary Dalrymple, Robert Keller, Peter Ludlow, Richard O'Keefe, Ray Perrault, and Ivan Sag all provided invaluable comments, corrections and improvements. We attempted to use as much of their advice as time permitted. We only wish that we had enough time to accomodate more of the changes that we now realize are needed.

Editorial assistance from Dikran Karagueuzian of CSLI and Valerie Maslak of SRI was also invaluable. Their efforts are especially appreciated given the stiff time constraints under which they were forced to work. The project was further expedited by the efforts of Emma Pease, Lynn Ruggles and Nancy Etchemendy, who aided us in the formatting of the book, especially the figures and index.

Many drafts of the manuscript and the final camera-ready copy were typeset with the help of Leslie Lamport's LaTeX document preparation system and Donald Knuth's TeX typesetting system on which it is based. We thank them for creating and making freely available those fine tools.

Finally, we want to thank Ana Pereira and Linda Sarnoff who bore the brunt of our idiosyncratic behavior during the genesis of these notes. This book is dedicated to them.

1

Introduction

1.1 Purpose

This book is an introduction to elementary computational linguistics from the point of view of logic programming. The connection between computational linguistics and logic programming has both formal and utilitarian aspects. On the formal side, we shall explore the restricted logical language of *definite clauses* as a means of expressing linguistic analyses and representations. On the utilitarian side, we shall introduce the logic-programming language Prolog, whose backbone is the definite-clause formalism, as a tool for implementing the basic components of natural-language-processing systems.

The main goal of the book is to enable the reader to acquire, as quickly as possible, a working understanding of basic computational linguistic and logic programming concepts. To achieve this goal, the book is organized around specific concepts and programming techniques, with examples supported by working programs. Most of the problems involve programming and also supplement the material in the main text. Although we have emphasized experimental rather than analytic or comparative questions, all concepts and techniques covered are given rigorous, if informal, theoretical justification.

1.2 Logic Programming and Language

One of the main goals of the development of symbolic logic has been to capture the notion of logical consequence with formal, mechanical, means. If the conditions for a certain class of problems can be formalized within a suitable logic as a set of premises, and if a problem to be solved can be stated as a sentence in the logic, then a solution might be found by constructing a formal proof of the problem statement from the premises.

For instance, in the linguistic case the premises might provide constraints on the grammaticality of classes of utterances, and the problems to solve would have the general form "there is some *a* such that *a* is an analysis (or interpretation) of the grammatical utterance *u*." A *constructive* proof of this statement would not only show that an analysis *a* exists but also find actual values for *a*.

A constructive proof procedure that not only creates proofs but also builds values for the unknowns in the problem statement can thus be seen as a computational device for determining those unknowns. From this perspective, the premises can be seen as a program, the problem statement as an invocation of the program with certain input values and output unknowns, and a proof as a computation from the program. This is the basic intuition behind logic programming.

However, it is not enough to have some sound and complete set of rules of inference and some procedure to apply them systematically to have a logic programming system. To be satisfactory as a computation device, a proof procedure should not leave proof possibilities unchecked (*search completeness*), that is the procedure should terminate without a proof only if no proof exists. We do not want our programs to terminate with no answer if there is one (except possibly for running out of computational resources such as computer memory). Furthermore, a set of premises has many consequences that are definitely irrelevant to the proof of a given consequence. The proof procedure should be *goal directed* in that derivations of irrelevant consequences are avoided. We do not want the computations of a program to include subcomputations that do not at least potentially contribute in some way to the program's output.

In fact, search completeness and goal directedness are very difficult to achieve in general, but become more feasible in weaker logical languages. The problem then becomes one of finding a good compromise between expressiveness of the logical language and the constraints of sound and efficient computation. The development of logic programming stemmed from the discovery of a reasonable compromise, *definite clauses*, and its partial implementation in Prolog, the first practical logic programming language.

Almost from its origin, the development of logic programming has been closely tied to the search for computational formalisms for expressing syntactic and semantic analyses of natural-language sentences. One of the main purposes in developing Prolog was to create a language in which phrase-structure and semantic-interpretation rules for a natural-language question-answering system could be easily expressed.

Phrase-structure rules for a language state how phrases of given types combine to form larger phrases in the language. For example, a (simplistic) phrase-structure rule for declarative sentences in English might state that a declarative sentence consists of a noun phrase (the subject of the sentence) followed by a verb phrase (the predicate of the sentence). Such rules have a very simple expression in first-order logic:

$$(\forall u, v, w) NP(u) \land VP(v) \land conc(u, v, w) \Rightarrow S(w)$$

where *NP* represents the class of noun phrases, *VP* the class of verb phrases, *S* the class of sentences, and *conc* holds of any strings u, v and w such that w is u followed by v, that is, the concatenation of u and v. This expression in first-order logic thus states that any noun phrase u and verb ph ase v can be concatenated to form a declarative sentence $w = uv$. The term *logic grammar* has come to refer to such uses of logic to formalize grammatical rules.

The above formula is an example of a definite clause. We shall see that many important classes of linguistic rules and constraints can be put in this general form, which states that any objects satisfying certain constraints (properties or relationships) also satisfy some other constraint (property or relationship). The fact that linguistic rules can be put in this format is the basis for the usefulness of definite clauses in language analysis. This fact has not only theoretical but also practical importance, in that linguistic rules encoded as definite clauses can be run directly by Prolog, providing an efficient and direct computational realization of grammars and interpretation rules.

1.3   Programming In Prolog

Logic programming languages in general, and Prolog in particular, differ from conventional programming languages (such as Pascal or Fortran) in several important ways. First of all, Prolog can be thought of as a largely *declarative* language; that is, a Prolog program can be viewed as stating *what* is computed, independent of a particular method for computation. Pascal, on the other hand, is *procedural*, in that what a Pascal program computes is definable only in terms of how it performs the computation.[1] Of course, Prolog also has a procedural interpretation; it uses a particular method for computing the relations which a program can be viewed as declaratively stating. Furthermore, certain "impure" portions of the Prolog

---

[1]This is not to say that Pascal can have no denotational semantics but only an operational semantics. Rather, any denotational semantics must make explicit reference to the state of the computation as encoded, for instance, in an environment.

language defeat its declarative interpretation. But Prolog, as a first step toward a logic programming language, can to a great extent be seen as a declarative language.

Second, Prolog programs are structured in terms of *relations* whereas traditional languages for the most part are structured in terms of *functions*. The notions of calling a function, returning a value, and so forth are foreign to Prolog. Instead, Prolog expresses relations among entities. Function calls correspond to queries as to whether a particular relation holds or not and under what conditions. This difference has tremendous ramifications. For instance, it means that *variables* play a completely different role in Prolog than they do in conventional languages.

From this relational structure, it follows that Prolog programs are *nondeterministic*, since several elements can be in a particular relation to a given element. Because conventional languages are geared toward functions, that is, relations in which one element is uniquely defined in terms of the others, computation proceeds *deterministically* in such languages.

These three properties of Prolog make it quite different from other programming languages. Consequently, a different way of thinking about programs and programming is necessary in using Prolog. Learning a new programming language can often be aided by analogy with previously learned languages. But Prolog might be most easily learned by ignoring previous experience with other programming languages and trying to absorb the Prolog gestalt from first principles.

Unfortunately, learning a language in this way requires many illustrative examples of the language and much detailed explanation about how they work and how they were derived. Since the goal of this book is to concentrate on natural-language processing applications, we must often forego such detailed analysis. Therefore, as part of a first course on Prolog, it is probably best to supplement the material here with one of the texts discussed in the bibliographic notes below.

All the particulars of the interaction with a Prolog system that are used in the present work are those of the Edinburgh family of Prolog systems, and when used without qualification, the term "Prolog" means any system of that family.

1.4   Overview

The Prolog language is presented in this book through a graded series of sublanguages. Chapter 2 presents *database Prolog*, a limited subset of Prolog that can express relationships between named individuals and constraints between those relationships. We then describe how phrase-structure rules can be represented in this subset. Database Prolog is extended in Chapter 3 to *pure Prolog*, the largest subset of Prolog that can be viewed as a logic programming language. This extension allows us to represent more complex kinds of linguistic rules and, in particular, the *definite-clause grammar* formalism. Techniques for linguistic analysis in definite-clause grammars are developed further in Chapter 4, where issues of syntactic coverage and semantic interpretation are discussed. Extralogical extensions to the pure subset of Prolog lead to the full Prolog language, which is presented in Chapter 5. These facilities are used to develop a simple natural-language question answering system which demonstrates the application of many of the techniques developed in earlier chapters. Finally, in Chapter 6 we explore the metalevel programming capabilities of Prolog, showing how to implement logic-programming language and logic-grammar interpreters exhibiting different control strategies from that provided directly by Prolog.

Throughout the book we have included exercises and problems. Exercises are interspersed throughout the text and are intended to help readers verify their understanding of the concepts covered. Problems, collected into separate problem sections, extend the material in the book and are appropriate for assignments in a course based on this text. It should be noted that problems vary widely in difficulty; instructors should take this variation into account.

Given the orientation of the book, we limited the discussion of issues of a more general nature, such as comparisons with other computational linguistic techniques or formal mathematical results. Three areas stand out among the omissions. First, we do not compare the logic programming approach with other approaches to natural-language processing, in particular the closely related unification-based grammar formalisms. Second, we do not present or compare the plethora of grammar formalisms based on logic programming. Finally, we do not address formal-language-theoretic issues of generative power and computational complexity for the formalisms and analysis mechanisms we present.

One of the major insufficiencies remaining in the text is a lack of linguistic sophistication and coverage evinced by the analyses we use. The reader should not think that such naiveté inheres in Prolog as a tool for natural-language analysis; the bibliographic notes at the end of the chapters often cite work with more convincing analyses.

1.5   Bibliographic Notes

In these bibliographic notes we give both the original sources for our material and other works that elaborate or supplement topics discussed in this book. As is often the case, the original source for a topic may no longer be the best place to learn about it. Unless otherwise specified, the most recent reference we give for a topic, and in particular a recent textbook, is to be preferred to other sources in a first approach to a topic.

Prerequisites

This book presupposes some acquaintance with elementary notions from logic, formal-language theory, computer science and linguistics.

The textbook *Mathematical Methods for Linguistics* by Partee, ter Meulen and Wall (1987) covers much of the background material we require in logic, formal-language theory and semantics (concepts such as first-order logic, quantifier scope, extension and intension).

For a more computation-oriented introduction to logic and deduction, Robinson's book *Logic: Form and Function* (1979) covers in detail all the concepts from logic and automated theorem proving used in this book. Gallier's *Logic for Computer Science* (1986) contains a mathematically more demanding coverage of the same material. Kowalski's *Logic for Problem Solving* (1980) gives an informal introduction to the use of logic in a logic programming setting for representing computational problems. The example problems are mostly taken from artificial intelligence applications including simple examples of syntactic analysis by deduction. Finally, *Automated Reasoning: Introduction and Applications* by Wos, Overbeek, Lusk and Boyle (1984) gives a comprehensive and readable discussion of many automated-deduction methods and their applications to knowledge-representation tasks.

Most of the concepts we use from formal-language theory and theoretical computer science (automata, context-free grammars, etc.) can be found in Hopcroft and Ullman's *Introduction to Automata Theory, Languages and Computation* (1979) or in Harrison's *Introduction to Formal Language Theory* (1978). Aho and Ullman's encyclopedic *Theory of Parsing, Translation and Compiling* (1972) covers specific parsing algorithms not included in the two preceding references.

Many of the basic concepts and terminology of modern [generative] syntactic theory are used informally in this book. For an introduction to them, the first two chapters of Baker's *Introduction to Generative-Transformational Syntax* (1978) should be sufficient. For readers interested in further background in the generative grammar tradition, the terminology of which has now become standard in modern syntax and has occasionally crept into this text, the remainder of Baker's book and the clear and elegant arguments of the volume by Soames and Perlmutter *Syntactic Argumentation and the Structure of English* (1979) are good sources.

Winograd's *Language as a Cognitive Process. Volume I: Syntax* (1983) gives a computationally oriented introduction to some of the basic concepts from natural-language syntax (e.g., parse tree, labeled bracketing, noun phrase, relative clause) used in this book, in addition to much other related material. Chapter 3 is particularly relevant.

Although this book is intended to be self-contained in its coverage of Prolog and basic logic-programming concepts, it could be usefully supplemented with a Prolog textbook. Sterling and Shapiro's *The Art of Prolog* (1986) is particularly suitable since it amplifies many of the concepts used here with further discussion, examples, and exercises. Except for divergences in some minor typographical conventions, the dialect of Prolog used in that book is compatible with the one used here.

Historical Material

The basic ideas of logic programming emerged in the late 1960s and early 1970s from work on automated deduction. Proof procedures based on Robinson's *resolution principle* (1965) operate by building values for unknowns that make a problem statement a consequence of the given premises. Green (1968) observed that resolution proof procedures could thus in principle be used for computation. Resolution on its own is not a sufficient basis for logic programming, because resolution proof procedures may not be sufficiently goal-directed. Thus, Green's observations linking computation to deduction (1968) had no effective realization until the development of more goal-oriented *linear resolution* proof procedures, in particular Kowalski and Kuehner's SL resolution (1971). This development allowed Kowalski (1974a) to suggest a general approach to goal-directed deductive computation based on appropriate control mechanisms for resolution theorem provers and the further specialization of SL resolution to Horn clauses, and the corresponding procedural interpretation of Horn clauses, was first described in principle by Kowalski (1974a; 1974b).

Even the SL resolution procedure and related theorem-proving methods were not efficient enough for practical computation, mainly because they had to cope with the full generality of first-order logic, in particular disjunctive conclusions. Further progress required the radical step of deliberately weakening the language to one that could be implemented with efficiency comparable to that of procedural languages. This step was mainly due to Colmerauer and his colleagues at Marseille in the early 1970s. Their work proceeded in parallel with (and in interaction with) the theoretical developments from the automated theorem-proving community. Inspired by his earlier Q-systems, a tree-matching phrase-structure grammar formalism (Colmerauer, 1970), Colmerauer started developing a language that could at the same time be used for language analysis and for implementing deductive question-answering mechanisms. It eventually became clear that a particular kind of linear resolution restricted to definite clauses had just the right goal-directness and efficiency, and also enough expressive power for linguistic rules and some important aspects of the question-answering problem. Their approach was first described as a tool for natural-language processing applications (Colmerauer et al., 1973). The resulting deductive system, supplemented with a few other computational devices, was the first Prolog system, known as "Marseille Prolog". The first detailed description of Prolog was the language manual for the Marseille Prolog interpreter (Roussel, 1975).

As noted above, Prolog was originally developed for natural-language processing. Besides the original application (Colmerauer et al., 1973), other early influential work includes systems by Colmerauer (1982; 1978), Pasero (1973) and Dahl (1981). Many other natural-language-processing systems and techniques based on logic programming have since been developed, which we will refer to when the relevant topics are discussed.

The collection *Readings in Natural Language Processing* (Grosz et al., 1986) reprints papers covering a wide variety of topics in natural-language processing, including some of the papers referred to in this book. In the bibliography, we use the original publication data, but we also indicate when the paper has been reprinted in that collection.

Besides natural-language processing, logic programming and Prolog have been used in many other application areas, particularly in artificial intelligence. For an idea of the current areas of application, the reader is directed to the collection edited by van Caneghem and Warren (1986) and the extensive logic-programming bibliography prepared by Balbin and Lecot (1985).

Since the original implementation in Marseille, Prolog implementation techniques, including compilation and various space-saving devices, have progressed to the point that Prolog is today at least comparable with other symbolic-processing languages, such as LISP, for a variety of problems areas, in particular natural-language processing (Warren et al., 1977; Warren, 1979; Warren, 1983).

2

Database Prolog: A Prolog Subset

2.1 Databases and Queries

We will start by seeing how simple tables of information can be expressed in Prolog. This may seem an odd way to start discussing a programming language (texts on, say, Pascal, start by discussing numbers and expressions), but it is revealing of the nature of Prolog as a language for *declarative* information, whether that information be simple relationships between individuals or complex constraints between types of individuals.

2.1.1 A Simple Database

Recall that Prolog programs are written in a subset of first-order logic (FOL). Like FOL, the language includes *constant symbols* naming entities and *predicate symbols* naming relations among the entities. Our first examples will use just this much Prolog notation, which is actually only useful to encode the type of information one might find in a relational database. For this reason, we call this subset *database Prolog*.

In Prolog, both predicate and constant symbols are written as tokens starting with a lower-case alphabetic character. Predication is notated in the normal way for logical languages using parentheses surrounding the arguments following the predicate, thereby forming an *atomic formula*. With this much notation we can already state some simple information in Prolog. For instance, a simple database of professors and the books and computer programs they have written might be expressed by the following Prolog program:

Program 2.1
```
wrote(terry, shrdlu).
wrote(bill, lunar).
wrote(roger, sam).

wrote(gottlob, begriffsschrift).
wrote(bertrand, principia).
wrote(alfred, principia).

book(begriffsschrift).
book(principia).

program(lunar).
program(sam).
program(shrdlu).
```

Each line in this program is a *clause* formed from a single atomic formula and ending with a period. As the clauses in this program have only a single atomic formula, they are referred to as *unit clauses*. Later, we will see that clauses with several atomic formulas are also allowed. In Program 2.1, an atomic formula wrote(X,Y) is intended to mean that person X wrote entity Y, book(X) is intended to mean that X is a book, and program(X) is intended to mean that X is a program. Thus the first clause in the program states the fact that Terry wrote SHRDLU, and the last clause, that SHRDLU is a program.

2.1.2   Querying the Database

Now that we have given some facts to the Prolog system as a set of axioms expressed as clauses (which is really all that a Prolog program is) we can answer questions about the information by having Prolog try to prove theorems from the axioms. We do this by prefixing a *goal G* with the Prolog symbol for implication, the ":-" symbol, thereby forming the *query* :- *G*. In this way we are asking Prolog "Does anything in the axioms imply an answer to our question?"

For example, here is how the queries "Did Terry write SHRDLU?" and "Is *Principia* a program?" are written.[1]
```
:- wrote(terry, shrdlu).
yes
:- program(principia).
no
```

---

[1]Throughout this text, user's input is typeset in a `typewriter font`, the Prolog system's answer is typeset in a *`slanted typewriter font`*.

It should be observed that the reply to the second query does not indicate that "*Principia* is not a program" is true, but rather that Prolog could not prove "*Principia* is a program" from the axioms in Program 2.1. This subtle distinction is the basis of much logic programming research on what assumptions about a database warrant the conclusion that "*P* is false in the database" from "*P* is not provable from the database" and we will have more to say about it in Section 5.1.3.

2.2   Extending the Query Language

Such limited potential for querying a Prolog program would of itself hardly constitute a useful programming language. Prolog extends this potential through the use of *variables*, *complex queries*, and *rules*.

Variables

We can ask open-ended questions of Prolog by using variables in place of constants in a query. To distinguish variables from constants, Prolog uses tokens that begin with upper-case letters for variables. We can ask whether *anyone* wrote SHRDLU with the following query:

```
:- wrote(Who,shrdlu).
yes
```

Since there exists an *assignment* to the variables in the query that makes it a consequence of the program axioms (namely, the assignment in which `Who = terry`,[2] Prolog replies "*yes*". Such assignments to variables are also called *bindings*.

Of course, we are usually interested not only in whether such an assignment exists but also in what it looks like. To request Prolog to indicate what assignment led to the proof of the goal, we simply use "?-" instead of ":-" to introduce the goal. For instance,

```
?- wrote(Who,shrdlu).
Who = terry
yes
```

The assignment is printed, along with the "*yes*" that means that a solution was found.

If there are several different ways to assign values to variables that make the   goal   statement   a   consequence   of   the   program,   the   Prolog

---

[2]The `slanted typewriter font` will be used for assignments as well as Prolog output to emphasize the fact that they are computer-generated structures.

execution mechanism will generate alternative bindings to the goal variables. Prolog prints one such solution at a time and then waits for a one-character command: a semicolon (";") to produce the next solution, or a newline to stop generating solutions for the query. For example, the query "Who wrote *Principia*?" has two satisfying assignments:

```
?- wrote(Who, principia).
Who = bertrand ;
Who = alfred ;
no
```

Notice that the final Prolog reply is *"no"* meaning that after this second assignment, no more solutions could be found.

Complex Queries

More complex queries can be constructed from goals consisting of multiple conditions, interpreted conjunctively, by separating the conditions by commas (","). For example, suppose we define an author as a person who has written a book. Then, if we want to discover who the authors are according to the database, we might ask the conjunctive query "What person `Person` is such that there is a book `Book` *and* `Person` wrote `Book`?", which can be phrased as a Prolog query as

```
?- book(Book), wrote(Person, Book).
Person = gottlob, Book = begriffsschrift ;
Person = bertrand, Book = principia ;
Person = alfred, Book = principia ;
no
```

Rules

The query above demonstrates that the property of being an author is implicit in the given database. The utility of the database can be increased by making this property explicit through the addition of a unary predicate `author` corresponding to this property. But this predicate is best defined not in terms of an exhaustive list of unit clauses—as previous predicates have been—but rather as a general rule for determining whether the property of being an author holds. In fact, the conjunctive query above gives just such a rule. A person `Person` is an author just in the case that the goal `book(Book)`, `wrote(Person, Book)` holds. The Prolog implication symbol ":-" (read "if") allows the encoding of this general rule.

```
author(Person) :-
    book(Book),
    wrote(Person, Book).
```

This clause can be read "Person is an author if there is a book Book and Person wrote Book," or, more simply, "an author is a writer of a book." Because clauses such as this one are composed of several atomic formulas, they are referred to as *nonunit clauses*. The left-hand side of the clause is often called the *head* of the clause, the right-hand side the *body*. Some people take the anatomical analogy a step further, referring to the :- operator itself as the *neck* of the clause.

The author clause defines a simple property. However, multiplace relations can be defined in this way as well. Consider the relation of a person Person being the author of a book Book. This author_of relation can be axiomatized similarly.

```
author_of(Person, Book) :-
    book(Book),
    wrote(Person, Book).
```

Exercise 2.1 *Write a Prolog clause that defines a programmer as a person who wrote a program.*

Exercise 2.2 *Consider the following augmentation of the sample database:*

```
professor(terry).
professor(roger).
professor(bertrand).
professor(gottlob).

concerns(shrdlu, blocks).
concerns(lunar, rocks).
concerns(sam, stories).

concerns(principia, logic).
concerns(principia, mathematics).
concerns(begriffsschrift, logic).
```

Write a Prolog clause that defines a logician as a professor who wrote a book concerning logic.

2.3   The Logic of Prolog

We have alluded to the relationship between database Prolog and first-order logical languages. In this section we describe this relationship in more detail, although still at an informal level.

First-order logic (FOL) is a logical language that includes predicate and function symbols and constants, from which are formed *atomic formulas* representing primitive propositions. An atomic formula is an expression of the form $p(t_1, \ldots, t_k)$, where p is a predicate symbol of *arity* k applied to *terms* t_i. A term is a *constant*, a *variable*, or a *compound term* $f(t_1, \ldots, t_m)$, where f is a function symbol of arity m and the t_i are terms. Following standard practice, we will use letters p, q, r, etc. and upper case letters for predicate symbols and letters f, g, h, etc. for function symbols. Variables will be denoted by (possibly subscripted) x, y, z, etc. A term without variables is called a *ground term*. For the nonce, we will ignore the role of function symbols and compound terms in FOL, returning to them when we discuss the relation between FOL and full Prolog in the next chapter.

The well-formed formulas of FOL are defined inductively, starting with the atomic formulas and combining simpler formulas into larger formulas with operators from some sufficiently rich set, e.g., conjunction ($\wedge$), disjunction ($\vee$), negation ($\neg$), implication ($\Rightarrow$), and universal ($\forall$) and existential ($\exists$) quantification. If ϕ and ψ are well-formed formulas and x is a variable, $\phi \wedge \psi$ (ϕ and ψ), $\phi \vee \psi$ (ϕ or ψ), $\neg\phi$ (not ϕ), $\phi \Rightarrow \psi$ (ϕ implies ψ) $(\forall x)\phi$ (for every x, ϕ) and $(\exists x)\phi$ (there is an x such that ϕ), with extra parenthesization to avoid ambiguity if necessary, are well-formed formulas. Both in $(\forall x)\phi$ and $(\exists x)\phi$, the formula ϕ is the *scope* of the quantifier, and x is the variable *bound* by the quantifier. *Closed* well-formed formulas are those in which every variable occurrence is within the scope of a quantifier binding that variable.

Many important automated deduction methods, and in particular those from which Prolog is derived, do not operate on general FOL formulas, but only on formulas in *clausal form* (*clauses*). A formula is in clausal form if it is a disjunction of *literals*, where a literal is an atomic formula or the negation of an atomic formula. All variables in the disjunction are universally quantified by quantifiers whose scope includes the whole disjunction. Thus, a clause can be written in the form

$$P_0 \vee P_1 \vee \cdots \vee \neg N_0 \vee \neg N_1 \vee \cdots$$

The P_i are positive literals; the $\neg N_i$ are negative literals. Note that we have left off the quantifiers, under the convention that all variables are quantified universally at the outermost level unless specified otherwise. The usefulness of clausal form stems from the fact that any closed formula ϕ

can be mechanically transformed into a conjunction of clauses $\mathcal{P}$ such that ϕ is inconsistent if and only if $\mathcal{P}$ is. Notice that in general ϕ and $\mathcal{P}$ are not equivalent, because the transformation into clausal form may require the introduction of auxiliary functions to remove existential quantifiers (so-called *Skolem functions*).[3] However, as we will see below, the intended use of clausal form is in proofs by contradiction, so preservation of inconsistency is all we need.

Using deMorgan's law

$$\neg P \vee \neg Q \text{ if and only if } \neg(P \wedge Q)$$

and the definition of implication in terms of negation and disjunction, i.e.,

$$P \Rightarrow Q \text{ if and only if } \neg P \vee Q \qquad ,$$

we can reexpress clauses as a single implication

$$(N_0 \wedge N_1 \wedge \cdots) \Rightarrow (P_0 \vee P_1 \vee \cdots) \qquad .$$

The left-hand side of the implication is its *antecedent*, the right-hand side its *consequent*. Henceforth, we will refer to the N_i and P_i as the literals composing the clause, although, strictly speaking, the negative literals in the clause are of the form $\neg N_i$, rather than N_i.

By expressing a clause as an implication as explained above, we see that a clause states that at least one of the atomic formulas in the consequent holds whenever all the atomic formulas in the antecedent hold. In particular, if a clause contains no negative literals, it will have an empty antecedent when written as an implication. Therefore an empty antecedent should be interpreted as standing for truth: The clause states that under all conditions at least one of the atomic formulas in the consequent holds. Conversely, if a clause has no positive literals, it asserts that at least one of the formulas in its antecedent is false, that is, the conjunction of the atomic formulas in the antecedent is false. When written as an implication, such a clause has an empty consequent. An implication is equivalent to the negation of its antecedent provided that its consequent is false. Thus an empty consequent corresponds to falsity. Finally, the *empty clause*, with empty antecedent and consequent, corresponds to the implication *true* $\Rightarrow$ *false*, which is equivalent to *false*.

Theorem-proving in first-order logic—and hence clausal form FOL— is a computationally difficult task and an area of active research. As we

---

[3]Thus even a formula without function symbols may be transformed into a clause with function symbols, outside the database subset we have been considering. But since the subset is just a stopping-off point to full Prolog, and the arguments are meant to be indicative only, we will ignore this subtlety.

indicated in Section 1.2, for computational feasibility Prolog is not based on full clausal form, but on a strictly less expressive subset, *Horn clauses*, which are clauses with *at most one positive literal.* Thus there are only three types of Horn clauses:

- *Unit clauses:* with one positive literal, no negative literals, i.e., of the form P_0 (or, equivalently, $\Rightarrow P_0$).

- *Nonunit clauses:* with one positive literal, one or more negative literals, i.e., of the form $P_0 \vee \neg N_0 \vee \neg N_1 \vee \cdots$ (or, equivalently, $N_0 \wedge N_1 \wedge \cdots \Rightarrow P_0$).

- *Negative clauses:* with no positive literals, one or more negative literals, i.e., of the form $\neg N_0 \vee \neg N_1 \vee \cdots$ (or, equivalently, $N_0 \wedge N_1 \wedge \cdots \Rightarrow$).

The first two types of Horn clauses are collectively referred to as *definite clauses* because they have exactly one positive literal—a single definite conclusion to the implication—unlike general clauses with their potentially disjunctive, indefinite, consequent.

Each type of Horn clause plays a different role in an axiomatization of a particular problem. Unit clauses, of the form P_0, assert the truth of their consequents. We might call such clauses *facts.*

A nonunit clause states that its consequent is true if its antecedent is true. Such clauses thus serve as general *rules* by which the consequent can be determined to hold.

Finally, a negative clause

$$N_0 \wedge N_1 \wedge \cdots \Rightarrow$$

has the equivalent form

$$\neg(N_0 \wedge N_1 \wedge \cdots) \qquad .$$

That is, a negative clause denies the truth of its antecedent. Negative clauses can be seen as *queries* as to under what conditions their antecedent is true, by the following reasoning. Suppose we have a set of facts and rules $\mathcal{P}$ (a *program*) and a conjunction

$$N_0 \wedge N_1 \wedge \cdots \qquad . \tag{2.1}$$

We want to determine values for the variables in (2.1) that make it a consequence of $\mathcal{P}$. In other words, we want a constructive proof, from $\mathcal{P}$, of

$$(\exists x_0, \ldots, x_k)(N_0 \wedge N_1 \wedge \cdots) \qquad . \tag{2.2}$$

One way of attempting to prove (2.2) is by contradiction, that is, by showing that the conjunction of the clauses in $\mathcal{P}$ and the negation of (2.2) is inconsistent. From the inconsistency of the conjunction, we can infer that (2.2) follows from $\mathcal{P}$ because $\mathcal{P}$ itself, being a set of definite clauses, cannot be inconsistent on its own.

Now, the negation of (2.2) can be put in the form

$$(\forall x_0, \ldots, x_k)\neg(N_0 \wedge N_1 \wedge \cdots) \qquad (2.3)$$

which is just another notation for the negative clause

$$N_0 \wedge N_1 \wedge \cdots \Rightarrow \qquad . \qquad (2.4)$$

A constructive proof of the inconsistency of (2.3) with $\mathcal{P}$ will provide a counterexample for the universal statement (2.3). It will yield values $v_0, \ldots, v_k$ for the variables $x_0, \ldots, x_k$ such that

$$\mathcal{P} \wedge \neg(N_0 \wedge N_1 \wedge \cdots) \qquad (2.5)$$

with each v_i substituted for x_i is false.

The proof of falsity comes about because we are proving inconsistency of (2.3) with $\mathcal{P}$. The actual values for the variables follows from the fact that the proof is constructive. It is easy to see from the proof of the falsity of (2.5) that (2.1) under that same substitution of values for variables is a consequence of $\mathcal{P}$. Assume $\mathcal{P}$ is true. Then $\neg(N_0 \wedge N_1 \wedge \cdots)$ must be false, and therefore (2.1) true, under the given values for variables. This concludes the constructive proof of the original existential query (2.2) from the program $\mathcal{P}$. Thus (2.4) can be seen as a query about the truth of its antecedent (2.1) relative to the program.

This method of proving an existential statement is called *refutation*, because the proof proceeds by refuting the negation of the statement.

As we have seen, Prolog programs follow this paradigm exactly. Facts and rules, presented with the Prolog implication and conjunction operators ":-" and ",", respectively, are queried using a negative clause. The only difference is that the Prolog :- operator puts its antecedent and consequent "backwards", that is, :- corresponds to $\Leftarrow$, so that $P \Rightarrow Q$ is written as Q :- P and $P \Rightarrow$ is written as :- P. A Prolog proof of a goal includes an assignment of values to variables in the goal which makes it a consequence of the program. It becomes apparent, then, why the notation ":- G" was chosen for queries. We are merely presenting the goal statement to Prolog directly in its negated form.

Exercise 2.3 *(For the logically inclined.) Recall that the discussion above assumed that any set of definite clauses is consistent. Why is this so?*

2.4   The Operation of Database Prolog

Intuitively, our definition of, for instance, `author_of` in terms of subsidiary predicates seems correct from the logical standpoint just outlined. But how does the Prolog system make use of this predicate? Suppose we ask Prolog for the writings of Bertrand Russell with the following query:

```
?- author_of(bertrand, What).
What = principia
yes
```

How does Prolog determine that a correct assignment to satisfy the goal (i.e., disprove its negation) is `What = principia`? What is the *procedural* interpretation of Horn clauses that Prolog uses in actually *executing* a goal? In this section we describe the execution of a Prolog goal informally, returning to a more precise discussion of the execution mechanism, and its relation to the logical basis for Prolog through a technique called *resolution*, in Section 3.5.

To execute a goal, Prolog searches forward from the beginning of the program for the first clause whose head matches the goal. We will have more to say about this matching process, called *unification*, when we further discuss the theory of Prolog in Section 3.5. For the time being, think of two literals matching if there exists an assignment to the variables in them under which they become identical. For instance, the literal `author_of(bertrand, What)` matches the literal `author_of(Person, Book)` under the assignment `Person = bertrand, Book = What`, because if the literals are modified by replacing the variables in the assignment with their assigned value, both literals become `author_of(bertrand, What)`.

If a match is found, the selected clause is *activated*. The matching assignment is applied to both the goal and a copy of the clause by replacing variables with their binding value, e.g., replacing `Person` with `bertrand` and `Book` with `What`. The literals in the body of the instantiated clause (if any) are then executed in turn, from left to right. If at any time the system fails to find a match for a goal, it *backtracks*, that is, it rejects the most recently activated clause, undoing any substitutions made by applying the assignment engendered by the match to the head of the clause. Next it reconsiders the original goal that activated the rejected clause, and tries to find another clause whose head also matches the goal. When finding alternative clauses, Prolog always works from the top of the program to the bottom, trying earlier clauses first.

We will trace through the operation of the system for the "writings of Russell" example. We begin by executing the goal `author_of(bertrand,`

What). Prolog finds a clause in its database whose head matches the goal. In this case, the only matching clause is

```
author_of(Person, Book) :-
    book(Book),
    wrote(Person, Book).
```

The head of this clause matches the goal under the bindings *Person = bertrand, Book = What* as described above. Under these bindings, the body of the rule becomes book(What), wrote(bertrand, What). Prolog activates the clause taking this conjunction on as its new goal, executing the conjuncts one by one, working from the left to the right.

Executing book(What) requires finding a clause whose head matches it. But in this case there are two such clauses, namely the unit clauses book(begriffsschrift) and book(principia). When faced with several clauses to choose from, Prolog chooses the textually earliest one that has not been considered in satisfying this goal; in this case, none have been considered, so the first matching clause book(begriffsschrift) is chosen, which matches the goal book(What) under the binding *What = begriffsschrift*. Under this binding, the second conjunct is wrote(bertrand, begriffsschrift), and this becomes the next goal.

However, no clause head matches this goal, so the goal fails. Prolog backtracks to its last choice among alternative clauses. In this case, the choice was between the two unit clauses matching book(What). This time, in satisfying the goal, the next matching clause is chosen, namely book(principia); the second conjunct then becomes wrote(bertrand, principia). This goal matches the identical unit clause in the database.

Thus we have satisfied all of the conjuncts in the antecedent of the author_of clause, thereby satisfying the original goal itself. Perusing the bindings that were necessary to satisfy the goal, we note that the variable What in the original goal was bound to principia; the binding *What = principia* is therefore reported.

2.4.1   Proof Trees and Traces

Often it is useful to have a method for summarizing the execution of a goal. We describe two such methods here. The first one, the *proof tree*, describes the literals that were proved in the course of the proof of the main goal and the dependencies between them. For the "writings of Russell" example, the main goal proved, under the satisfying assignment, was author_of(bertrand, principia). It depended on the proofs of two subsidiary literals, namely, book(principia) and wrote(bertrand, principia). These literals were proved primitively with no dependent literals. Thus the proof tree for this example is as given in Figure 2.1.

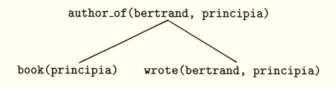

Figure 2.1. A proof tree

This proof tree makes explicit the steps in the execution of Prolog that led to a successful proof of the goal under a given assignment. However, it abstracts away from the parts of the execution that led down blind alleys, not becoming part of the final proof. A second method of summarizing Prolog executions, the *trace*, is useful when this higher level of detail is desired.

The particular tracing method we shall use is called the *box model* (Byrd, 1980), since it models a predicate as a box with certain *ports* through which the computation passes. The box model underlies the tracing and debugging facilities of most Edinburgh Prolog systems.

In a box-model trace, each step the system takes—whether it be the recursive proving of a literal, the activating of a clause to prove it, or the subsequent success or failure of the subproof—is sequentially listed using the following general format:

(*i*) *d p*:   *G*

Each goal *G* is given a *goal number i* which uniquely identifies it throughout the execution. As the goal progresses through the execution, trace lines with the given goal number show the state of instantiation of the goal at different points. The *recursion depth* is given as *d*. The main goal has recursion depth 0, its subgoals, recursion depth 1, their subgoals, 2, and so forth.[4] Trace lines correspond to different kinds of steps in the execution of a Prolog query. The *port name p* specifies the type of step in the execution that the trace line records. The execution of a literal is started at a *Call* port corresponding to the activation of the first matching clause. When the proof using this clause is successful, a trace line with the port name *Exit* is listed. If the first clause activated does not yield a successful proof, a *Redo* port line is added for each later clause that is invoked. Finally, if all clauses fail to provide a proof for the given goal, a *Fail* port trace line is used.

---

[4]We will also sometimes use indentation to reflect the depth of recursion of the execution in order to aid readability.

The following trace of the "writings of Russell" example may elucidate the Prolog trace facility. Note especially the changing instantiation of the variables during the trace. The Prolog tracing facility is invoked with the literal "trace".

```
?- trace.
Debug mode switched on.
yes

?- author_of(bertrand, What).
   (1) 0 Call :  author_of(bertrand,What)
   (2) 1 Call :    book(What)
   (2) 1 Exit :    book(begriffsschrift)
   (3) 1 Call :    wrote(bertrand,begriffsschrift)
   (3) 1 Fail :    wrote(bertrand,begriffsschrift)
   (2) 1 Redo :    book(begriffsschrift)
   (2) 1 Exit :    book(principia)
   (4) 1 Call :    wrote(bertrand,principia)
   (4) 1 Exit :    wrote(bertrand,principia)
   (1) 0 Exit :  author_of(bertrand,principia)
What = principia
yes
```

Note that the exit lines leading to the final proof contain the same information as a proof tree for the goal.

Not only does the trace make explicit the ordering in which the proof tree was traversed by Prolog, it also shows all the blind alleys that Prolog tried before finding an actual proof. These two phenomena are related. For example, if the second branch of the proof tree (corresponding to the second literal in the clause defining author_of) had been tried first, the only satisfying assignment for it would have been *Book = principia*. Under this assignment, the first clause becomes book(principia), which is immediately proved from the database. Thus no blind alleys are tried. This behavior would be engendered by the following alternative definition of author_of:

```
author_of(Person, Book) :-
    wrote(Person, Book),
    book(Book).
```

This example shows that although the ordering of literals within a clause does not affect the logical meaning of the clause as a definition of a relation, it can have far-reaching effects in terms of the control flow of the program.

That is, although Prolog can be viewed as a subset of a logical language, we cannot forget that it is still a programming language, and issues of control are still important.

2.5   Recursive Predicate Definitions

The relations discussed above—author, logician, and so forth—are defined directly in terms of other relations, which ultimately are defined in terms of the original database. However, it is not possible to give such definitions for relations that involve chains of relationships of arbitrary lengths. To define such relations, we need to use *recursive* definitions in which a predicate is defined (possibly indirectly) in terms of itself.

As a simple illustration of the need for recursive definitions, consider the following database, which encodes a portion of the family tree of Bertrand Russell.

```
parent(katherine, bertrand).  parent(amberley, bertrand).
parent(katherine, frank).     parent(amberley, frank).
parent(katherine, rachel).    parent(amberley, rachel).

parent(dora, kate).           parent(bertrand, kate).
parent(dora, john).           parent(bertrand, john).
parent(peter, conrad).        parent(bertrand, conrad).

female(katherine).       male(amberley).
female(rachel).          male(frank).
female(dora).            male(bertrand).
female(peter).           male(conrad).
female(kate).            male(john).
```

Here a literal parent(X,Y) is intended to mean that X is a parent of Y. The information in this database is conveniently factored among the parent, male, and female predicates so that there is no duplication as there would be if the same information were expressed in terms of, for instance, father, mother, male and female.

Exercise 2.4 *Write Prolog clauses defining* father, grandmother, uncle, cousin, *etc., in terms of the primitives* parent, male, *and* female.

Suppose we wanted to define a notion of ancestor. Intuitively, a person Old is an ancestor of a person Young if there is some chain of parent relationships of arbitrary length connecting Old to Young. We could start by writing clauses like:

```
ancestor(Old, Young) :-
    parent(Old, Young).
ancestor(Old, Young) :-
    parent(Old, Middle),
    parent(Middle, Young).
ancestor(Old, Young) :-
    parent(Old, Middle),
    parent(Middle, Middle2),
    parent(Middle2, Young).
...
```

Clearly, no finite axiomatization in this style is possible. Instead, we define ancestor recursively. At the base, one's closest ancestors are parents. All other ancestors are parents of closer ancestors. Stating this in Prolog, we have

Program 2.2
```
ancestor(Old,Young) :-
    parent(Old,Young).
ancestor(Old,Young) :-
    parent(Old,Middle),
    ancestor(Middle,Young).
```

The execution of the query ancestor(katherine, kate), under this definition of ancestor, proceeds as follows:

```
?- ancestor(katherine, kate).
    (1) 0 Call: ancestor(katherine, kate)
    (2) 1 Call:   parent(katherine, kate)
    (2) 1 Fail:   parent(katherine, kate)
    (3) 1 Call:   parent(katherine, Middle_3)
    (3) 1 Exit:   parent(katherine, bertrand)
    (4) 1 Call:   ancestor(bertrand, kate)
    (5) 2 Call:     parent(bertrand, kate)
    (5) 2 Exit:     parent(bertrand, kate)
    (4) 1 Exit:   ancestor(bertrand, kate)
    (1) 0 Exit: ancestor(katherine, kate)
yes
```

The reader should confirm that this definition of ancestor works appropriately by following the trace and executing similar queries.

Exercise 2.5 *What is the proof tree corresponding to this execution?*

The reader with some knowledge of model theory for first-order logic might be wondering about our use of recursive predicate definitions like the one above. In general, the transitive closure of a binary relation is not *first-order definable* (Boolos and Jeffrey, 1980). That is, given a binary predicate p there is no first-order formula $T(x, y)$ with free variables x and y such that for all interpretations of predicate symbols, constants and free variables, $T(x, y)$ holds in the interpretation if and only if the values for x and y in the interpretation are in the transitive closure of the relation interpreting the predicate p. Thus, the above definition, and others like it used in the rest of this book, seem not to really define what they are supposed to define. The solution of this conundrum is that definite-clause programs must be interpreted with a specific model in mind, the *least Herbrand model* (van Emden and Kowalski, 1976; Lloyd, 1984) for the program, rather than in terms of arbitrary first-order models. In the intended model, a program like the above indeed defines the transitive closure of the base relation.

2.5.1   Variable Renaming

In previous examples we have ignored the issue of the scope of variable names. We have been implicitly assuming that several occurrences of variables with the same spelling all occurring in one clause are to be considered instances of the same variable. Thus, in the first clause of Program 2.2, the two occurrences of Young are intended to notate the same variable. When one is bound in an assignment, they both are. However, these two occurrences and the two in the second clause are not intended to notate the same variable. For instance, in the trace above, each of these rules is used once in the proof, the first under the assignment Old = bertrand, Young = kate and the second under the assignment Old = katherine, Middle = bertrand, Young = kate. These two assignments are incompatible, assigning different values to Old. Yet their use in the execution of the query is not inconsistent because they arose from different invocations of clauses. Thus we need some way of distinguishing variables in different clauses—or different invocations of the same clause—that happen to be spelled the same.

One way of doing so would be to require that the programmer always use different variables in each clause. But not only would this be cumbersome, it would not solve the problem for different invocations for the same clause, which recursive definitions make possible. Therefore, each invocation of a given clause in a proof conceptually requires the renaming of the variables in the clause to new variables. In this book, we will represent the variables in a clause invocation resulting from renaming by x_i where x is the textual name of the original variable and i is the number of the invocation. For instance, in the execution trace above, the third clause invocation has a variable that is an instance of the variable `Middle` from the second clause of Program 2.2. It is therefore listed as `Middle_3` in the trace. Thus variables from different invocations are guaranteed to be unique.

In practice, Prolog systems use less obvious (but more efficient) variable-renaming mechanisms. Typically, new variables are internally represented as an index into Prolog's working storage, and are displayed with the notation "_i" where i encodes the index.

2.5.2 Termination

In `ancestor` we find our first example of a predicate whose definition has to be carefully designed to avoid nontermination. The idea of the definition of `ancestor` given above is that in the recursive second clause the proof procedure will have to follow a specific `parent` link in the family tree or graph before recurring to follow other links. As the family graph is finite and acyclic, at some point we will run out of `parent` links to explore and the procedure will terminate.

In contrast, the following definition is possibly more natural but causes nontermination problems for the Prolog interpreter.

Program 2.3
```
ancestor(Old,Young) :-
    ancestor(Old,Middle),
    ancestor(Middle,Young).
ancestor(Old,Young) :-
    parent(Old,Young).
```

The definition can be read "an ancestor is a parent or an ancestor of an ancestor" and includes directly an instance of the *transitivity* axiom schema which would be expressed in FOL as

$$R(x,y) \land R(y,z) \Rightarrow R(x,z)$$

However, when Prolog tries to prove `ancestor`(x,z) for any terms x and z, it falls into an infinite loop, because the first subgoal it attempts to prove is `ancestor`$(x,\text{Y\_1})$, which in turn leads to an attempt to prove `ancestor`$(x,\text{Y\_2})$ and so on.

If the two clauses are interchanged, we have

```
ancestor(Old,Young) :-
    parent(Old,Young).
ancestor(Old,Young) :-
    ancestor(Old,Middle),
    ancestor(Middle,Young).
```

In this case, Prolog will first try to use `parent` facts and therefore produce a solution in finite time if one exists. However, if we ask for more solutions by backtracking, there will come a point when all the `parent` facts will have been used in all possible ways, and Prolog will go into a loop using the recursive clause alone.

The source of the difficulty in these cases is that one of the clauses is *left recursive*, that is, the leftmost antecedent literal in a clause defining a predicate is itself a reference to that same predicate. In general, left recursive predicates cause problems for the left-to-right, depth-first control regime that Prolog uses. In fact, the left recursion need not even be direct. If by following a chain of leftmost literals we can cycle back to a predicate previously used, the Prolog proof procedure may follow this chain depth-first, fruitlessly searching for a way out. It should be noted that there are more sophisticated Horn-clause proof procedures that will not loop with transitive relation definitions. Unfortunately, those procedures are in general so expensive that it is infeasible to use them for general programming tasks. However, some of them are useful for certain parsing problems as we will see in Chapter 6.

Thus, in the avoidance of termination by clause and literal ordering, just as in the previous discussion of using such ordering to reduce search, we see that control issues must be carefully considered in writing Prolog programs, very much as when programming in other languages. In Prolog we can ignore some low-level details of data representation and execution control, but that does not mean that we can ignore *all* issues of data representation and control. Each programming language places this kind of abstraction barrier in a different place. One of the main difficulties in learning Prolog after learning other programming languages is Prolog's particular placement of the barrier.

2.6   Problem Section: Semantic Networks

Semantic networks are graph structures often used for knowledge representation in artificial intelligence. The simplest form of semantic network consists of *nodes* representing individuals and *directed arcs* representing binary relationships between nodes. For example, the network in Figure 2.2 contains several types of arcs representing relationships between nodes. For instance, the `isa` arcs represent membership relations, e.g., Ole Black *is a* Mustang (that is, is a member of the class of Mustangs). Similarly, `ako`, which stands for *a kind of*, represents the inclusion relation between classes. For instance, Mustangs are a kind of automobile.

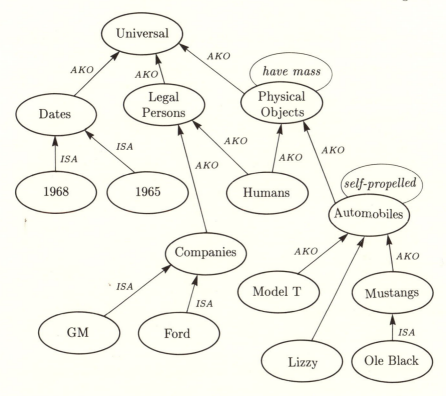

Figure 2.2. A semantic network

Problem 2.6 *Find a way of representing this simple semantic network in Prolog using unit clauses. It should be possible with your representation to answer queries paraphrasable as "What class is Ole Black a member of?" (the answer should be* mustang*) or "What companies are there?" (the answers should be* gm *and* ford*). Demonstrate that your representation can handle these queries.*

We can ask Prolog what individuals satisfy a given relation. However, we cannot ask directly what relations hold between given individuals. In semantic network representations, we often want to ask the latter kind of question, for instance, "What relationships hold between Ford and the class of companies?"

Problem 2.7 *Modify your representation of semantic networks to allow both this new kind of question and the kind in the previous problem. (HINT:*

Treat semantic network relations as Prolog individuals. This is an important Prolog programming technique, sometimes called reification *in philosophical circles.)*

Semantic networks are often used to represent *taxonomies* with *property inheritance*. A taxonomy, like the one in the example above, places individuals in classes, and specifies which classes are subclasses of other classes. If all the members of a class necessarily have a certain property, we say (abusing language slightly) that the class has the property. Further, we say that all individuals in the class, and all subclasses of the class, *inherit* the property. The following three conventions are usually followed for economy of representation:

- Class containment statements are given only between a class and the smallest classes in the taxonomy that contain it. (For instance, we do not have an explicit representation of the fact that Mustangs are physical objects.)

- Class membership statements are given between an individual and the smallest classes in the taxonomy that contain it. (For instance, we do not explicitly represent that Ford is a legal person.)

- Properties are associated with the largest class in the taxonomy that has them. (For instance, we explicitly associate the property of being self-propelled with automobiles but not with Mustangs).

The transitivity of class containment is then used to deduce from the explicit data whether specific individuals or classes have certain properties or are in certain classes, for example, that Mustangs are physical objects.

Problem 2.8 *Use your Prolog encoding of semantic networks for a general encoding of taxonomies of the kind described. Define the following Prolog predicates in terms of your representation:*

- `is_instance(Individual, Class)` *holds when* `Individual` *is an element of* `Class`.

- `has_property(Individual,Property)` *holds when* `Individual` *has* `Property`.

- `subclass(Class1, Class2)` *holds when* `Class1` *is a [possibly improper] subclass of* `Class2`.

Test your program by demonstrating that GM is a legal person, that Ole Black is self-propelled, and that Mustangs are physical objects.

In Prolog, we can have predicates of any number of arguments. We may, for example, represent the fact that Ford built Ole Black in 1965 by the clause built(ford,ole_black,1965). However, in the simple form of semantic network discussed so far, we can only represent directly binary relations.

Problem 2.9 *Find a way of representing n-ary predicates using nodes and labeled arcs in a semantic network. How would you represent "Ole Black was built by Ford in 1965" with this encoding? How would you ask Prolog to determine which company built Mustangs in 1967?*

2.7 Context-Free Grammars

We begin the discussion of natural-language analysis and the role Prolog can play therein with a discussion of context-free grammars and their axiomatization in the database subset of Prolog.

Context-free grammars (CFG) constitute a system for defining the expressions of a language in terms of *rules*, which are recursive equations over expression types, called *nonterminals*, and primitive expressions, called *terminals*. The standard notation for a context-free rule is

$$N_0 \rightarrow V_1 \cdots V_n$$

where N_0 is some nonterminal and the V_i are nonterminals or terminals. Such a rule has the following informal interpretation: "if expressions $w_1, \ldots, w_n$ match $V_1, \ldots, V_n$, respectively, then the single expression $w_1 \cdots w_n$ (the concatenation of the w_i) is itself of expression type N_0." By an expression w_i matching a V_i we mean that either V_i is a terminal (a primitive expression) and identical to w_i, or V_i is a nonterminal (an expression type) and w_i is of that type (presumably by virtue of some rule in the grammar).

Consider, for example, the following context-free grammar for a fragment of English:

$$S \rightarrow NP\ VP$$
$$NP \rightarrow Det\ N\ OptRel$$
$$NP \rightarrow PN$$
$$OptRel \rightarrow \epsilon$$
$$OptRel \rightarrow that\ VP$$
$$VP \rightarrow TV\ NP$$
$$VP \rightarrow IV$$

$$PN \rightarrow terry$$
$$PN \rightarrow shrdlu$$
$$Det \rightarrow a$$
$$N \rightarrow program$$
$$IV \rightarrow halts$$
$$TV \rightarrow writes$$

We have notated nonterminals with upper-case names and terminals with lower-case. The nonterminal names we have used here are, for the most part, standard in current linguistics. For reference, we include below a table of the terms they abbreviate.

symbol	abbreviates
S	Sentence
NP	Noun Phrase
VP	Verb Phrase
IV	Intransitive Verb
TV	Transitive Verb
PN	Proper Noun
Det	DETerminer[5]
N	Noun
OptRel	OPTional RELative clause

The grammar above classifies strings as being of zero or more of these types. For instance, by virtue of the ninth rule, the expression "SHRDLU" is classified as a *PN*. An alternate terminology is often used in which the nonterminal *PN* is said to *cover* the string "SHRDLU". Similarly, the string "halts" is covered by the nonterminal *IV*. Furthermore, by the twelfth rule, "halts" is also classified as a *VP*. The first and third rules allow the conclusion that the entire phrase "SHRDLU halts" is an *S*.

This classification of an expression and its subexpressions according to a context-free grammar can be summarized in a *phrase-structure tree* or *parse tree*. The tree for the sentence "SHRDLU halts" is given in Figure 2.3. Each local set of nodes, consisting of a parent node and its immediate children, corresponds to a rule application. For instance, the top set of nodes corresponds to an application of the rule $S \rightarrow NP\ VP$. The leaves of the tree, that is, the symbols at the bottom with no children, correspond to the primitive expressions, the terminals, and the interior nodes correspond to nonterminals. The expression covered by a given node is just the fringe

---

[5]Determiners (like *the* and *a*) are also sometimes called articles.

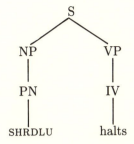

Figure 2.3. Parse tree for a simple sentence

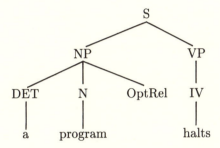

Figure 2.4. Parse tree including empty constituent

of the subtree whose root is that node. Such a phrase-structure tree for a string provides a sort of proof that the string is classified as the nonterminal at the root.

The symbol "ϵ", which occurs in the first rule for optional relative clauses, is used to mark a rule with zero elements on the right-hand side, hence, covering the "empty string". For example, the string "a program halts" is classified as an S as illustrated by the parse tree of Figure 2.4. Note that since the OptRel rule has no elements on the right-hand side, it requires no dependents in the parse tree and covers no portion of the string.

Any procedure for determining the parse tree corresponding to an expression must perform the rule applications in a given order. Such an ordering of the applications summarized in the tree is called a *derivation* of the string. In the particular example "SHRDLU halts", we might derive the string performing lower applications in the tree before those higher up, as we did in the informal description above. Alternatively, we might start by applying the first rule to the root symbol S, then expanding the *NP* and *VP* and so forth, working down from the top of the tree. Derivations of the former sort are referred to as *bottom-up* derivations, those of the latter type as *top-down* derivations. On an orthogonal dimension, we can have *depth-first* or *breadth-first* derivations, depending on whether an entire subtree is or is not derived before the derivation of its siblings begins. Many other possible derivation orderings are possible, combining facets of top-down versus bottom-up, depth- versus breadth-first, left-to-right versus right-to-left orderings, and so forth. The parse tree abstracts away from all these ordering issues manifested in particular derivations, just as a proof tree abstracts away from ordering issues manifested in particular traces.

As a side note, it is traditional to separate a grammar of this sort into two parts, one which contains the grammar rules proper and one which contains the rules with a single terminal on the right hand side. The latter part is called the *dictionary* or *lexicon* for the grammar. Dictionary rules correspond to the lines in the parse tree connecting a *preterminal*—a nonterminal immediately covering a terminal—and the terminal it covers.

Exercise 2.10 *What expression types are the following expressions classified under according to the context-free grammar just given?*

1. halts
2. writes a program
3. a program that Terry writes
4. Terry writes a program that halts
5. a program that halts writes a program that halts
6. Terry halts a program
7. a program that Terry writes halts

Exercise 2.11 *For each classification of each expression in the preceding exercise, give the parse tree for the derivation of that expression under that classification.*

2.7.1   Axiomatizing Context-Free Grammars

In parse trees like the one given in Figure 2.4, nonterminals can be interpreted not only as a classification of expressions (viz., the expressions that are the fringes of trees labeled with the given nonterminal) but also as binary relations on *positions* in the expression, where a position divides an expression into two subexpressions which concatenated together form the

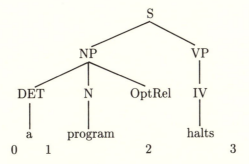

Figure 2.5. Parse tree with string positions

original expression. For example, string positions for the the sample parse tree of Figure 2.4 are shown in Figure 2.5. Position 2, for example, divides the expression into the two subexpressions "a program" and "halts".

The nonterminals can now be seen as binary relations on the positions. The pair of positions $\langle 0, 2 \rangle$ is in the *NP* relation because the nonterminal *NP* covers the subexpression between positions 0 and 2. Using logical notation for the relation, this fact can be notated as *NP*(0,2). Similarly, *S*(0,3) holds because the nonterminal *S* covers the expression between positions 0 and 3. The empty optional relative clause covers the string between position 2 and itself, i.e., *OptRel*(2,2).

In fact, the general statement made by the context-free rule

$$S \rightarrow NP \; VP$$

can be summarized using relations on positions with the following logical statement:

$$NP(p_0, p_1) \wedge VP(p_1, p) \Rightarrow S(p_0, p)$$

that is, if there is an *NP* between positions p_0 and p_1 and a *VP* between positions p_1 and p, then there is an *S* between positions p_0 and p. Indeed, any context-free rule of the form

$$N_0 \rightarrow V_1 \cdots V_n$$

can be axiomatized as

$$V_1(p_0, p_1) \wedge \cdots \wedge V_n(p_{n-1}, p) \Rightarrow N_0(p_0, p)$$

2.7.2   Context-Free Grammars in Prolog

To express a context-free grammar in Prolog, then, we merely note that this general form for axiomatizing rules is itself in definite clause form. Thus,

it can be directly stated in Prolog. For instance, the sentence formation
rule is expressed

```
s(P0, P) :- np(P0, P1), vp(P1, P).
```

A full axiomatization of the English fragment would be as follows:

Program 2.4
```
s(P0, P) :- np(P0, P1), vp(P1, P).
np(P0, P) :- det(P0, P1), n(P1, P2), optrel(P2, P).
np(P0, P) :- pn(P0, P).
vp(P0, P) :- tv(P0, P1), np(P1, P).
vp(P0, P) :- iv(P0, P).
optrel(P, P).
optrel(P0, P) :- connects(that, P0, P1), vp(P1, P).

pn(P0, P) :- connects(terry, P0, P).
pn(P0, P) :- connects(shrdlu, P0, P).
iv(P0, P) :- connects(halts, P0, P).
det(P0, P) :- connects(a, P0, P).
n(P0, P) :- connects(program, P0, P).
tv(P0, P) :- connects(writes, P0, P).
```

We have used the literal connects(Terminal, Position1, Position2)
to mean that the terminal symbol Terminal lies between consecutive positions Position1 and Position2.

This axiomatization of a CFG in Prolog can be seen as the output of
a general mapping or algorithmic translation from CFGs into Prolog. The
mapping takes any CF rule and forms a corresponding Prolog clause as
follows:

- For each nonterminal, construct a literal applying a binary predicate
  for that nonterminal to two position arguments (e.g., the nonterminal
  NP becomes the literal np(P1, P2)).

- For each terminal, construct a literal applying the predicate connects
  to three arguments, viz., the terminal symbol expressed as a Prolog
  constant and two position arguments (e.g., the terminal *halts* becomes
  the literal connects(halts, P1, P2)).

Furthermore, as exemplified above, the position arguments for each constituent form a sequence $p_0, \ldots, p_n$ such that the constituent defined by the
rule relates p_0 to p_n and subconstituent i in the right-hand side of the rule
relates p_{i-1} to p_i. The ability to describe this mapping algorithmically is

the basis for interpreters for this and other grammar formalisms. We will investigate such formalisms and interpreters in Chapter 6.

2.7.3   Prolog as Parser

Given our usage of the `connects` predicate, an expression can be axiomatized by stating which terminal symbols in the string connect the string positions. For instance, the string "a program halts" is represented by the following unit clauses:

```
connects(a, 0, 1).
connects(program, 1, 2).
connects(halts, 2, 3).
```

This axiomatization of expressions and context-free grammars in definite clauses allows any Horn-clause proof procedure to serve as a *parser* (or, strictly speaking, a *recognizer*) for expressions.[6] The Prolog proof procedure, in particular, gives us a *top-down, depth-first, left-to-right* parsing mechanism because the derivations Prolog assigns to a string by its execution correspond to top-down, depth-first, left-to-right traversal of the parse tree. A query of the form s(0, 3) will hold if the string between positions 0 and 3 is a sentence according to the grammar.

```
?- s(0, 3).
yes
?- s(0, 2).
no
```

Tracing the execution by Prolog explicitly exhibits the derivation order implicit in using Prolog as a parser of grammars encoded in this way. The execution trace of the grammar given above with the input sentence "a program halts" represented by unit clauses clearly shows Prolog's top-down, depth-first, left-to-right behavior.

```
?- s(0,3).
    (1) 0 Call :  s(0,3)
    (2) 1 Call :    np(0,P1_2)
    (3) 2 Call :      det(0,P1_3)
    (4) 3 Call :        connects(a,0,P1_3)
    (4) 3 Exit :        connects(a,0,1)
```

---

[6] A recognizer is a program that determines whether or not an expression is grammatical according to the grammar. A parser is a recognizer that furthermore determines the structure under which grammatical strings are admitted by the grammar.

```
 (3) 2 Exit :      det(0,1)
 (5) 2 Call :      n(1,P2_5)
 (6) 3 Call :        connects(program,1,P2_5)
 (6) 3 Exit :        connects(program,1,2)
 (5) 2 Exit :      n(1,2)
 (7) 2 Call :      optrel(2,P1_2)
 (7) 2 Exit :      optrel(2,2)
 (2) 1 Exit :    np(0,2)
 (8) 1 Call :    vp(2,3)
 (9) 2 Call :      tv(2,P1_9)
(10) 3 Call :        connects(writes,2,P1_9)
(10) 3 Fail :        connects(writes,2,P1_9)
 (9) 2 Fail :      tv(2,P1_9)
(11) 2 Call :      iv(2,3)
(12) 3 Call :        connects(halts,2,3)
(12) 3 Exit :        connects(halts,2,3)
(11) 2 Exit :      iv(2,3)
 (8) 1 Exit :    vp(2,3)
 (1) 0 Exit : s(0,3)
yes
```

The trace shows that Prolog parses by searching for a derivation of the expression starting at the top node in the parse tree and working its way down, choosing one rule at a time and backtracking when dead ends in the search are reached. For pure context-free grammars, many other better parsing mechanisms are known, so this parsing technique is not very interesting for CFGs. It becomes more interesting for the more general grammars discussed in Section 3.7. Furthermore, alternative axiomatizations of CFGs can engender different parsing mechanisms, and Prolog interpreters for grammars can make use of alternative algorithms for parsing. These possibilities are explored further in Chapter 6.

The axiomatization of grammars just presented makes more precise the sense in which a parse tree provides a kind of proof of the grammaticality of an expression, as the parse tree for a sentence corresponds directly to the proof tree that Prolog develops in recognizing the expression. This can be readily seen for the sample sentence whose proof tree is given in Figure 2.6 (cf. Figure 2.5). In fact, this isomorphism is exploited further in Section 3.7.1, in developing a grammar that builds the parse tree corresponding to a given derivation.

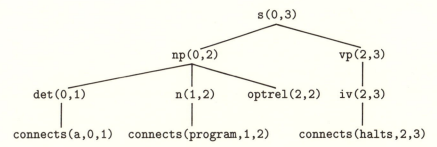

Figure 2.6. Proof tree for parse of sentence

2.8 Problem Section: Grammars

In this problem section, we will develop alternative ways of encoding languages in Prolog. First, we will consider how to encode the syntax of database Prolog itself using the encoding technique described in Section 2.7.2 but with a much freer encoding of the primitive expressions. Then we will look at various other mechanisms for encoding languages based on adding operations like intersection or using different data structures like graphs.

2.8.1 A Syntactic Analyzer for Database Prolog

We will consider here the question of how to build a syntactic analyzer for a programming language, in this case the database subset of Prolog we have seen so far. This subset has a very simple syntax:

- o A clause is a *clause term* followed by a period.

- o A clause term is an *atomic formula* (a unit clause) or an atomic formula followed by an implication followed by a sequence of atomic formulas separated by commas (a nonunit clause).

- o An atomic formula is a *predicate symbol* (a constant) optionally followed by a parenthesized list of comma-separated *arguments*.

- o An argument is a constant or a variable.

Prolog syntactic analyzers, like those for other programming languages, do not usually analyze character strings directly but rather strings of lexical *tokens* produced by a lexical analyzer (Aho and Ullman, 1977). We will assume in this problem that the results of lexical analysis of a string are expressed not by `connects` clauses but rather by Prolog unit clauses of the following forms:

o `constant(Constant,From,To)`, meaning that there is a constant to-
ken between points `From` and `To` in the string with spelling `Constant`.

o `variable(Variable,From,To)`, meaning that there is a variable to-
ken between points `From` and `To` in the string with spelling `Variable`.

o `punctuation(Punct,From,To)`, meaning that there is a punctuation
mark between points `From` and `To` in the string with "spelling" `Punct`.

For example, for the Prolog clause

```
ancestor(Old,Young) :- parent(Old,Young).
```

we can assume that the following assertions will be in the Prolog database:

```
constant(ancestor,1,2).
punctuation('(', 2,3).
variable('Old',3,4).
punctuation(',',4,5).
variable('Young',5,6).
punctuation(')',6,7).
punctuation((:-),7,8).
     ...
punctuation('.',14,15).
```

Note that punctuation and capitalized constants (denoting the spelling
of variables) must be in quotes so they are read as constants by Prolog, and
not as operators or variables, respectively. Also note the extra parentheses
in the seventh clause. These are required by Edinburgh Prolog syntax because of the precedences of operators in order to prevent the interpretation
of :- as a prefix operator.

Problem 2.12 *Write a context-free grammar for dbProlog. Translate it to
Prolog, and test it with some of its own clauses as data. (We recommend
choosing short clauses for the data as the encoding is tedious. Chapter 3
discusses better string position encodings.)*

2.8.2 Extending CFGs with Intersection

Context-free grammars can be generalized by using the *intersection* operator "&". A rule of the form

$$X \to \alpha \,\&\, \beta \qquad (2.6)$$

is interpreted as saying that a string is an X if it is simultaneously an α and a β. This extended notation thus represents *intersections* of context-free languages, which in general are not context-free (Hopcroft and Ullman, 1979, pages 134-135).

Problem 2.13 *Extend the standard mapping of context-free rules to Prolog (discussed in Section 2.7.2) to allow for rules with the intersection operator. Demonstrate the mapping by writing and testing a Prolog program defining a grammar for the non-context-free language made of all strings of the form* $a^n b^n c^n$ *for* $n \geq 0$.

2.8.3   Transition Networks

Transition networks are an alternative to formal grammars for defining formal languages (i.e., sets of strings). Whereas a formal grammar defines a language in terms of combinations of types of strings, a transition network for a language is a kind of abstract machine for recognizing whether strings are in the language. The machine can be in one of a set of states, and the transitions from state to state correspond to processing successive symbols in the string to be recognized. Certain special states correspond to acceptance or recognition of the string. If the machine finishes processing when in such a state, the string is accepted as being in the language recognized by the machine. If the machine does not end up in such a state, the string is not accepted. The problems in this section cover the writing of interpreters for transition networks of both nonrecursive and recursive varieties.

Graph Languages

The states and state transitions of a machine like the kind just described form a kind of graph or network with the states as the nodes and the transitions as the arcs. For this reason, we will start by looking at a simple way to recognize languages using graphs, and move on to the more complex networks in later problems.

A *finite directed labeled graph* is a finite set G of triples (n, l, m), where n and m are elements of a set of *nodes* and l is an element of a set of *labels*. A *path* through the graph is a string of labels $l_1 \cdots l_k$ such that there exist graph nodes $n_0, \ldots, n_k$ for which the triples $(n_0, l_1, n_1), \ldots, (n_{k-1}, l_k, n_k)$ are in the graph. The graph's *path language* is the language whose strings are all paths in g.

For example, the graph $\{(1, a, 2), (2, b, 3), (3, c, 2)\}$ can be depicted as in Figure 2.7. This graph describes a language containing, among other strings, ϵ, a, ab, bc, $cbcbc$, and so forth.

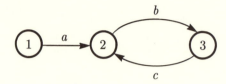

Figure 2.7. A graph

Problem 2.14 *Write a Prolog program that can be combined with a Prolog representation of an arbitrary finite directed labeled graph and a Prolog representation of a string to recognize that string as belonging to the path language of the graph.*

Nonrecursive Transition Networks

Transition networks can be seen as a kind of graph where the nodes are called *states* and the arcs *state transitions*. More formally, a nonrecursive transition network is a labeled directed graph N (as in the previous problem) together with a distinguished *initial state i* and a set of *final states* F. A string $s = l_1 \ldots l_k$ is *accepted* by the network (or is in the *language* of the network) if and only if there is a path in N given by the triples $(n_0, l_1, n_1), \ldots, (n_{k-1}, l_k, n_k)$ such that n_0 is the initial state and n_k is a final state.

For example, Figure 2.8 depicts a transition network with initial state 1 (signified by the arrow ">") and final state 5 (signified by the concentric circles). This network will accept strings such as "every professor's professor's program halts", but not "program halts" (because it does not start at the start state) or "every professor's professor" (because it does not end in a final state).

Problem 2.15 *Write a Prolog program that will recognize the strings in the language of an arbitrary transition network described by an appropriate set of unit clauses. Test the program at least on the example in Figure 2.8. (Your solution of Problem 2.14 might be useful here.)*

Recursive Transition Networks

A *recursive* transition network (RTN) is a transition network with a set of *labeled initial states* each labeled by a different label, instead of a single initial state. Initial state labels play the same role as nonterminals in CFGs. Of all the initial state labels, we distinguish a *start label* (or start symbol).

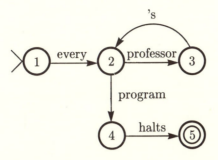

Figure 2.8. A nonrecursive transition network

A string s is *recognized* as an X by RTN N if and only if

1. X is the label of an initial state x, and

2. there is a path (string of labels) $l_1 \cdots l_k$ that is accepted by N seen as a nonrecursive transition network with initial state x, and

3. there are strings $s_1, \ldots, s_k$ such that $s = s_1 \cdots s_k$, and

4. for each s_i, either $s_i = l_i$ or s_i is recognized (recursively) as an l_i by N. (We will extend this part of the definition shortly.)

A string s is recognized by an RTN N with start label S if and only if s is recognized as an S by N. The *language* of an RTN is the set of strings it recognizes.

Consider the sample RTN in Figure 2.9. A labeled initial state n with label l is represented in the example by $l : n$. By convention in such drawings of transition networks, terminal symbols are written in lower case and nonterminal symbols (subnetwork labels) are written in upper case. Of the nonterminal symbols in the example, only S, NP, VP and REL have corresponding subnetworks. Rather than give subnetworks for the other nonterminals which correspond to preterminal categories (DET, N and TV), we treat them specially. A preterminal P will match a word w in the string if w is listed as a p in a dictionary external to the network. That is, we are extending Part 4 of the definition given above of what it means for a string element to match a label to allow a case where s_i is listed in a dictionary under the preterminal category l_i.

The network of Figure 2.9 would therefore recognize sentences like

every professor's student wrote a program

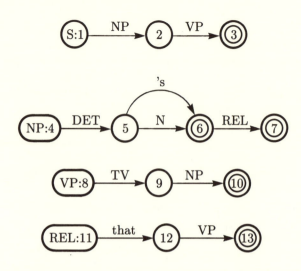

Figure 2.9. A recursive transition network

assuming that 'every' and 'a' are listed as *DET*s; 'professor', 'program', and 'student' are *N*s; and 'wrote' is a *TV* in the dictionary.

Problem 2.16 *Extend your solution of the previous problem to recognize the strings in the language of an arbitrary recursive transition network plus dictionary, represented by appropriate unit clauses for both the network and the dictionary. Test it at least on the example RTN of Figure 2.9.*

2.9   Bibliographic Notes

The database subset of Prolog (Section 2.1) is discussed in more detail by Sterling and Shapiro (1986). The relationship between first-order logic and Prolog is covered to some extent in that book, and is also addressed in the books by Kowalski (1980), Gallier (1986) and Clocksin and Mellish (1981). The dual interpretation of logic programs, declarative and procedural, was first discussed by Kowalski (1974a; 1974b), and related to denotational semantics for programming languages by van Emden and Kowalski (1976). Lloyd's book (1984) gives a detailed mathematical account of the semantics of definite-clause programs.

The family tree of Bertrand Russell (Section 2.5) was derived from Katherine Tait's biography of her father (1975).

The more general question of the relationship between clausal form and full first-order logic (Section 2.3) is discussed in detail in every book on automated theorem-proving, a few of which were mentioned in Section 1.5. The concepts underlying clausal form and Skolem functions were used in logical investigations for several decades, as can be seen in the papers by Skolem (1920) and Herbrand (1930) in the van Heijenoort collection (1967). Building upon Herbrand's work, Robinson (1965) developed the resolution inference procedure for clausal form.

The tracing and debugging of Prolog programs (Section 2.4.1) has unique difficulties that can be attributed to the nondeterminacy of clause selection. Proof trees are commonly used in logic to represent the relationship between premises and conclusions in a proof. The space of alternatives in the search for a proof can also be represented by a tree, and the combination of the two trees forms an and-or tree. These concepts are discussed by Kowalski (1980).

Tree representations are convenient in proof theory and for heuristic purposes, but are unwieldy when tracing large Prolog executions. Byrd's box model (1980), the first practical framework for debugging Prolog programs, has been implemented in many Prolog systems. More advanced models have since been proposed, in particular the family of *algorithmic debugging* methods that started with Shapiro's dissertation (1983).

Semantic networks (Section 2.6) were originally proposed by Quillian (1967). They have been the object of much work in artificial intelligence, including that of Hendrix (1979), from which we derived our example. The connections between semantic networks and logic are discussed, for instance, by Woods (1975) and by Deliyanni and Kowalski (1979).

Context-free grammars (Section 2.7) originated in the formalization of the notions of immediate constituent and phrase structure in structural linguistics, in particular with the work of Chomsky (1956). A detailed history of the development of these ideas is given by Greibach (1981), who also supplies a comprehensive bibliography of formal-language theory. A linguistically oriented overview of context-free grammars can be found in the book by Partee et al. (1987). A full mathematical treatment of context-free grammars, their properties, and parsing algorithms is given, for instance, by Harrison (1978). The representation of context-free grammars in first-order logic has been in the folklore for a long time, but the first reference to the idea in print that we know of is by Kowalski (1974a).

The problem in Section 2.8.1 requires the text of Prolog programs to be given in a "predigested" tokenized form. The techniques of lexical analysis required to produce that form are discussed in any compiler-design reference, e.g., (Aho and Ullman, 1977).

The problem in Section 2.8.2 introduces intersections of context-free languages, which in general are not context free. Classes of languages are partly characterized by how languages in the class behave under set operations such as intersection. Proofs that a certain language is not in a certain class (e.g. context free) often depend on the closure properties of language classes under set operations (Ginsburg, 1966; Harrison, 1978). Such results can be useful in linguistic argumentation (Shieber, 1985b).

Transition networks (Section 2.8.3) are a common representation of abstract string-recognition devices. In the nonrecursive case, they are just another notation for nondeterministic finite-state acceptors, which are discussed in any introductory book on compilers or formal-language theory (Hopcroft and Ullman, 1979; Aho and Ullman, 1972; Harrison, 1978). Recursive transition networks are closely related to the nondeterministic pushdown acceptors, which are the abstract machine counterparts of context-free grammars (Hopcroft and Ullman, 1979; Aho and Ullman, 1972; Harrison, 1978). However, the actual notion of recursive transition network used here comes from Woods's work on transition networks for natural-language analysis (1970). Woods extends recursive transition networks with data registers that can be set by actions and tested by conditions on arcs. The resulting formalism, *augmented transition networks* (ATNs), is very powerful; in fact, an ATN can be written to recognize any recursively enumerable language. Bates (1978) gives a very good tutorial on ATNs and their application in natural-language processing. Pereira and Warren (1980) have compared ATNs with logic grammars in detail.

3

Pure Prolog:
Theory and Application

In the database subset of Prolog we have seen so far, the arguments to predicates have been constants or variables. Like FOL, however, Prolog allows arbitrary *terms* to serve as arguments of predicates, of which constants and variables are but two subclasses. Terms also include recursive structures formed by applying *function symbols* to other terms, using the parenthesized syntax familiar from logic.

The extension of database Prolog to include terms of arbitrary complexity is called *pure Prolog* because it is a pure subset of FOL, containing no extralogical features (except for those in Section 3.4.1). Full Prolog, discussed in Chapter 6, does have such features; consequently, its declarative semantics and procedural operation diverge. But pure Prolog is a pure logic programming language. It has a procedural interpretation that is potentially sound (though not complete) with respect to its declarative interpretation.[1]

3.1 Prolog Notation Revisited

At this point, let us review the notation for Prolog that we have been using and augment it to include compound terms formed with function symbols, as mentioned in Section 2.3. We give a simplified CFG for the Prolog syntax introduced so far, augmented to include functions and terms formed from them.

---

[1]However, because of the lack of the "occurs check" in Prolog systems (Section 3.5.2), this potential soundness is not realized in most implementations.

$$Program \rightarrow Clause$$
$$Program \rightarrow Clause\ Program$$

$$Clause \rightarrow AtForm :- Condition\ .$$
$$Clause \rightarrow AtForm\ .$$

$$Condition \rightarrow AtForm$$
$$Condition \rightarrow AtForm\ ,\ Condition$$

$$AtForm \rightarrow Predsym$$
$$AtForm \rightarrow Predsym\ (\ TermSeq\ )$$

$$TermSeq \rightarrow Term$$
$$TermSeq \rightarrow Term\ ,\ TermSeq$$

$$Term \rightarrow Constant$$
$$Term \rightarrow Number$$
$$Term \rightarrow Variable$$
$$Term \rightarrow Funcsym\ (\ TermSeq\ )$$

The primitive types of expressions, then, are *constants, function symbols* (*Funcsym*), *predicate symbols* (*Predsym*), and *variables*. Constants are either *numbers* (such as 0, 99.99, -129) or *atoms*. Atoms are tokens beginning with a lower-case alphabetic or composed of a sequence of special characters or composed of any characters surrounded by single quotes. For instance, the following are atoms: a, bertrand, =, :=, 'Bertrand Russell', [].

Function symbols and predicate symbols (often collectively referred to as *functors*) are also notated with atoms.

Compound expressions (a functor applied to a sequence of term arguments) are by default represented in parenthesized prefix notation as in *Funcsym* (*TermSeq*) or *Predsym* (*TermSeq*) above.

3.2   Terms and Unification

To illustrate the notation, here is an example program that axiomatizes addition in successor notation:

Program 3.1

```
add(0, Y, Y).
add(succ(X), Y, succ(Z)) :- add(X, Y, Z).
```

In this program, the simple term 0 is intended to represent the number 0, the term succ(0) the number 1, succ(succ(0)) the number 2, and so forth. (The function symbol succ is so-called because it corresponds to the integer successor function.) Thus, the first clause states that 0 added to any number is that number. The second clause states that the successor of any number x added to y is the successor of the sum z of x and y.

Unlike in imperative languages, the succ function symbol when applied to a term will not "return a value"; the term succ(0) does not equal (reduce to, return, evaluate to, etc.) the term 1 or any other structure. The only relationship between the terms and the numbers is the meaning relationship we, as programmers and users, attribute to the terms. The program respects this attribution because it holds of three terms just in case the numbers they represent are related by the addition relation. We can see this in the following queries:

```
?- add(0, succ(0), Result).
Result = succ(0)
yes

?- add(succ(succ(0)), succ(succ(0)), Result).
Result = succ(succ(succ(succ(0))))
yes
```

These queries correspond to computing that $0 + 1$ is 1 and $2 + 2$ is 4.

Prolog augmented with terms works in exactly the same way as the database subset discussed in the previous chapter. The only difference is that the matching of a goal literal with the head of a rule, the process of *unification* informally defined in Section 2.4 and more fully discussed in Section 3.5.2, must in general apply to arbitrary compound terms. Recall the informal definition of unification given previously. Two atomic formulas unify if there exists an assignment to the variables in them under which the two formulas become identical. Applying this definition to an example, consider the unification of the two atomic formulas

```
add(succ(succ(0)), succ(succ(0)), Result)
```

and

```
add(succ(X), Y, succ(Z))      .
```

This unification succeeds because the assignment

```
X = succ(0), Y = succ(succ(0)), Result = succ(Z)
```

transforms both formulas into

```
add(succ(succ(0)), succ(succ(0)), succ(Z))      .
```

The execution of a goal to add 2 and 2 (encoded in successor notation) would then proceed as follows: The initial goal is

```
add(succ(succ(0)), succ(succ(0)), Result)      .
```

This fails to unify with the first clause for `add`, but unifies with the head of the second clause with the unifying assignment as above. Under this assignment, the body of the clause becomes

```
add(succ(0), succ(succ(0)), Z)      .
```

Now this clause also matches the head of the second clause (which we will write with variables renamed to `X_1`, `Y_1` and `Z_1` to avoid confusion as per Section 2.5.1). This time the unifying assignment is

$$X\_1 = 0, \ Y\_1 = succ(succ(0)), \ Z = succ(Z\_1)   .$$

The body of this second activation of the clause becomes

```
add(0, succ(succ(0)), Z_1)      .
```

This goal matches the unit clause `add(0,Y,Y)` under the assignment

$$Y\_2 = succ(succ(0)), \ Z\_1 = Y\_2   ,$$

and the execution is complete. In looking at the assignments that were involved in the proof, we note that `Result` was bound to `succ(Z)`, Z to `succ(Z_1)`, `Z_1` to `Y_2`, and `Y_2` to `succ(succ(0))`. Thus, aggregating assignments, we have $Result = succ(Z) = succ(succ(Z\_1)) = succ(succ(Y\_2)) = succ(succ(succ(succ(0))))$. The query thus computes that $2 + 2 = 4$.

3.3   Functions in Prolog and Other Languages

In logics that include equality between terms as a primitive notion, the reducibility of one term to another enables a powerful technique for reasoning about functions. Conventional programming languages—and even more so, so-called functional programming languages—make use of this by basing their constructs on equalities (usually in the guise of function definitions). These equalities are typically interpreted as rewriting rules that can be used to reduce terms to simpler ones, and eventually to irreducible terms that are identified with "values". In imperative programming languages, this notion is implicit in the notion of a function call that returns a value. All of this, of course, depends on the language in some sense embodying axioms of equality. For instance, reduction corresponds to the substitutivity of equality. In fact, proof procedures for equality could be used as the basis for functional computation very much as Horn-clause proof procedures are the basis for relational computation.

General proof procedures for logics with equality are very difficult to control, and therefore have to date been too inefficient to use in logic programming. It was observed, however, that much of the work of equations and function symbols could be done instead by relations. For example, instead of representing addition as a function $+$ with axioms

$$
\begin{aligned}
succ(x) + y &= succ(x + y) \\
0 + x &= x
\end{aligned}
$$

we can use the ternary predicate **add** with the Prolog definition given in Program 3.1.

The simple observation that subject-domain functions can be represented as relations was a crucial step in making logic programming practical. However, this step is not without losses. For example, the uniqueness of function values, a consequence of the equality axiom schemata in FOL with equality, is not available for reasoning when the relational encoding of functions is used. It may be that the Prolog definition of a function gives only one output for each input (as is the case with **add** above), but this is a contingent property of a particular predicate definition rather than a necessary property as it is with functional notation. Another disadvantage is that relational syntax requires the introduction of intermediate variables for function composition, often impairing the readability of programs.

Of the standard equality axioms and their consequences, the only one that is left in Prolog, because it is definable in the language, is the reflexivity axiom $x = x$, which can be implemented in Prolog with the unit clause

Program 3.2
```
X = X.
```

In fact, the infix $=$ operator is built in to most Prolog systems.

The lack of more powerful equality axioms in Prolog means that in Prolog it is not possible to reason about whether two distinct terms denote the same object. In other words, the value of applying a function to some arguments can only be represented by the term expressing that application and not by some other (presumably simpler) term representing the "value" of the function on those arguments. Thus, in Prolog we look at functions as *constructors*, one-to-one functions with disjoint ranges. Each ground term is seen as denoting a distinct element in the domain, and function symbols are means of constructing new elements from old, analogous to constructor functions such as cons in LISP or record constructors in Ada. Compound terms in Prolog have the same role as record structures in other languages, namely, representing structured information. For instance, in the addition example above, the succ function symbol applied to an argument α does not "return" the successor of the argument. It merely constructs the larger term succ(α). We may choose to interpret the terms 0, succ(0), succ(succ(0)), ... as representing the nonnegative integers (which they are isomorphic to). We can then compute with these terms in ways consistent with their interpretation as integers, as we did in the addition example.

To extend our analogy between Prolog terms and data structures, note that unification between terms plays both a structure *selection* role, picking up the arguments of functions, and a structure *construction* role, instantiating variables to compound terms. For example, recall the query

```
add(succ(succ(0)), succ(succ(0)), Result)    .
```

This literal matched the head of the second clause for add under the assignment

$$X = succ(0), \; Y = succ(succ(0)), \; Result = succ(Z)   .$$

Note how unification between the first arguments of the goal and head has decomposed the argument, performing a selection role. The body of the clause, the new goal, was

```
add(succ(0),succ(succ(0)),Z)    ,
```

which succeeded with the unifying assignment

$$Z = succ(succ(succ((0)))   .$$

Thus the original goal succeeds with

$$Result = succ(Z) = succ(succ(succ(succ(0))))   .$$

The unification between the third arguments of goal and head are this time playing a construction role, building the representation of the result succ(succ(succ(succ(0)))) from succ(succ(succ(0))), the intermediate result. This simple example of addition demonstrates that computations that might have been formulated in functional-equational terms in another language can be formulated as a relational computation over terms in Prolog.

Compound terms in Prolog thus play the same role as complex data structures such as lists, trees, or records in other programming languages. But whereas in LISP, for example, every list (S-expression) is fully specified once it is built, terms with variables in Prolog stand for *partially specified* data structures, possibly to be further specified by variable instantiation in the course of a proof. This role of variables as "stand-ins" for as yet unspecified structures is very different from the roles of variables as formal parameters or updatable locations in functional and imperative languages like LISP and Pascal. To distinguish Prolog variables from variables in other languages, the Prolog type of variable has often been called a *logical variable*.

3.3.1   Alternate Notations for Functors

We digress here briefly to discuss a useful extension to Prolog notation. In addition to the default parenthesized prefix notation for compound terms, Prolog allows unary functors to be used with a prefix or postfix notation, and binary functors in infix notation, given appropriate *operator declarations*. For example, the expressions

succ succ 0   3+4   f * *

are convenient notations for

succ(succ(0))   +(3,4)   *(*(f))   .

Prefix, postfix, and infix operators must be declared to Prolog. For Prologs of the Edinburgh family, the system can be informed about the operators used in this example by executing the following queries:

```
:- op(500, yfx, +).
:- op(300, fy,  succ).
:- op(300, yf,  *).
```

The final argument of the op predicate is simply the operator being declared. The first argument is the relative precedence of the operator, with larger numbers indicating lower precedence, that is, weaker binding and wider scope. Thus * will have a lower precedence number than +. The second argument provides its position (prefix, infix, postfix). In addition, it determines the iterability or associativity of the operator. We call a unary operator *iterable* if it can apply to an expression whose main functor has the same precedence. Noniterable can only apply to expressions whose main functor has lower precedence. Thus, succ above is an iterable operator, whereas the standard prefix operator ?- is noniterable. Nonassociative operators are defined analogously.

The affixing behavior of operators is determined according to the following table:

symbol	position	associativity
fx	prefix	noniterable
fy	prefix	iterable
xf	postfix	noniterable
yf	prefix	iterable
xfx	infix	nonassociative
yfx	infix	left associative
xfy	infix	right associative

The intuition behind these symbols is that in the case of an expression with two operators of equal precedence, one will be chosen as main functor such that the other occurs to the same side of the main functor as the y occurs to the side of the f. For example, since the + operator is declared yfx in Prolog, X+Y+Z will be parsed as (X+Y)+Z. The subordinate + comes on the left side of the main +. If the symbol associated with an operator has no y in it, expressions where it occurs with scope immediately over an operator of equal precedence will not be allowed at all.

Clearly, operator declaration queries are being executed for their side effects. As such, op is extralogical, and hence, not part of pure Prolog. These declarations should therefore be thought of as imperative *commands* to the system, not as part of the logical structure of a program. For further information about such declarations, refer to the manual for your Prolog system.

3.4 Lists

Returning to the main topic of the use of compound terms in Prolog programming, we consider a particular kind of data structure, lists, that will be especially useful in later programs.

The abstract notion of a finite sequence is a basic notion in mathematical descriptions of many concepts. For example, the sentences of a language can be represented as sequences of words. Formally, a sequence can be seen as a function from an initial segment of the natural numbers to some set, the elements of the sequence. Another view of sequences, which will be more useful here, is an inductive one following closely the inductive definition of the natural numbers. Given some set Σ of sequence elements, the set Σ^* of finite sequences of elements of Σ can be informally characterized as the smallest set satisfying the following conditions:

○ The *empty sequence* ⟨⟩ is a sequence.

o If s is a sequence and e an element of Σ, the pair (e, s) is a sequence with *head e* and *tail s*.

Thus $(1, (2, (3, \langle \rangle)))$ is a sequence of three elements: 1, 2, and 3. Notationally, of course, the more common expression of this sequence is $\langle 1, 2, 3 \rangle$. In the angle bracket notation, $\langle e_1, \ldots, e_n \rangle$ expresses the list whose head is e_1 and whose tail is expressed by $\langle e_2, \ldots, e_n \rangle$.

Sequences are represented in Prolog by *lists*. In Edinburgh Prolog, the empty sequence is represented by the *empty list* constant [ ], and the sequence (e, s) with head e and tail s is represented by the expression [e | s]. More generally, the sequence $(e_1, (\cdots (e_n, s) \cdots))$ is represented by the term [e_1, \ldots, e_n | s]. This can be abbreviated when s is the empty sequence to [e_1, \ldots, e_n].

For example,

[Head|Tail]   [a,b|X]   [a,b]

are respectively the Prolog representations of a sequence with head **Head** and tail **Tail**, a sequence with head **a** and tail the sequence with head **b** and tail **X**, and the sequence $\langle \text{a}, \text{b} \rangle$. The inductive conditions defining lists given above can then be represented by the Prolog program

```
list([]).
list([Head|Tail]) :- element(Head), list(Tail).
```

where the predicate **element** tests whether its argument belongs in the element domain. More generally, lists with any Prolog terms (including lists!) as elements can be characterized by the following program.

```
list([]).
list([_Head|Tail]) :- list(Tail).
```

In this program we used the common Prolog notational convention of giving a name beginning with an underbar to variables whose role is not to pass a value but merely to be a place holder, as the variable **_Head** is in the preceding program. Prolog further allows so-called *anonymous variables*, notated by a single underbar. Each occurrence of "_" as a variable name in a clause represents a distinct place-holder variable. For example, the two anonymous variables in **f(_,_)** are distinct, so the unification of that term with **f(a,X)** does not bind **X** to **a**. Anonymous variables are used for place-holder variables for those rare occasions in which naming the variable would detract from program readability.

Although we have introduced lists as a special notation for sequences, lists are Prolog terms like any other. Our inductive conditions for sequences involve two ingredients: the empty sequence and the pairing function that puts together an element and a sequence to make a longer sequence. As we have seen, the empty sequence is represented by the empty list constant [], which is just a Prolog constant. The pairing function is represented by the special notation [e | s], but in fact corresponds to a binary function symbol which in most Prolog systems is named ".". Thus, the lists shown earlier are shorthand notation for the Prolog terms

.(Head,Tail)   .(a,.(b,X))   .(a,.(b,[]))   .

Exercise 3.1 *What terms (expressed using the binary operator ".") do the following Prolog expressions abbreviate?*

1. [a,b,c]

2. [a|[b,c]]

3. [[a,b],c]

4. [[a,b]|c]

5. [[A|B]|C]

3.4.1   List Processing

Lists and the list notations above play an important role in the remainder of these notes. As examples of the definition of predicates over lists, we will give Prolog programs to concatenate, shuffle, and sort lists. Along the way, we will introduce some useful Prolog concepts—modes of use of Prolog predicates and Prolog arithmetic tests.

The basic form of list processing programs has been demonstrated by the list predicate itself, namely, the separating of two cases, one for the empty list, and one for nonempty lists of the form .(Head,Tail) or, equivalently, [Head|Tail].

List concatenation

The definition of the concatenation of two lists to form a third divides similarly into two cases. The base case occurs when concatenating the empty list to any list, which yields the latter unchanged. For nonempty lists, the concatenation is the head of the first list added to the recursive concatenation of the tail of the first list and the entire second list. The concatenation relation is implemented in Prolog by the predicate conc, which holds of three lists *l*, *r*, and *c* if *c* is the concatenation of *l* and

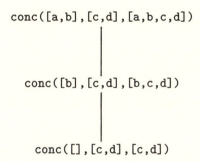

conc([a,b],[c,d],[a,b,c,d])

conc([b],[c,d],[b,c,d])

conc([],[c,d],[c,d])

Figure 3.1. Proof tree for concatenation query

r. Using juxtaposition to represent concatenation, the constraint can be stated $c = lr$.

Program 3.3
```
conc([], List, List).
conc([Element|Rest], List, [Element|LongRest]) :-
    conc(Rest, List, LongRest).
```

As an example of the operation of conc, consider the following goal:

```
?- conc([a,b],[c,d],Result).
Result = [a,b,c,d]
yes
```

Its proof tree is given in Figure 3.1. Note that although list concatenation is functional, in the sense that the third argument is uniquely defined by (hence functionally dependent on) the other two, it is implemented relationally in Prolog. We will see an advantage of this relational view of concatenation in the next example.

Shuffling lists

The shuffle of two lists consists of taking a few elements from the first list, the next few from the second, some more from the first, and so forth until the lists are exhausted. More formally, the shuffle relation holds between three lists l, r and s (i.e., s is a *shuffling* of l and r) if and only if there are (possibly empty) lists $l_1, \ldots, l_k$ and $r_1, \ldots, r_k$ such that $l = l_1 \cdots l_k$, $r = r_1 \cdots r_k$ and $s = l_1 r_1 \cdots l_k r_k$. That is, s contains interspersed all the elements of l and r, but maintains the original order of elements of l and r.

We can break this definition down recursively by considering the concatenation of l_1 and r_1 separate from the concatenations for the rest of l and r. In particular, we define s to be the shuffle of l and r if $s = l_1 r_1 s_{rest}$, where $l = l_1 l_{rest}$ and $r = r_1 r_{rest}$ and s_{rest} is a shuffle of l_{rest} and r_{rest}. To guarantee that this definition is well-founded, i.e., that the recursive shuffle is a smaller problem than the original, we require that one of l_1 and r_1 be nonempty. In fact, without loss of generality, we can assume that it is r_1 that is nonempty. Further, we can assume that r_1 contains exactly one element; call it e.

Exercise 3.2 *Why are these assumptions valid?*

We still must settle on the base case for the recursion. Because each recursive shuffle decreases the length of the second list by exactly one element, we can stop when this list is empty. In this case, the shuffle of l with the empty list is simply l. This definition can be translated directly into Prolog as follows:

Program 3.4

```
shuffle(L, [], L).
shuffle(L, [E|Rrest], S) :-
    conc(L1, Lrest, L),
    shuffle(Lrest, Rrest, Srest),
    conc(L1, [E|Srest], S).
```

In this program, the last argument is the shuffle of the first two. It is conventional in Prolog programming to place the arguments that tend to be thought of as inputs before those that are outputs.

Nondeterminism and modes

The shuffle program exhibits several important facets of Prolog programming. First, the notion of a shuffle of two lists, unlike the notion of concatenation, is intrinsically nondeterministic. But this causes no problem for the Prolog definition. Our definition will merely compute all the various shuffles by backtracking, e.g.,

```
?- shuffle([a,b], [1,2], Shuffle).
Shuffle = [1,2,a,b] ;
Shuffle = [1,a,2,b] ;
Shuffle = [1,a,b,2] ;
Shuffle = [a,1,2,b] ;
Shuffle = [a,1,b,2] ;
Shuffle = [a,b,1,2] ;
no
```

Second, `shuffle` demonstrates the *reversibility* of Prolog programs. In particular, the predicate `conc` is used in `shuffle` not only to concatenate two lists together (i.e., combining `L1` and `[R1|Srest]`), but also to take a list apart into two sublists (i.e., splitting `L` into `L1` and `Lrest`). Because Prolog programs like `conc` can be used to compute any of their arguments from any others, they are said to be reversible.

To capture the idea of which arguments are being computed on the basis of which others, the notion of a *mode* for a Prolog predicate can be defined. A mode tells which arguments are used as inputs and which as outputs. That is, it specifies which arguments on execution of the predicate are nonvariables and which are variables. Modes are typically notated by marking the input arguments with the symbol + and the outputs with -. Thus, the normal mode for `conc` in its use as a program for concatenating lists is `conc(+,+,-)`. But the mode of the first use of `conc` in the `shuffle` program is `conc(-,-,+)`. By reversibility of Prolog programs, we merely mean that the same program can be used in different modes, whereas in other languages, different programs must be designed for each mode.

Although the third argument to `conc` is functionally dependent on the other two, inverses of functions are not in general themselves functional. Thus using `conc` in mode `conc(-,-,+)` is nondeterministic. Indeed, this is the source of the nondeterminism of the `shuffle` predicate itself.

There are severe restrictions on the reversibility of Prolog programs. Pure Prolog programs that terminate when used in one mode may no longer terminate when used in another mode. Full Prolog programs with their metalogical facilities can exhibit completely different behavior when executed in different modes. Nonetheless, the use of Prolog programs with different modes is often a useful technique, and it is important to note that pure Prolog programs will never allow contradictory solutions just on the basis of being used in different modes. The worst that can happen is that execution in certain modes will not terminate.

Arithmetic tests and operations

While on the subject of mode limitations, we will mention some useful built-in predicates that are restricted to operate only in certain modes. These restrictions arise for reasons of efficiency or implementation ease but are in no way part of the logic. One may think of the restricted predicates as *approximations* to ideal, logically correct predicates, which the Prolog system has not implemented in their full generality.

The situation that arises when a restricted predicate is called in the wrong mode, that is, with improperly instantiated arguments, is called an *instantiation fault*. Different Prolog systems handle instantiation faults differently, but most will at least produce some kind of error message and stop the execution of the faulting goal. Therefore, when using restricted predicates, it is important to keep track of calling patterns for predicates to make sure that the restricted ones are called with the correct modes. This is shown clearly by the mergesort example in the next section.

Among the constants that Prolog allows are numbers. Numbers can be compared using a set of built-in Prolog predicates. For instance, the binary infix operator "<" holds of two numbers if the first is less than the second. The "<" operator operates only in the mode + < +, that is, neither argument may be a variable. Other arithmetic tests include ">" (greater than), "=<" (less than or equal to), and ">=" (greater than or equal to) and have the same mode restrictions. Without these mode restrictions, Prolog would either have to be able to backtrack through all pairs of numbers satisfying an arithmetic comparison, leading to combinatorial explosion, or to delay the execution of the comparisons until both arguments are instantiated. The latter approach has actually been implemented in a few experimental Prolog systems.

In fact, in Edinburgh Prolog the arithmetic predicates are sensitive not only to the modes of their arguments but also to their types, since only *arithmetic expressions* are allowed as the arguments of comparisons. An arithmetic expression is a term built from numeric constants and variables with various *arithmetic* operators such as +, *, -,and /, which is to be evaluated according to the usual arithmetic evaluation rules to produce a number. When an arithmetic-predicate goal is executed, all the variables in its expression arguments must be bound to numbers so that the expression may be evaluated to a number.

The best way to understand arithmetic expressions is to think of them as shorthand for sequences of calls to arithmetic relations defining the basic arithmetic operations. Thus, the goal

```
X*X + Y*Y > Z*Z
```

could be read as an abbreviation of

```
times(X, X, V1),
times(Y, Y, V2),
plus(V1, V2, V),
times(Z, Z, W),
V > W
```

where `times` and `plus` are hypothetical predicates that compute the obvious functions of their first two arguments.

For arithmetic calculations, Edinburgh Prolog provides the binary infix predicate `is` with mode ? `is` + (where ? in a mode is intended to mean that the input/output distinction is not being determined for this argument). The second argument of is is some arithmetic expression, and the first argument (typically a variable) is unified with the result of evaluating the second argument.

It should be noted that type restrictions on the arguments of a predicate are of a different nature from mode restrictions. Mode restrictions indicate that the implementation of a predicate is not able to cope with uninstantiated arguments, usually because the implementation needs to know more about the arguments to do anything sensible. The appropriate action for Prolog to take is therefore an instantiation-fault report. In contrast, failure to prove is the conceptually correct action in the face of arguments of incorrect type (e.g., non-numbers given to an arithmetic comparison predicate), since these arguments are merely outside the extension of the predicate. However, many Prolog systems signal an error on type restriction violations as an aid to debugging.

Sorting numbers

The final example is a program to sort lists of numbers. The algorithm we will use is called *mergesort* because the basic operation is the merging of two previously sorted lists. The merge of two sorted lists is a shuffle of the lists in which the output list is sorted.

Program 3.5
```
merge(A, [], A).
merge([], B, B).
merge([A|RestAs], [B|RestBs], [A|Merged]) :-
    A < B,
    merge(RestAs, [B|RestBs], Merged).
merge([A|RestAs], [B|RestBs], [B|Merged]) :-
    B =< A,
    merge([A|RestAs], RestBs, Merged).
```

Note that this merge operation is redundant, in the sense that there are two proofs for the goal merge([], [], Merged). As a result, we get the following behavior.

```
?- merge([], [], Merged).
Merged = [] ;
Merged = [] ;
no
```

We will carefully avoid invoking the merge predicate in this way, so that the redundancy will not affect the behavior of other programs.

Sorting using the merge operation consists of splitting the unsorted list into two smaller lists, recursively sorting the sublists, and merging the results into the final answer. The recursion bottoms out when the list to be sorted is too small to be split into smaller lists, that is, it has less than two elements, in which case the sorted list is identical to the unsorted.

Program 3.6
```
mergesort([], []).
mergesort([A], [A]).
mergesort([A,B|Rest], Sorted) :-
    split([A,B|Rest], L1, L2),
    mergesort(L1, SortedL1),
    mergesort(L2, SortedL2),
    merge(SortedL1, SortedL2, Sorted).
```

A simple (though nonoptimal) method for splitting a list into two lists of roughly equal size is to add alternate elements in the list to the sublists. Again, the base case of the recursion occurs when the list is too short.

Program 3.7
```
split([], [], []).
split([A], [A], []).
split([A,B|Rest], [A|RestA], [B|RestB]) :-
    split(Rest, RestA, RestB).
```

We can demonstrate the mergesort program and its various ancillary predicates with the following queries.
```
?- mergesort([3,1,4,2], [1,2,3,4]).
yes

?- mergesort([3,1,4,2], Sorted).
Sorted = [1,2,3,4]
yes
```

Note that `mergesort` cannot be used to "unsort" a sorted list (i.e., to generate permutations of a sorted list); it cannot be used in mode `sort(-,+)`. If it were so used, the execution of `merge` inside would be with mode `merge(?,?,-)`. Then the third clause of merge would execute < with mode ? < -. But < must be executed in mode + < +. Consequently, `mergesort` will not execute correctly in an "unsorting" mode. The impurity of < infects all programs that are built using it. Thus, the merging and sorting programs are not in the pure subset of Prolog.

Exercise 3.3 *Rewrite* merge *so that it does not generate redundant solutions.*

Exercise 3.4 *Write a definition for the binary predicate* member, *which determines whether its first argument is an element in the list that is its second argument. For instance, the following queries should work:*

```
?- member(a, [a,b,c]).
yes
?- member(d, [a,b,c]).
no
?- member(f(X), [g(a),f(b),h(c)]).
X = b
yes
```

Exercise 3.5 *Write a definition for the binary predicate* reverse, *which holds of two arguments if one is a list that is the reverse of the other. For instance, the following queries should work:*

```
?- reverse([a,b,c], [c,b,a]).
yes
?- reverse([a,b,c], [c,b,b,a]).
no
?- reverse([a,X,c], [Y,b,a]).
X = b, Y = c
yes
```

Exercise 3.6 *Write an alternative definition of* split *which works by placing the first half of the elements on one list and the rest on another. (HINT: The difficult part is determining when you have reached the middle of the list. Use a copy of the list as a counter to help you determine when you have moved half the elements.)*

3.4.2 Representing String Positions with Lists

An application of lists which we will use extensively is their use in representing string positions. This representation can serve as the basis of an alternative method for axiomatizing phrase-structure grammars. Instead of a specific set of connects clauses representing an input string as in Section 2.7.3, we have a single general clause:

Program 3.8
```
connects(Word, [Word|Rest], Rest).
```

Effectively, this clause induces a representation of each string position by *the substring following the position*. In particular, the position after the last word is represented by the empty list `[]`. For example, to use the grammar of Program 2.4 to parse the sentence

Terry writes a program that halts.

we need not put in unit clauses for the individual words. Instead, we use the list encoding of the string itself as the initial position and the empty list as the final position:

```
:- s([terry,writes,a,program,that,halts],[]).
yes
```

The single `connects` clause then describes the relation between the words and their surrounding positions.

3.5   The Logic and Operation of Prolog Revisited

The operation of pure Prolog should by now be relatively familiar. It seems appropriate, then, to return to the logical foundations of Prolog, the presentation of which was begun in Section 2.3, and extend it to the operation of Prolog presented informally in Sections 2.4 and 3.2.

For a logical language to be used for logic programming, we must have an effective *proof procedure* to test whether a goal statement is a consequence of the program.[2] This proof procedure must be efficient enough to make a proof step analogous in computational cost to, say, a function call in a traditional programming language; only in this way is the program execution (proof generation) sufficiently predictable in performance to qualify the proof procedure as a program execution mechanism.

Because of the strict requirements on the computational behavior of programs in the language, Prolog programs are restricted to definite clauses and queries to negative clauses. In this section, we discuss the proof procedure that this restriction makes possible, an instance of a class of Horn-clause proof procedures known as *SLD resolution*. First, however, we clarify some terms that have been used in the informal discussions of Prolog execution, namely *substitution* and *unification*.

---

[2] Actually, if the logical language is powerful enough to express all the kinds of relationships normally expressed by programs (i.e., all recursive relations), then the proof procedure will be only a *semidecision procedure*: If the goal statement is a theorem, the procedure will terminate with success, but it may loop for nontheorem goal statements—corresponding to the fact that the language can express partial recursive functions that are not total.

3.5.1   Substitutions

A *substitution* is a function from a set of variables $x_1, \ldots, x_k$ to terms $t_1, \ldots, t_k$. Such a function is notated $\{x_1 = t_1, \ldots, x_k = t_k\}$. The *application* of a substitution σ to an expression e, notated $[e]\sigma$, is the expression with all instances of the x_i replaced by the corresponding t_i. For example,

$$[f(x, g(y))]\{x = a, y = h(a, z)\} = f(a, g(h(a, z)))$$

If, for some σ, $[e_1]\sigma = e_2$, then e_2 is said to be an *instance* of e_1 and e_1 is said to *subsume* e_2. Thus $f(x, g(y))$ subsumes $f(a, g(h(a, z)))$. If e_1 subsumes e_2 but not vice versa, then e_1 is *more general than* e_2. Thus $f(x, g(y))$ is more general than $f(a, g(h(a, z)))$, but is not more general than $f(z, g(w))$.

3.5.2   Unification

Given two expressions e_1 and e_2, some substitutions σ may have the property that $[e_1]\sigma = [e_2]\sigma$; the substitution σ serves to transform the expressions into identical instances. Such a substitution is called a *unifying substitution* or *unifier* for e_1 and e_2. Not all pairs of expressions have unifiers. For example, there is no unifier for the expressions $f(a, x)$ and $f(b, y)$. However, when two expressions do have a unifier, they have one that can be considered most general. A *most general unifier* is a unifier that, intuitively speaking, makes no commitments that are not called for by the expressions; no extra variables are instantiated, nor are variables instantiated to more complex terms than is necessary. More formally, σ is a most general unifier for e_1 and e_2 if and only if for every unifier σ' of e_1 and e_2, $[e_1]\sigma$ subsumes (is no less general than) $[e_1]\sigma'$. When two expressions have a most general unifier, then that unifier applied to either of the two expressions is a *unification* of the two expressions.

The effect of most general unifiers is *unique up to renaming of variables*, in the sense that if σ and θ are most general unifiers of e_1 and e_2, then $[e_1]\sigma$ and $[e_1]\theta$ either are identical or differ only in the names of variables. Since the naming of variables in an expression is really an incidental property—unlike the sharing structure of the occurrences of the variables—we can think of uniqueness up to renaming as being, for all intents and purposes, actual uniqueness.

An algorithm that computes the most general unifier of two expressions is called a *unification algorithm*, and many such have been designed. We will not discuss the details of unification algorithms here, but mention one aspect of their design. A unification algorithm constructs a unifying substitution by finding "mismatches" between the two expressions and adding appropriate bindings to alleviate them. But consider the case of two expressions $f(x)$ and $f(g(x))$. Although there is no unifying substitution for these terms, a naive unification algorithm might note the mismatch between the variable x and the term $g(x)$ and construct the substitution $\{x = g(x)\}$. But applying this substitution to the two terms, we have $f(g(x))$ and $f(g(g(x)))$ respectively, which are not identical. Thus, the substitution is not a unifier for the expressions. This example demonstrates that an algorithm to compute most general unifiers must be careful not to construct substitutions in which a variable is assigned a term in which that variable occurs. For a unification algorithm to be correct, it must check that such occurrences do not exist; this test is typically referred to as the *occurs check*.

3.5.3   Resolution

Given the tools of substitutions and unification, we can return to the issue of proof procedures for Prolog. The use of refutation to construct proofs, as discussed in Section 2.3, is characteristic of Robinson's resolution principle. We will not discuss resolution in general here, but merely present its specialization to Horn clauses, which for historical reasons is called *SLD resolution*.

SLD Resolution: From a *query* (a negative Horn clause)

$$N_0 \wedge \cdots \wedge N_i \wedge \cdots \wedge N_m \Rightarrow$$

and a definite clause

$$C_0 \wedge \cdots \wedge C_k \Rightarrow P_0$$

where σ is a most general unifier of P_0 and N_i, produce the new query

$$[N_0 \wedge \cdots \wedge N_{i-1} \wedge C_0 \wedge \cdots \wedge C_k \wedge N_{i+1} \wedge \cdots \wedge N_m]\sigma \Rightarrow \qquad .$$

The new query is called the *resolvent* of the original query and clause, obtained by *resolving* P_0 and N_i. If the resolvent contradicts the program from which the definite clause was taken, then the original query does also.

As we have seen in Section 2.3, to find an instance of a goal G of atomic formulas that follows from a program, we try to show that the query $G \Rightarrow$ contradicts the program. We show such a contradiction with SLD resolution by constructing an *SLD derivation* of G, a sequence $R_0, \ldots, R_n$ of queries such that R_0 is $G \Rightarrow$, R_n is the empty clause and each element of the sequence is obtained from the preceding one by an SLD resolution step. Since the empty clause indicates contradiction, we have shown that the original query $G \Rightarrow$ contradicts the given definite-clause program.

Each step in the derivation, from R_{i-1} to R_i, has an associated substitution σ_i. The goal instance $[G \Rightarrow]\sigma_1 \cdots \sigma_n$ is a counterexample to the query, which as we have seen means that $[G]\sigma_1 \cdots \sigma_n$ is a consequence of the program. Because the substitutions are most general unifiers, this consequence is the most general instance of the goal that follows by using this particular sequence of program clauses. The derivation sequence can be seen as a traversal of a proof tree for the goal.

3.5.4   Prolog's proof procedure

Prolog's proof procedure, then, amounts to a particular instance of SLD resolution. As described above, resolution is nondeterministic in that there are many resolvents that follow from a given query, corresponding to the choice of literal in the query to resolve, and the choice of rule to resolve the query literal against. The Prolog proof procedure makes these choices as follows: literals in a query are resolved from *left to right*, and rules are tried in order from *top to bottom* in a *depth-first, backtrack* search.

The proof procedure is depth-first because all ways of refuting a given resolvent are tried before backtracking to try a different resolvent (by choosing a different rule to resolve against). As should be apparent, the discussions of Prolog execution in Sections 2.4 and 3.2 were merely informal descriptions of the Prolog variant of SLD resolution.

3.5.5   Semantics of Prolog

Because of their relationship to Horn-clause logic, Prolog programs have both a declarative and a procedural semantics. The declarative semantics of a program plus query is derivative on the semantics of the Horn-clause subset of FOL. A goal follows from a program just in case the conjunction of its negation and the program is unsatisfiable.

Note that the declarative semantics makes no reference to the sequencing of literals within the body of a clause, nor to the sequencing of clauses within a program. This sequencing information is, however, very relevant for the procedural semantics that Prolog gives to Horn clauses.

The procedural semantics reflects SLD resolution. A goal follows from a program just in case the negated goal and program generate the empty clause by the Prolog proof procedure, that is, left-to-right, top-to-bottom, depth-first, backtracking SLD resolution.

The Prolog proof procedure gives Horn-clause programs an interpretation in terms of more usual programming constructs. The set of clauses with a particular predicate in the consequent is the *procedure* that *defines* the predicate. Each clause in a procedure is like a case in a *case* or *conditional* statement. Each literal in the antecedent of a clause is a *procedure call*.

This analogy with programming concepts for Algol-like languages is the basis of very efficient implementation techniques for Prolog. However, this efficiency is bought at some cost. The two semantics for Prolog diverge at certain points. The procedural semantics lacks *completeness* and *soundness* relative to the declarative semantics.

The lack of completeness in the Prolog proof procedure results from the fact that Prolog's depth-first search for a proof may not terminate in some cases where in fact there is a proof. We saw this problem in Program 2.3.

The lack of soundness comes from a property of the Prolog proof procedure that we have heretofore ignored, namely, the lack of an occurs check (Section 3.5.2) in Prolog's unification algorithm. The occurs check is too expensive for general use in a basic operation of a computation mechanism as unification is in Prolog; thus the unification algorithm used by Prolog is not sound. However, this unsoundness is not a problem for the great majority of practical programs.[3]

Further divergence of the two semantics results from extralogical mechanisms that have been introduced into Prolog. Some of these are discussed in Chapter 5.

3.6 Problem Section: Terms and Lists

Tree Manipulation

Suppose we encode trees like the parse trees of Section 2.7 using Prolog terms in the following way. Internal tree nodes will be encoded with the binary function symbol node whose first argument is the node label, and whose second is a list of the children of the node. Leaves of the tree will be encoded with the unary function symbol leaf whose single argument is the label at the leaf. Thus the tree of Figure 2.4 would be encoded as the Prolog term

```
node(s, [node(np, [node(det, [leaf(a)]),
                   node(n, [leaf(program)]),
                   node(optrel, [])]),
         node(vp, [node(iv, [leaf(halts)])])])
```

Although this method for encoding trees is more complex than the one we will use for parse trees in Section 3.7.1, this method is preferable for general tree-manipulation programs because it limits the number of functors introducing tree nodes to two.

---

[3]There is also a way to reinterpret the Prolog proof procedure in a domain of [conceptually] infinite terms such that it is sound with respect to that class of interpretations (Colmerauer, 1986; Jaffar and Stuckey, 1986.)

The fringe of a tree is just the leaves of the tree in order. Thus, the fringe of the example tree is the list [a, program, halts]. In formal-language theory, the fringe of a parse tree is called the *yield* of the tree.

Problem 3.7 *Write a program implementing the relation* fringe(Tree, List), *which holds just in case* Tree, *a tree encoded as above, has fringe* List.

Simplifying Arithmetic Expressions

Terms can represent arithmetic expressions. Using function symbols + and * and representing variables by the term x(V) and constants by c(C), we can represent the expression

$$x_1 + x_2 * (0 + 1)$$

by the term

    +(x(1), *(x(2), +(c(0), c(1))))

or, using the fact that + and * are infix operators in most Prologs,

    x(1) + x(2) * (c(0) + c(1))   .

However, this arithmetic expression can be simplified using certain identities. Because zero is the additive identity, $0 + 1$ can be simplified to 1. Because one is the multiplicative identity, $x_2 * 1$ can be simplified to x_2. Thus the whole expression can be simplified to $x_1 + x_2$.

Problem 3.8   *Write a program that implements the binary relation* simplifies_to *such that the following behavior is engendered:*

    ?- simplifies_to(x(1) + x(2) * (c(0) + c(1)), S).
    S = x(1) + x(2)
    yes

You can use simplifications such as the multiplicative and additive identities, distributivity of multiplication over addition, multiplication by zero, and so forth. (HINT: In general it is preferable to simplify an expression after simplifying its arguments.)

Tree Grammars[4]

In the same way as phrase-structure grammars define sets of strings in terms of rules that rewrite nonterminal symbols, one may define certain classes of trees in terms of rules that rewrite certain nonterminal tree nodes into other trees. This is best explained in terms of the representation of trees as logic terms.

Let Σ be a set of function symbols and X a set of variables. Then the set of Σ-terms over X $\mathcal{T}_\Sigma(X)$ is the least set of terms satisfying the following inductive conditions:

o If $x \in X$ then $x \in \mathcal{T}_\Sigma(X)$.

o If $f \in \Sigma$ is a n-ary function symbol and $t_1, \ldots, t_n$ are terms in $\mathcal{T}_\Sigma(X)$, then $f(t_1, \ldots, t_n) \in \mathcal{T}_\Sigma(X)$.

That is, $\mathcal{T}_\Sigma(X)$ is the set of terms built from the variables in X with the function symbols in Σ. In this definition and in what follows, constants are identified with nullary function symbols.

Let $\Sigma = N \cup T$ where N (the *nonterminals*) and T (the *terminals*) are two disjoint sets of function symbols. Nonterminals stand for tree nodes that may be rewritten into subtrees, terminals for nodes of the final trees. A tree all of whose nodes are terminal is called a *terminal* tree.

Tree rewriting is done by *productions* that are the tree analog of phrase-structure grammar rules. A production over Σ is a pair $(A(x_1, \ldots, x_n), t)$ (which is conventionally written $A(x_1, \ldots, x_n) \rightarrow t$). A is an n-ary non-terminal, $x_1, \ldots, x_n$ are variables and $t \in \mathcal{T}_\Sigma(\{x_1, \ldots, x_n\})$. This production states that a term with main function symbol A and subterms $t_1, \ldots, t_n$ may be rewritten into the new term $[t]\sigma$, where σ is the substitution $\{x_1 = t_1, \ldots, x_n = t_n\}$. Notice that by definition every variable that occurs in t is one of the x_i.

For example, consider $N = \{S_3\}$, $T = A_2, B_2, C_2, a_0, b_0, c_0$ and the production $S(x_1, x_2, x_3) \rightarrow S(A(a, x_1), B(b, x_2), C(c, x_3))$. Figure 3.2 shows the application of this rule to a node of a tree to derive a new tree.

In general, productions can apply to any node of a tree and not only to the root node. To define this formally, consider a set of productions Π, a ground term t, and one of its subterms s. Clearly, there is a unique nonground term $c \in \mathcal{T}_\Sigma(\{x\})$ such that $t = [c]\{x = s\}$. Assume that there is a rule $s' \rightarrow u$ in Π such that s' and s unify with most general unifier σ. Then we say that t *rewrites* into $t' = [c]\{x = [u]\sigma\}$, in symbols $t \Rightarrow t'$. Informally, we have applied the production to the subtree s of t

---

[4]This section and the included problems are intended primarily for the formally inclined reader.

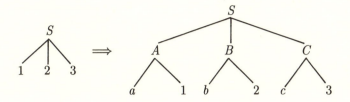

Figure 3.2. A tree rewrite

and replaced s in t by the result $[u]\sigma$ of the production. As usual, we will use the notation $t \stackrel{*}{\Rightarrow} t'$ for the reflexive-transitive closure of the rewriting relation.

Formally, a *context-free tree grammar* is a triple (Σ, S, Π) of a finite function symbol (tree node) alphabet divided in terminals and nonterminals as above, a finite set Π of productions over Σ and a finite set S of *start trees*, which are ground terms over Σ. A terminal tree (term) t is the *tree language* generated by the grammar if there is a start tree $s \in S$ such that $s \stackrel{*}{\Rightarrow} t$. Finally, the *string language* yielded by a tree grammar is the set of the yields of the trees generated by the grammar.

Context-free tree grammars are so called because productions apply freely to tree nodes without regard for the form of the tree above or below the node. One should carefully distinguish this notion of context-freeness from the one for string grammars. The string languages yielded by context-free tree grammars are in general in the class of *indexed languages*, which is a larger class than that of context-free languages (Aho, 1968; Rounds, 1969).

Problem 3.9 *Write a context-free tree grammar whose yield is the set of strings $a^n b^n c^n$ for $n > 0$.*

In the problems that follow, you may want to take advantage of the encoding for trees used in the previous section.

Problem 3.10 *Define an encoding of context-free tree grammars in Prolog. You should give encodings for terminals, nonterminals, start trees, and productions.*

Problem 3.11 *It can be shown (Maibaum, 1974) that when constructing a derivation of a terminal tree from a start tree of a context-free tree grammar it is only necessary to consider production applications to* outermost *nonterminal nodes, that is, nodes whose ancestors are all terminals. This strategy* *is called* outside-in *(O-I) rewriting. Using the encoding from the last problem, write a program that performs O-I rewriting to nondeterministically generate terminal trees in the tree language of an arbitrary context-free tree grammar. In this problem, you must use the search order of Prolog to avoid looping without producing any answers. Use the grammar of Problem 3.9 to test your program.*

3.7   Definite Clause Grammars

In Section 2.7 we saw how to translate CFGs into Horn clauses, in fact into definite clauses. This translation method can be used as the basis for an extension of CFGs based on definite clauses, *definite-clause grammars* (DCGs).

The general form of the definite clause associated with a context-free grammar rule

$$N_0 \rightarrow V_1 \cdots V_n$$

is (in Prolog notation)

```
n0(P0, P) :- v1(P0, P1), ..., vn(Pn-1, P).
```

We can generalize such an axiom by allowing, in addition to the two predicate arguments for the string positions, additional arguments that further specify the expression type. For instance, suppose we want to distinguish the *number* of noun and verb phrases—whether they are singular or plural—so as to guarantee that sentences are composed of NPs and VPs *with the same number.* We might extend the axiomatization of the grammar and dictionary with an additional argument in certain predicates (e.g., np, vp, pn) encoding number. A fragment of such a grammar would look like this:

Program 3.9
```
s(P0, P) :-
    np(Number, P0, P1),
    vp(Number, P1, P).
np(Number, P0, P) :-
    pn(Number, P0, P).
vp(Number, P0, P) :-
    tv(Number, P0, P1),
    np(_, P1, P).
vp(Number, P0, P) :-
    iv(Number, P0, P).
```

```
pn(singular, P0, P) :- connects(shrdlu, P0, P).
pn(plural,   P0, P) :- connects(they, P0, P).
iv(singular, P0, P) :- connects(halts, P0, P).
iv(plural,   P0, P) :- connects(halt, P0, P).
tv(singular, P0, P) :- connects(writes, P0, P).
```

As an example, the first rule in this grammar encoding states that an s
(sentence) may be an np (noun phrase) with number value **Number** followed
by a vp (verb phrase) with the same number. Note the use of an anonymous variable (Section 3.4) for the object NP in the transitive verb rule
as a way of ignoring the number of the object. This grammar admits the
sentence "SHRDLU halts" but not "*SHRDLU halt"[5] even though both verbs
are intransitive.

```
:- s([shrdlu,halts], []).
yes
:- s([shrdlu,halt], []).
no
:- s([they,halt], []).
yes
```

Just as the two-argument-predicate clauses can be seen as encoding
context-free grammars, these multiple-argument-predicate clauses can be
seen as encoding a generalization of context-free grammars, called *definite-
clause grammars* (DCG). DCGs differ from CFGs just in the way this
extended encoding of rules in Horn clauses differs from the simple two-
argument encoding: A DCG nonterminal may have *arguments* just like
the arguments of a predicate, and a terminal symbol may be an arbitrary
term. For instance, the extended Prolog encoding above axiomatizes the
following definite-clause grammar. (We here use the FOL conventions for
variables and constants discussed in Section 2.3.)

$$S \rightarrow NP(x_{num}) \ VP(x_{num})$$
$$NP(x_{num}) \rightarrow PN(x_{num})$$
$$VP(x_{num}) \rightarrow TV(x_{num}) \ NP(y_{num})$$
$$VP(x_{num}) \rightarrow IV(x_{num})$$

---

[5] We are here using the convention from the linguistics literature that in discussions
of grammaticality, ungrammatical strings are prefixed with asterisks to highlight the
fact that they are not expressions of English. Of course, this is just an expository
device; the asterisks themselves have no place in grammars that people write.

$$PN(s) \rightarrow shrdlu$$
$$PN(p) \rightarrow they$$
$$IV(s) \rightarrow halts$$
$$IV(p) \rightarrow halt$$
$$TV(s) \rightarrow writes$$

The meaning of a DCG rule is given by translating the rule into a definite clause using the same mapping as for context-free rules except that now an n-argument nonterminal is translated into an $n + 2$-argument literal in which the final two arguments represent string positions.

Definite-clause grammars are so useful that Prolog systems often include a special notation for encoding them directly, rather than having to go through the clumsy translation described above. In particular, the notation used within Prolog to notate a DCG rule is the following:

- Predicate and function symbols, variables, and constants obey normal Prolog syntax.

- Adjacent symbols in the right-hand side of a DCG rule are separated by the "," operator, just like literals in a clause.

- The arrow in a DCG rule is "-->".

- Terminal symbols are written inside Prolog list brackets "[" and "]".

- The empty string is represented by the empty list constant "[]".

For example, the DCG grammar painstakingly encoded in Program 3.9 could be directly stated *in Prolog* using the Prolog DCG notation as:

```
s --> np(Number), vp(Number).
np(Number) --> pn(Number).
vp(Number) --> tv(Number), np(_).
vp(Number) --> iv(Number).

pn(singular) --> [shrdlu].
pn(plural) --> [they].
iv(singular) --> [halts].
iv(plural) --> [halt].
tv(singular) --> [writes].
```

The Prolog DCG notation allows context-free grammars to be stated directly in Prolog as well, since CFGs are a special case of DCGs. In so

doing, the Prolog statements of the grammars are considerably more succinct. For instance, the English fragment of Program 2.4 could be directly
stated in Prolog as:

Program 3.10
```
s --> np, vp.
np --> det, n, optrel.
np --> pn.
vp --> tv, np.
vp --> iv.
optrel --> [].
optrel --> [that], vp.

pn --> [terry].
pn --> [shrdlu].
iv --> [halts].
det --> [a].
n --> [program].
tv --> [writes].
```

In fact, Prolog systems typically perform the appropriate translation from
DCG rules like these to Prolog clauses immediately upon reading the program, and the clauses are stored internally in the fully expanded form.
Consequently, queries will receive the same replies as the expanded version, e.g.,

```
:- s([terry,writes,a,program,that,halts],[]).
yes
```

The connection between definite-clause grammars and Prolog is a close
one. But it is important to keep in mind that DCGs are a formal language independent of their Prolog encoding just as Horn clauses are of
their instantiation in Prolog programs. For instance, just as Prolog is an
incomplete implementation of Horn-clause theorem-proving, the DCG notation as interpreted by Prolog is incomplete for DCGs in the abstract. We
have tried to emphasize the difference by using a different notation (akin
to that of CFGs) for DCGs in the abstract, before presenting the Prolog
notation. The distinction between DCGs in the abstract and their statement in Prolog using the special notation is important to keep straight as
it has, in the past, been the source of considerable confusion.

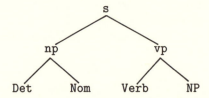

Figure 3.3. A partially specified tree

3.7.1   Trees for Simple Sentences

The DCG ability to add arguments to the nonterminals in a grammar is useful in a variety of ways. The addition of more detailed syntactic information such as agreement features, which we saw in the previous section and which will be explored in more detail in later problems, is just one of these. Indeed, much of the remainder of these notes is merely elaboration on this basic capability.

As a simple example of the utility of argument-passing in DCGs we will develop a grammar which not only recognizes the strings in the fragment of English of Program 3.10, but also builds a representation of the parse tree for the sentence, encoded as a Prolog term.

Terms can be seen as partially specified trees in which variables correspond to as yet unspecified subtrees. For example, the term

    s(np(Det,Nom),vp(Verb,NP))

corresponds to the (partial) tree of Figure 3.3 in which the variables may be replaced by any trees.

It is therefore only natural to use terms to represent parse trees in definite clause grammars. To do this, every nonterminal predicate will have an argument representing the parse tree for that portion of the string covered by the nonterminal. For each nonterminal there will be a homonymous function symbol to represent a node of that type. Finally, we will use a constant, epsilon, to represent an empty subtree.

The following DCG covers the same fragment of English as the CFG axiomatized in Program 3.10, but it adds an argument to each nonterminal predicate to carry the parse tree. Once the DCG is translated into a Prolog program, the execution of the resulting program is very similar to that of the earlier one, except that unification incrementally builds the tree for the sentence being analyzed.

Program 3.11
```
s(s(NP,VP)) --> np(NP), vp(VP).
np(np(Det,N,Rel)) --> det(Det), n(N), optrel(Rel).
np(np(PN)) --> pn(PN).
vp(vp(TV,NP)) --> tv(TV), np(NP).
vp(vp(IV)) --> iv(IV).
optrel(rel(epsilon)) --> [].
optrel(rel(that,VP)) --> [that], vp(VP).

pn(pn(terry)) --> [terry].
pn(pn(shrdlu)) --> [shrdlu].
iv(iv(halts)) --> [halts].
det(det(a)) --> [a].
n(n(program)) --> [program].
tv(tv(writes)) --> [writes].
```

For example, the analysis of "Terry writes a program that halts" would be as follows:

```
?- s(Tree, [terry,writes,a,program,that,halts],[]).
Tree = s(np(pn(terry)),
         vp(tv(writes),
            np(det(a),
               n(program),
               rel(that,
                   vp(iv(halts))))))
yes
```

Notice that the parse tree for a noun phrase without a relative clause still includes a relative clause node covering the symbol epsilon representing the empty string.

```
?- np(Tree, [a, program], []).
Tree = np(det(a),
          n(program),
          rel(epsilon))
yes
```

3.7.2   Embedding Prolog Calls in DCGs

The abstract DCG formalism augments CFGs by allowing nonterminals to take extra arguments which, through the sharing of logical variables, allow passing of information among subphrases. However, no other form of computation other than this sharing of information is allowed. The Prolog notation for DCGs goes beyond this limited form of computation in DCGs by providing a mechanism for specifying arbitrary computations over the logical variables through direct execution of Prolog goals. Prolog goals can be interspersed with the terminals and nonterminals on the right-hand side of a DCG rule. They are distinguished from the grammatical elements notationally by being embedded under the bracketing operator "{···}".

Removing extraneous tree nodes

As a simple example, we will modify the parse-tree-building grammar in such a way that noun-phrase parse trees do not include nodes for empty relative clauses. There are several methods for achieving this behavior. We take the simple expedient of building the parse tree for the NP using a separate Prolog program for this purpose. Thus, the only change to the grammar involves a modification of the NP formation rule.

```
np(NP) --> det(Det), n(N), optrel(Rel),
              {build_np(Det,N,Rel,NP)}.
```

The `build_np` predicate operates in mode `build_np(+,+,+,-)`, building the parse tree for an NP from the trees for the subconstituents. In the case where the relative-clause tree is empty, no node is included in the output parse tree.

```
build_np(Det, N, rel(epsilon),
         np(Det,N)).
build_np(Det, N, rel(that,VP),
         np(Det,N,rel(that,VP))).
```

Using this modified grammar, the behavior of the grammar on simple noun phrases becomes:

```
?- np(Tree, [a, program], []).
Tree = np(det(a),
          n(program))
yes
```

Simplifying the lexicon

One of the most common uses for adding Prolog goals to a DCG is the simplification of the encoding of the lexicon. Imagine a DCG with a large lexicon. Rather than encoding the lexicon with separate DCG rules for each lexical item, e.g.,

```
...
n --> [problem].
n --> [professor].
n --> [program].
...
```

it is much simpler and less redundant to have a single DCG rule:

```
n --> [Word], {n(Word)}.
```

that says that the nonterminal n can cover any terminal symbol that is an n. Along with this single rule, we need a *dictionary* like this:

```
...
n(problem).
n(professor).
n(program)
...
```

The utility of this technique is magnified in the context of lexical items associated with extra arguments. If an argument is directly computable from the word itself, the lexical entry can perform the computation and the dictionary entry need not give a value for the argument. Such is the case for the parse trees associated with terminal symbols. Thus, for the parse-tree-building grammar, the lexical entries might look like

```
n(n(Word)) --> [Word], {n(Word)}.
```

And for arguments that are idiosyncratically related to the word, for example, grammatical number, the dictionary entry will contain this information in tabular form.

```
n(Number) --> [Word], {n(Word, Number)}.
...
n(professors, plural).
n(program,   singular).
n(programs,  plural).
...
```

In fact, a more succinct encoding of grammatical paradigms uses unit clauses to list the entries in the paradigm as a table and uses the lexicon rules to decode the table. For instance, for nouns we might have

```
n(singular) --> [Word], {n(Word, _)}.
n(plural  ) --> [Word], {n(_, Word)}.
...
n(professor, professors).
n(project,   projects).
n(program,   programs).
...
```

For verbs, the table might include entries for each form of the verb, as is done in Appendix A.

Using this technique in the English fragment we have been developing, we have the following grammar, with dictionary augmented to include some lexical items we will find useful in later examples.

Program 3.12

```
s --> np, vp.

np --> det, n, optrel.
np --> pn.

vp --> tv, np.
vp --> iv.

optrel --> [].
optrel --> [that], vp.

det --> [Det], det(Det).
det(a).     det(every).
det(some).  det(the).

n --> [N], n(N).
n(author).      n(book).
n(professor).   n(program).
n(programmer).  n(student).

pn --> [PN], pn(PN).
pn(begriffsschrift).  pn(bertrand).
pn(bill).             pn(gottlob).
pn(lunar).            pn(principia).
pn(shrdlu).           pn(terry).
```

```
tv --> [TV], tv(TV).
tv(concerns).   tv(met).
tv(ran).        tv(wrote).

iv --> [IV], iv(IV).
iv(halted).
```

3.8   Problem Section: DCGs

3.8.1   The Syntax of First-Order Logic

First-order formulas are built from the following *vocabulary*:

o A countable set of *variables* V,

o Countable sets F_n of n-ary *function symbols* for each $n \geq 0$ (the elements of F_0 are also called *constants*),

o Countable sets P_n of n-ary *predicate symbols* for each $n \geq 0$,

o The *connectives* $\forall, \exists, \vee, \wedge, \neg$, and

o The punctuation marks (,) and ,.

The set of first-order *terms* is the smallest set satisfying the following conditions:

o Each variable is a term.

o If f is an n-ary function symbol (an element of F_n) and $t_1, \ldots, t_n$ are terms, then $f(t_1, \ldots, t_n)$ is a term. As a special case, if $n = 0$, f as a term can be written without parentheses. In such a case, f is referred to as a *nullary function* or, more simply, a *constant*.

The set of *well-formed* formulas (*wffs*) is the smallest set satisfying the following conditions:

o If p is an n-ary predicate symbol (an element of P_n) and $t_1, \ldots, t_n$ are terms, $p(t_1, \ldots, t_n)$ is a wff.

o If p is a wff and x is a variable, $(\forall x)p$ and $(\exists x)p$ are wffs.

o If p_1 and p_2 are wffs, $(p_1 \vee p_2)$ and $(p_1 \wedge p_2)$ are wffs.

o If p is a wff, $\neg p$ is a wff.

For example
$$(\forall x)(= (x, 0) \vee (\exists y) = (s(y), x))$$
is a wff assuming that x and y are in V, 0 is in F_0, s is in F_1 and $=$ is in P_2.

Problem 3.12 *Define an encoding of the vocabulary of first-order logic as Prolog terms. Your encoding should represent each vocabulary item as a distinct Prolog term in such a way that the representation of each type of item (variable, function symbol, predicate symbol, etc.) is distinguishable from all the others. Using this representation, write a DCG defining the set of wffs. (HINTS: Make sure you can distinguish function and predicate symbols of different arities; if for your solution you need an encoding of numbers, you can either use the successor notation for numbers or the built-in arithmetic facilities of Prolog discussed in Section 3.4.1).*

A term or wff *occurs* in a wff iff the term was used in constructing the wff according to the inductive definition of wffs given above. A string of one of the forms '$(\forall x)$' or '$(\exists x)$' is a *binder* for x. In a wff of the form $B\ p$ where B is a binder and p is a wff, p is the *scope* of B. An occurrence of a variable x is *bound* in a wff if and only if the variable occurrence occurs within the scope of a binder for x. A wff is *closed* if and only if every one of its variable occurrences is bound. For example,

$$(\forall x)p(x, x)$$

is closed but

$$(\forall x)p(x, y)$$

is not.

Problem 3.13 *Modify your wff analyzer to accept only closed wffs.*

A binder for x in a wff is *vacuous* if there is no occurrence of x in the scope of the binder. For example, the binder $(\exists x)$ is vacuous in

$$(\exists x)p(a) \qquad .$$

Problem 3.14 *Modify your wff analyzer to accept only closed wffs without vacuous binders.*

3.8.2   Extending Syntactic Coverage

The following problems deal with extending the sophistication of the syntactic treatments in the grammars we are developing.

Possessives

The grammar of Program 3.12 does not accept sentences using the English possessive construction, such as "Every student's professor's book concerns some programmer's program". In general, a noun phrase followed by the possessive suffix *'s* plays the same syntactic role as a determiner. Thus, an appropriate parse tree for the sentence above would be Figure 3.4.

Problem 3.15 *Extend the DCG above to accept the English possessive construction according to the analysis exemplified in this analysis tree. Assume that the possessive suffix is represented by the constant s in the input string. Testing the DCG will probably be unsuccessful as the analysis will undoubtedly be left-recursive.*

The analysis of possessives illustrated in the tree of Figure 3.4 is *left-recursive*, that is, a phrase type X has a possible analysis as $X\alpha$. (In this particular case, the noun phrases may be analyzed as a noun phrase followed by an *'s* and a noun.)

As the discussion in the previous problem and Section 2.5.2 show, left-recursive analyses cause problems with the use of Prolog as a DCG parser. A possible technique to avoid this problem is to transform (by hand, or, in some cases, automatically) a left-recursive grammar into one without left-recursion that is *weakly equivalent* to the original one, that is, that accepts exactly the same strings even though it assigns them different structures.

Problem 3.16 *Develop a non-left-recursive grammar for the English sentences covered by the grammar in the last problem. To what extent are systematic methods for converting left-recursive CFGs to weakly equivalent non-left-recursive ones (such as are discussed by Hopcroft and Ullman (1979, pages 94–99)) applicable to definite-clause grammars?*

Problem 3.17 *(Easy) Modify your solution of the previous problem to produce a parse tree, as was done in the previous section.*

Problem 3.18 *(More difficult) Modify your solution of Problem 3.16 to produce left-recursive parse trees like the one given above. How general is your method?*

Problem 3.19 *Modify your solution so that so-called* heavy NPs, *e.g., noun phrases with relative clauses, are disallowed in possessives. For instance, the following NP should be ungrammatical according to the grammar: "* a program that halts's programmer".*

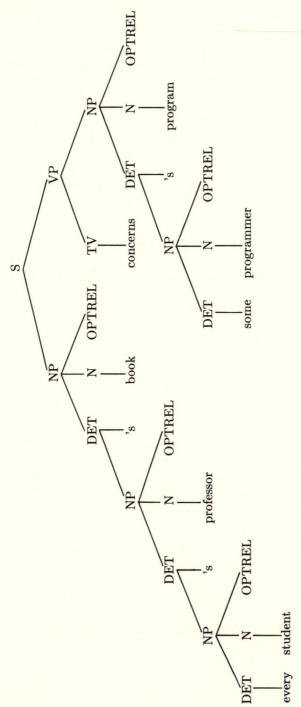

Figure 3.4. Parse tree with possessives

Prepositional Phrases

Prepositional phrases (PP) are used in English in a variety of ways. They can play the role of an adverbial phrase modifying the entire action described by a verb and its complements, as in

> Terry wrote a program with a computer.
> Every professor wrote a book for a dollar.

And like relative clauses, they can modify a class of objects given by a noun, e.g.,

> Every program in Bill's book halts.
> Alfred met a student with a problem.

In Problem 4.6, we will see yet another role for PPs.

Typical analyses of the structure of English sentences containing PPs place them as siblings to the constituent they modify. Thus, adverbial PPs are siblings of VPs (or, under certain conditions, Ss), and noun-modifying PPs are siblings of N (like relative clauses). There are two ways that such a configuration could come about. Consider the VP-modifying adverbial PPs. The PP could occur under the S node, just as the VP does. Alternatively, a new node under the S could cover both the VP and the PP. Usually, this node is considered to be a VP itself, thus allowing for a left-recursive VP structure. Linguistically, this analysis may be preferred because it allows for several adverbials to follow a VP. The left recursion, however, presents a problem for Prolog; therefore, we will assume the former analysis. Indeed, the positioning of relative clauses directly under NP as a sibling of the noun was chosen for the same reason, to avoid the left recursion implicit in the more traditional analysis.

Note that the first and last example sentences include the same categories of lexical items, i.e.,

> *PN TV Det N P Det N*

Yet intuitively the first PP modifies the verb phrase—it is the writing of the program that is performed with a computer—while the second does not modify the VP—it is not the meeting of the student that is performed with a problem. These two sentences are thus syntactically *ambiguous*, though semantically only one of the two *readings* seems plausible. This phenomenon of ambiguity in the structural placement of PPs is often called the *PP attachment problem*.

Problem 3.20 *Write DCG rules to allow adverbial and NP-modifier PPs such as those above. You will need rules not only for the prepositional* *phrases themselves but also for their use in modifying VPs and NPs. Is your grammar ambiguous, that is, does it display the PP attachment ambiguities discussed above? How might you augment the grammar (presumably with semantic information) so that spurious readings are filtered out?*

Subject-Verb Agreement

In Section 3.7 we alluded to the phenomenon of subject-verb agreement in English. This problem explores the phenomenon in greater detail.

In English, subjects agree with the verb they are the subject of both in person (first, second or third) and in number (singular or plural). For instance, the string "*I writes programs" is not a grammatical English sentence because the word "I" is a first-person, singular noun phrase, whereas the verb "writes" is third-person, singular. On the other hand, "I write programs" is grammatical because "write" is a first-person singular verb. Of course, it is also second-person singular as in "you write programs" and any-person plural as in "they write programs", "we write programs", etc.

The problem is compounded in that in complex noun phrases, such as "a programmer" or "all programmers", both the determiner and the noun carry agreement information. So we have "all programmers write programs" but not "* all programmers writes programs" or "* a programmers write programs" or "* a programmers writes programs". A final complication is the fact that certain determiners, nouns, and verbs are unmarked for person or number or both. For instance, as we have seen above, the word "write" viewed as a plural verb is unmarked for person. The determiner "the" is unmarked for number, as seen in "the programmer" and "the programmers". Rarer are nouns that are unmarked for number. Examples include so-called summation plurals (e.g., *scissors, binoculars, jeans*), certain foreign words (e.g., *corps, chamois*, although there is a difference in pronounciation despite identical spelling in the singular and plural), certain other words ending in *-s* (e.g., *crossroads, species, series*), some nationality terms (e.g., *Chinese, Eskimo*) and some other idiosyncratic nouns (e.g., *offspring, aircraft*), and certain zoological terms (e.g., *fish, sheep, salmon,* etc.

Thus, we have "a fish swims" and "all fish swim". We could handle this phenomenon by having separate lexical entries for the singular noun *fish* and the plural noun *fish* just as we would have separate entries for the noun *fish* and the verb *fish*, but a nicer solution is to allow entries to be unmarked for person and/or number. Nonetheless, the less elegant solution is still needed for the first/second-person singular verb *write*, since leaving it unmarked for person would allow the string "* he write a program" as a sentence.

Problem 3.21 *Extend the grammar so that it requires that subjects agree with verbs in sentences and that determiners and nouns agree as well. You should do this by adding a single extra argument to appropriate nonterminals to hold agreement information. Discuss the following facets of the solution:*

1. *How the various strings are or are not admitted (parsed) by the grammar.*

2. *How certain lexical entries can be underspecified for certain agreement information. Demonstrate at least the full paradigm of agreement of the verb* halt *and the verb* be, *that is, make sure you have sufficient lexical entries for all the forms of the verb.*

3. *What you do for proper nouns and pronouns.*

4. *Why it is preferable to use only one argument position for agreement.*

(For the purposes of these problems you can think of pronouns like I, we, he, *etc. as merely a type of proper noun.)*

Relative Clause Agreement

Agreement in English does not stop at the subject and the verb of the whole sentence. Even subclauses like relative clauses display this phenomenon. Thus the string

A program that concerns Bertrand halted.

is a grammatical sentence whereas

*A program that concern Bertrand halted.

is not, even though in both cases the subject "a program..." agrees with the verb *halted.* The problem, of course, is that the *implicit* subject of the verb phrase in the relative clause "concern Bertrand" is that same phrase "a program" (often called the *head* of the relative clause), but the verb *concern* is either plural or first- or second-person singular, whereas "a program" shows third-person singular agreement.

Problem 3.22 *Extend your grammar so that it captures the phenomenon of agreement between heads of relative clauses and the verbs in the relative clause. Again demonstrate that your solution interacts appropriately with normal subject-verb agreement, underspecified lexical entries, etc.*

Subcategorization

We have seen in previous grammars that different verbs require different *complements*, that is, phrases following them in the verb phrase. So, for instance, the verb *wrote* requires a single noun phrase following it as in the VP "met Bertrand". Thus the string "*met Bertrand a book" is not a grammatical VP (or anything else for that matter), nor is "*met". On the other hand, the verb *gave* requires (or, in the linguistics jargon, *subcategorizes for*) two NPs, not one, as in the VP "gave Bertrand a book", but not "*gave Bertrand". This phenomenon of *subcategorization* has been primitively encoded in previous grammars in the distinction between TVs (transitive verbs) and IVs (intransitive verbs). In this problem we will investigate subcategorization in more detail.

One possible solution to the subcategorization problem is to associate another argument to each verb, its subcategorization type. Then for each type, we would have a rule that admitted only verbs of the appropriate type. Here is a piece of a grammar using this method of subcategorization (but ignoring agreement, verb form, etc.):

Program 3.13

```
vp --> v(intransitive).
vp --> v(transitive), np.
vp --> v(ditransitive), np, np.
vp --> v(dative), np, pp.
...
v(intransitive) --> [halted].
v(transitive) --> [met].
v(ditransitive) --> [gave].
v(dative) --> [gave].
...
```

(By *dative* here we mean that the verb requires a noun phrase and a prepositional phrase with the preposition *to* as in "gave the book to Bertrand". Thus the verb *gave* has two subcategorization frames: ditransitive and dative.)

The phenomenon has been called subcategorization because the extra argument puts verbs into subclasses, or subcategories, of the main category *verb*. Estimates by linguists as to the number of different *subcategorization frames*, i.e., types of subcategorization, vary, but at least 30 such rules are postulated for English by Gazdar et al. (1985) and probably many more would be required. Estimates run as high as the tens of thousands (Gross, 1975). For this reason (and the fact that we have already given this solution), we will not use this sort of attack on the problem.

Instead, we will use a different technique for handling subcategorization. We will have a single rule allowing a verb phrase to be formed from a verb followed by a sequence of zero or more complements where a complement is either a noun phrase or a prepositional phrase. The verb will have a list of complement types in its lexical entry. For instance, the verb *gave* might have the list [np,np], the verb *halted* might have the empty list []. While building up the sequence of complements, the grammar will keep track of the types of the complements and make sure they match the list in the lexical entry for the verb. The sequence of complements "Bertrand a book" would have the associated list of types [np,np]. Since this matches the lexical entry for the verb *gave*, the grammar would allow "gave Bertrand a book" but since it doesn't match the empty list, the grammar would disallow "*halted Bertrand a book".

Problem 3.23 *Extend your grammar so that it handles subcategorization requirements of verbs in the way just described. Demonstrate that it allows appropriate verb phrases and sentences and conversely for non-sentences. Then extend the solution to capture the fact that the verb* gave *requires a prepositional phrase with the preposition* to *whereas* bought *requires a PP with the preposition* from, *e.g., "bought a book from Bertrand".*

Notice that in either of the subcategorization methods mentioned here a PP complement is (a subconstituent of) a sibling of the verb, rather than a sibling of the VP as adverbial PPs are. This can be a further source of the kind of grammatical ambiguity discussed in Problem 3.20.

3.9   Bibliographic Notes

Edinburgh Prolog syntax is so simple that a detailed account of the syntax is rarely required when programming. The manual for each particular Prolog implementation usually contains a full description of the syntax for reference purposes. Appendix I of the DEC-10 Prolog manual contains such a description for the Edinburgh family of Prologs (Bowen, 1982).

Functional programming (Section 3.3) has been developed for many of the same reasons as logic programming has been (Backus, 1978). Efforts to introduce functional and equational notions into logic programming languages have been numerous. A good cross-section can be found in the book by DeGroot and Lindstrom (1986). Equality (i.e., equational logic) as a sufficient basis for logic programming is developed by O'Donnell (1985).

The term "logical variable" (Section 3.3) was introduced by D. H. D. Warren (1977) to distinguish the specific procedural properties given to the variables in definite clauses by Prolog, or more generally by SLD proof procedures, from both the variables of imperative languages (names for assignable locations) and the variables of functional languages (names for values). The distinguishing characteristics of logical variables include their role in standing for as yet unfilled parts of a term and their ability to become coreferential through variable-to-variable bindings.

Lists as a data structure (Section 3.4) are heavily used in languages other than Prolog. In particular, the programming language LISP (which stands for LIST Processing) makes heavy use of lists. Many introductory LISP books are available, but few introduce the subject as simply and clearly as the original LISP 1.5 Programmers' Manual (McCarthy, *et al.*, 1965). The modern LISP dialect SCHEME is thoroughly discussed in an excellent textbook by Abelson and Sussman (1985).

The notion of modes (Section 3.4.1) for predicates in logic programs appeared first in the DEC-10 Prolog. Mode declarations allowed the DEC-10 Prolog compiler to generate better code for predicates known to be used only in certain modes (Warren, 1977; Warren, 1979). The concept has since then been explored as an additional control mechanism for logic programs (Clark and McCabe, 1981; Naish, 1986) and in global program-optimization techniques (Mellish, 1985).

Mode assignments depend on the particular order of calls in a program. Thus correct mode assignments are program properties tied to the program's procedural interpretation. Other properties, such as what types of arguments predicates accept, depend only on the declarative interpretation of programs (Mycroft and O'Keefe, 1984; Mishra, 1984). Type assignments to predicates can be useful both for program verification and for compilation. Methods to compute both declarative and procedural properties of Prolog programs, among them mode and type assignments, often rely on the techniques of *abstract interpretation*, a means of analyzing the properties of programs by interpreting them over simplified data domains in which the properties of interest are computable (Mellish, 1986; Jones and Søndergaard, 1987).

As we noted before, the resolution method (Section 3.5) is due to Robinson (1965). Resolution, substitutions, and unification are covered in any of the automated deduction books mentioned on Section 1.5; Robinson's treatment (1979) is particularly clear. The special case of SLD resolution is discussed by Lloyd (1984), who gives a detailed mathematical account of the semantics of Prolog.

Definite-clause programs define relations over the *Herbrand universe*, the set of all ground terms built from the constants and function symbols in the program. It is possible to represent the tape of a Turing machine as a term, and it is then not difficult to show that the relation betweeen initial and final configurations for any Turing machine can be represented by a definite-clause program (Tärnlund, 1977). Furthermore, it is possible to show that any computable function on terms, for a suitable definition of computation on terms, can be represented without encoding of the data by a definite-clause program (Andreka and Nemeti, 1976). The overall computation model given by SLD resolution is rather similar to the alternating Turing machine model (Shapiro, 1982). Background material on notions of computability and decidability from computer science and logical perspectives can be found in the books by Hopcroft and Ullman (1979) and Boolos and Jeffrey (1980) respectively.

The concept of definite-clause grammar (Section 3.7) was introduced by Pereira and Warren (1980). DCGs are a simplification of Colmerauer's *metamorphosis grammars* (1978), which were the first grammar formalism based on Horn clauses. Metamorphosis grammars and definite-clause grammars are two instances of *logic grammars*, grammar formalisms whose meaning is given in terms on an underlying logic. Even from a fixed logic such as definite clauses, one can construct distinct formalisms depending on what grammatical notions one chooses to make part of the formalism instead of representing explicitly by grammar rules. Examples of such formalisms include extraposition grammars (Pereira, 1981), definite-clause translation grammars (Abramson, 1984) and gapping grammars (Dahl and Abramson, 1984). The basic notion of logic grammar has also been instantiated within other logics, in particular Rounds's logics for linguistic descriptions, which formalize certain aspects of DCGs to give logical definitions for natural recognition-complexity classes of formal languages (Rounds, 1987).

The construction of efficient sorting algorithms (Section 3.4.1) is of course a very important problem in computer science. The most thorough design and analyses of sorting algorithms (Knuth, 1973) have usually been done for random-access memory machine models. It is possible to rewrite many of those algorithms (eg. bubblesort, quicksort) for Prolog's declarative model, but in general the computational cost of the algorithm will change, because the sequences to be sorted are encoded as lists rather than as arrays with direct access to all elements. Algorithms specifically designed to sort lists, such as mergesort, are more suitable for implementation in Prolog, which is the reason for our choice of example.

Tree grammars (Section 3.6) were introduced as the grammatical counterparts of generalized automata that operate on trees (Rounds, 1969). The yields of regular tree grammars (finite-state-tree automata) are exactly the context-free languages, and the yields of context-free tree grammars are exactly the indexed languages (Rounds, 1970). Indexed languages have another characterization, the *indexed grammars* introduced by Aho (1968; Hopcroft and Ullman, 1979), which are much closer in form to definite-clause grammars.

Arithmetic expression simplification is a particular case of the general problem of rewriting an expression according to a set of equations giving the algebraic laws of the operators in the expressions, e.g., associativity or commutativity. The rewriting method we suggest in Section 3.6 is rather simple-minded. More sophisticated approaches involve methods to determine an *orientation* for equations so that the result of applying an equation is in some appropriate sense simpler than the starting expression, and methods for *completing* a set of equations so that the order of application of oriented equalities does not matter. These techniques are surveyed by Huet and Oppen (1980) and Buchberger (1985).

Subcategorization has been a primary phenomenon of interest in modern linguistics, and there are as many analyses of the phenomenon as there are linguistic theories, if not more. We start by using a subcategorization method (Program 3.12) loosely based on the terminology of Montague grammar. The first augmentation (Program 3.13) is inspired by Gazdar et al. (1985). Section 3.8.2 works toward an analysis common in the logic programming field; it was first published by Dahl (1981) and extended by several authors such as McCord (1982). Similar analyses employing lists, but in slightly different ways, can be found in HPSG (Sag and Pollard, 1986) and PATR-II (Shieber, 1985a).

The PP attachment problem (Section 3.8.2) has received much attention in the computational linguistics literature. A particularly detailed discussion is that of Church (1980; Church and Patil, 1982). Pereira (1982) discusses the problem from a logic grammar perspective.

4

Further Topics in
Natural-Language Analysis

In this chapter, we will be concerned with extending the capabilities and coverage of grammars in two ways. First, we will explore grammars that express not only syntactic but also semantic relationships among constituents. These grammars incorporate constraints on how the meaning of a phrase is related to the meanings of its subphrases. Second, we will extend the range of syntactic constructions covered by previous grammars. Both of these kinds of extensions will prove useful in the next chapter in the development of a simple natural-language question-answering system.

4.1 Semantic Interpretation

First, we turn to the incorporation of semantic information into a DCG. A common way to model the semantics of a natural language is to associate with each phrase a *logical form*, that is, an expression from some logical language that has the same truth conditions as the phrase. A simple recursive method for maintaining such an association is possible if the logical form associated with a phrase can be composed out of the logical forms associated with its subparts. This *compositional* method for modeling the semantics of a natural language is the hallmark of the highly influential work by the logician Richard Montague and his students and followers.

Montague used a higher-order logic based on the typed lambda calculus, *intensional logic*, as the language for logical forms. We will describe a vastly simplified form of compositional semantics inspired by Montagovian techniques but using first-order logic extended with an untyped lambda calculus as the logical form language. Then we will show how such a semantics can be encoded in a DCG which builds logical forms in the course of parsing. A technique of general utility, *partial execution*, will be introduced as a method with which we can simplify the DCG. We will then proceed to discuss several topics in the encoding of semantics, namely, quantifiers, quantifier scope, and (after the appropriate syntactic background in Section 4.2) filler-gap dependencies.

4.1.1   The Lambda Calculus

In the semantics we will develop, logical forms for sentences will be expressions in first-order logic that encode propositions. For instance, the sentences "SHRDLU halts" and "Every student wrote a program" will be associated with the first-order logic expressions $halts(shrdlu)$ and $(\forall s)student(s) \Rightarrow (\exists p)(program(p)\&wrote(s,p))$, respectively.

We again emphasize the differences between the FOL notation we use here (see Section 2.3) and the notation for Prolog. The differences help to carefully distinguish the abstract notion of logical forms from the particular encoding of them in Prolog. FOL formulas will later be encoded in Prolog not as Prolog formulas, but as terms, because our programs are treating the formulas as *data*.

Most intermediate (i.e., nonsentential) logical forms in the grammar do not encode whole propositions, but rather, propositions with certain parts missing. For instance, a verb phrase logical form will typically be a proposition parameterized by one of the entities in the situation described by the proposition. That is, the VP logical form can be seen as a *function* from entities to propositions, what is often called a *property* of entities. In first-order logic, functions can only be specified with function symbols. We must have one such symbol for each function that will ever be used. Because arbitrary numbers of functions might be needed as intermediate logical forms for phrases, we will relax the "one symbol per function" constraint by extending the language of FOL with a special function-forming operator.

The lambda calculus allows us to specify functions by describing them in terms of combinations of other functions. For instance, consider the function from an integer, call it x, to the integer $x + 1$. We would like to specify this function without having to give it a name (like *succ* as we have done previously). The expression $x + 1$ seems to have all the information needed to pick out which function we want, except that it does not specify what in the expression marks the argument of the function. This problem may not seem especially commanding in the case of the function $x + 1$, but when we consider the function specified by the expression $x + y$, it becomes clear that we must be able to distinguish the function that takes an integer x onto the sum of that integer and y from the function that takes an integer y onto the sum of it and x.

Therefore, to pick out which variable is marking the argument of the function, we introduce a new symbol "λ" into the logical language (hence the name "lambda calculus"). To specify a function, we will use the notation

$$\lambda x.\phi \quad ,$$

where x is the variable marking the argument of the function and ϕ is the expression defining the value of the function at that argument. Thus we can specify the successor function as $\lambda x.x + 1$ and the two incrementing functions can be distinguished as $\lambda x.x + y$ and $\lambda y.x + y$. We will allow these *lambda expressions* anywhere a functor would be allowed. For instance, the following is a well-formed lambda calculus term:

$$(\lambda x.x + 1)(3) \quad .$$

Intuitively, such a function application expression should be semantically identical to the expression $3 + 1$. The formal operation called (for historical reasons) *β-reduction* codifies this intuition. The rule of β-reduction says that any expression of the form

$$(\lambda x.\phi)a$$

can be reduced to the (semantically equivalent) expression

$$[\phi]\{x = a\} \quad ,$$

that is, the expression ϕ with all occurrences of x replaced with a. We ignore here and in the sequel the problem of renaming of variables, so-called *α-conversion*, to avoid capture of free variables. In the examples to follow, we will always make sure that variables in the various lambda-calculus expressions being applied are distinct. The scoping rules of Prolog (Section 2.5.1), being geared toward logical languages in the first place, guarantee the appropriate scoping of variables in the case of the encoded logical language as well. In fact, this is one of the advantages of using Prolog variables to encode variables in the logical form language, as we will do in Section 4.1.3 below.

We will see in the next section how the lambda calculus and β-reduction can be used to provide a simple compositional semantics for a fragment of English.

4.1.2   A Simple Compositional Semantics

We will now consider how to specify a semantics for the fragment of English given as the context-free grammar in Section 2.7 and axiomatized in

Programs 2.4 and 3.10. We will associate with each context-free rule a corresponding rule for composing the logical forms of the subconstituents into the logical form for the parent constituent. For instance, associated with the rule

$$S \to NP \ VP$$

we will have the rule[1]

> **Semantic Rule 1:** If the logical form of the *NP* is *NP'* and the logical form for the *VP* is *VP'* then the logical form for the *S* is *VP'(NP')*.

and with the rule

$$VP \to TV \ NP$$

we will associate

> **Semantic Rule 2:** If the logical form of the *TV* is *TV'* and the logical form of the *NP* is *NP'* then the logical form for the *VP* is *TV'(NP')*.

For instance, the sentence "SHRDLU halts" can be decomposed into an NP and a VP. Suppose the logical form for the NP "SHRDLU" is *shrdlu* and that for the VP "halts" is *halts*. Then by Semantic Rule 1 above, the logical form for the whole sentence will be *halts(shrdlu)*, an expression which, under the natural interpretation and idealizations, has the same truth conditions as the sentence "SHRDLU halts". So far, no use of the lambda calculus extension to first-order logic has been needed.

Now consider the sentence "Bertrand wrote *Principia*". Again, we will have the logical forms for the proper nouns "Bertrand" and "*Principia*" be *bertrand* and *principia* respectively. The logical form for the transitive verb "wrote" will be the lambda expression $\lambda x. \lambda y. wrote(y, x)$. By the second rule above, the VP "wrote *Principia*" will be associated with the expression $(\lambda x. \lambda y. wrote(y, x))(principia)$, which by β-reduction is equivalent to $\lambda y. wrote(y, principia)$. Now by the first rule above, the sentence "Bertrand wrote *Principia*" is associated with the logical form $(\lambda y. wrote(y, principia))(bertrand)$, which, β-reducing again, is equivalent to $wrote(bertrand, principia)$. The derivation can be summarized in the parse tree of Figure 4.1, which has been annotated with appropriate logical forms. Similar semantic rules could be given to the other context-free rules in the grammar to allow the building of logical forms for a larger class of phrases.

---

[1] By convention, we will notate variables representing the logical form associated with a nonterminal by adding a prime suffix.

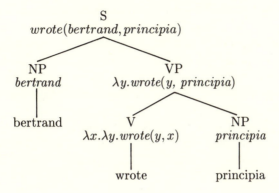

Figure 4.1. Parse tree with logical forms

Exercise 4.1   *What do the following lambda-calculus expressions reduce to?*

1. $(\lambda x.halts(x))(shrdlu)$
2. $((\lambda y.\lambda x.halts(x))(shrdlu))(lunar)$
3. $(\lambda y.\lambda p.\lambda x.wants(x, p(y))))(shrdlu)(\lambda z.halts(z))(terry)$
4. $(\lambda y.yy)(\lambda y.yy)$

4.1.3   Encoding the Semantic System in Prolog

We now turn to the issue of encoding such a grammar with compositional semantics in Prolog. Several problems face us. First, we must be able to encode logical forms in Prolog. Second, we must be able to associate with each constituent an encoded lambda expression. Finally, we must be able to encode the process of β-reduction.

As mentioned before, we will encode all FOL expressions—both formulas and terms—as Prolog terms, since we will be manipulating them as data within the DCGs. As it turns out, we will encode FOL variables in Prolog as Prolog variables, and FOL function symbols as Prolog function symbols, but this is where the isomorphism stops, for FOL quantifiers, predicate symbols, and connectives will also receive encodings as Prolog function symbols. In particular, we will encode the universal quantification $(\forall x)\phi$ with the Prolog term all(X, ϕ'), where ϕ' is the Prolog encoding of ϕ. Similarly, $(\exists x)\phi$ is encoded as exists(X, ϕ').[2] The implication and conjunction connectives are encoded with the binary infix functor symbols

---

[2] From a strict logical point of view, the use of Prolog variables to encode FOL variables is incorrect, being a case of confusion between object variables (those in the logical

"=>" and "&" respectively. All FOL predicate and function symbols are encoded by their homonymous Prolog function symbols.

Lambda expressions consist of a variable and a logical expression which uses that variable. We will encode the pairing of the variable with the expression with a new infix binary Prolog operator, the caret "^". Thus the lambda expression $\lambda x.x + 1$ would be encoded in Prolog as `X^(X+1)`. Similarly, the lambda expression $\lambda x.\lambda y.wrote(y, x)$ would be encoded as the Prolog term `X^Y^wrote(Y,X)`, assuming right associativity of "^".[3]

We solve the second problem—associating an encoded lambda expression with each constituent—using the by now familiar technique of adding an argument position to each nonterminal to hold the logical form encoding. So a skeletal DCG rule for combining an NP and VP to form an S (ignoring for the moment the constraints on the logical forms expressed in Semantic Rule 1) will be:[4]

```
s(S) --> np(NP), vp(VP).
```

which can be read as "a sentence with logical form S can be formed by concatenating a noun phrase with logical form NP and a verb phrase with logical form VP".

Finally, we model the application of a lambda expression and subsequent β-reduction with the predicate `reduce`. The intended interpretation of a literal `reduce(Function, Arg, Result)` is that `Result` is the β-reduced form of the application of the lambda expression `Function` to the argument `Arg`. We implement the predicate with the following single unit clause.

Program 4.1
```
reduce(Arg^Expr, Arg, Expr).
```

The earlier examples of β-reduction can now be handled by this Prolog encoding. For instance, corresponding to the reduction of the application

---

form) and metalanguage variables (those in Prolog, the metalanguage used here to describe the relation between strings and logical forms). It would be possible to avoid this confusion between object and metalanguage variables with a somewhat more complicated description. However, this particular abuse of notation, if properly understood, is unlikely to cause problems and brings substantial benefits in program simplicity.

[3] There is precedent for the use of the caret to form lambda expressions. The notation that Montague himself used for the lambda expression $\lambda x.\phi$ was (ignoring details of intensionality operators) $\hat{x}\phi$, which we have merely linearized.

[4] For ease of expression within the Prolog syntax, we drop the priming convention when writing Prolog clauses.

$(\lambda x.halts(x))(shrdlu)$ to the logical form $halts(shrdlu)$ we have the following Prolog dialogue:

```
?- reduce(X^halts(X), shrdlu, LF).
LF = halts(shrdlu)
```

The other examples are handled similarly.

The **reduce** predicate performs a single outermost reduction. It does not reduce a lambda expression until no further reductions can be performed. That is, it does not reduce to *canonical form*. For instance, consider an expression that has a variable bound by a λ used as a function in the body of the lambda expression, e.g., $\lambda p.p(a)$. When this lambda expression is itself applied to, say, $\lambda y.f(y)$, the result can be reduced to $f(a)$. The Prolog encoding of the former expression, `P^P(a)`, is not even well-formed. Even if it were, the **reduce** predicate does not perform internal reductions, but only the reduction associated with the outermost expression. When expressions with internal applications like this are needed, we will be forced to implement the internal applications with explicit **reduce** literals. For instance, the troublesome lambda expression $\lambda p.p(a)$ could be implemented as `P^Q` where `reduce(P,a,Q)` holds.

Using the **reduce** predicate, we can now directly encode the compositional semantic rules described above. For the first semantic rule applying the VP logical form to that of the NP, we add to the DCG an appropriate extra condition.

```
s(S) --> np(NP), vp(VP), {reduce(VP,NP,S)}.
```

Similarly, for the verb-phrase rules, we have,

```
vp(VP) --> tv(TV), np(NP), {reduce(TV, NP, VP)}.
vp(VP) --> iv(VP).
```

Lexical entries must now include semantic information.

```
tv(X^Y^wrote(Y,X)) --> [wrote].
iv(X^halts(X)) --> [halts].
np(shrdlu) --> [shrdlu].
np(terry) --> [terry].
```

Given this augmented grammar and lexicon, which is merely the direct encoding of the type of compositional semantic rules presented at the beginning of this section, we can parse simple sentences while building encodings of their logical forms in the process.

```
?- s(LF, [shrdlu, halts], []).
LF = halts(shrdlu)
yes

?- s(LF, [terry, wrote, shrdlu], []).
LF = wrote(terry, shrdlu)
yes
```

and so forth.

4.1.4 Partial Execution

In this section, we will introduce a technique called *partial execution* which is a device of general utility for the manipulation of Prolog (and other logic and functional) programs. Partial execution of a program involves the replacing of certain computations that would normally be performed at execution time by changes to the program itself.

Pure Prolog programs are particularly well suited for partial execution because this technique is just a different way of applying the basic Horn-clause computation rule, resolution, that is used for normal execution. For instance, consider the DCG rule

```
s(S) --> np(NP), vp(VP), {reduce(VP,NP,S)}.
```

The computation of the `reduce` condition is deterministic and involves only the mutual binding of several variables. If we change the clause by performing these bindings in the clause itself, we can actually remove the `reduce` literal, since its purpose has been fulfilled. In the case at hand, `reduce` merely requires that VP be of the form NP^S. If we guarantee this in the clause, i.e.,

```
s(S) --> np(NP), vp(NP^S).
```

we can leave off the application, as it is already implicit in the clause. The clause is said to have been *partially executed with respect to the* `reduce` *predicate*.

Similarly, we can partially execute the transitive VP clause to get

```
vp(VP) --> tv(NP^VP), np(NP).
```

Partial execution becomes more complex in the face of nondeterminism. If the literal we are removing from a clause by partial execution has several solutions, we must replace the original clause by all of the possible partial executions of the original. Clearly, partial execution of a clause with respect to a literal is useful only if there are a finite number of solutions to the literal in the context of the clause. If there are potentially an infinite number, then we must in general wait until run time to execute the literal, in the hope that the previous computation will provide enough restrictions on the goal literal to limit the search space.

From now on, we will often eschew explicit `reduce` literals by implicitly partially executing the clauses so as to remove them. We will discuss partial execution in more detail in Section 6.4.

4.1.5   Quantified Noun Phrases

In attempting to extend the technique of compositional semantics to the rest of the context-free grammar in Program 3.12, we immediately run into problems with the rule for quantified noun phrases. Consider a sentence such as "every program halts". The natural first-order logical form for this sentence is

$$(\forall x) program(x) \Rightarrow halts(x) \quad .$$

Using the encoding of FOL as Prolog terms, this would be

```
all(X, program(X) => halts(X))      .
```

Notice that the main functor of the expression is the universal quantifier, whereas the application of the logical form for "halts" will always result in the main functor of the output being the predicate *halts*. This problem in term manipulation is actually the formal reflex of a much deeper problem noticed by Montague, which led to a drastic reorganization of his compositional semantics. Unlike the simple two-rule grammar above, in which verb-phrase logical forms apply to noun phrases, Montague required noun phrases (which are, of course, the source of the quantifier functors) to apply to verb phrase arguments. For instance, for the sentence "every program halts", the verb "halts" will retain its logical form $\lambda x.halts(x)$, but the noun phrase will have the LF $\lambda q.(\forall p) program(p) \Rightarrow q(p)$. Applying the noun phrase LF to that of the verb phrase, we have

$$(\lambda q.(\forall p) program(p) \Rightarrow q(p))(\lambda x.halts(x)) =$$
$$(\forall p) program(p) \Rightarrow (\lambda x.halts(x))(p) =$$
$$(\forall p) program(p) \Rightarrow halts(p) \quad .$$

The DCG rule encoding this revised application direction is

```
s(S) --> np(VP^S), vp(VP).
```

The verb phrase logical forms will be encoded as before. Noun phrases, on the other hand will now be of the form

```
Q^all(M, (program(M) => R))        ,
```

where R is the application of Q to M, that is, `reduce(Q,M,R)` holds. (Recall that such internal applications would not be performed automatically by the `reduce` predicate, so we must list them explicitly.) In fact, we can remove this extra condition by partial execution with respect to the `reduce` predicate, yielding the rather more cumbersome

```
(M^R)^all(M, (program(M) => R))      .
```

The LF associated with the noun "program" we will take to be the simple property of being a program, that is, $\lambda x.program(x)$ encoded in Prolog as `X^program(X)`. Determiners will be functors from noun logical forms (simple properties) to the complex NP logical forms like that above. Thus, the determiner "every" will have the logical form

$$\lambda p.\lambda q.(\forall x)p(x) \Rightarrow q(x)$$

encoded in Prolog (with applications removed by partial execution) as

```
(X^P)^(X^Q)^all(X,(P => Q))      .
```

The lexical entry for "every" is therefore

```
det( (X^P)^(X^Q)^all(X,(P => Q)) ) --> [every].
```

As implied above, determiners will be functions on their noun arguments, so the DCG rule for NP formation (ignoring relative clauses for the moment) is:

```
np(NP) --> det(N^NP), n(N).
```

Exercise 4.2 *Check that these rules and lexical entries allow for the following parse, and give its proof tree.*

```
?- s(LF, [every, program, halts], []).
LF = all(X, (program(X) => halts(X)))
yes
```

Given the reorientation of application, we have developed an appropriate LF for determined noun phrases, but we must rework the encoding of proper noun meanings we were using before. Clearly, their LFs must be modified to respect the new application direction. In particular a proper noun like "SHRDLU" must, like all NPs, be a function from VP-type LFs to full sentence LFs; that is, it must be of the form

```
VP^S     ,
```

where `reduce(VP, shrdlu, S)` holds. By partial execution, we have the relatively unintuitive logical form

```
(shrdlu^S)^S     .
```

In any case, the lexical entry

```
np( (shrdlu^S)^S ) --> [shrdlu].
```

allows the parse

```
?- s(LF, [shrdlu, halts], []).
LF = halts(shrdlu)
yes
```

as before.

The logical form for "SHRDLU" seems unintuitive because it is not the encoding of any lambda expression. The position that should be occupied by a variable is occupied by a constant `shrdlu`. Actually, we have seen a similar phenomenon before in LFs for determiners and noun phrases, in which the same position is occupied by a full lambda expression. Partial execution of applications can yield bizarre expressions, exactly because the execution is partial. Only part of the work of β-reduction is done, the remainder being performed at run time when the appropriate variables are instantiated. Thus, we should not worry too much that the encoding of the lambda expressions we are using has certain properties that the calculus in the abstract does not have.

Finally, modifying the transitive verb phrase rule, again changing the direction of application, consider the verb phrase "wrote a program", which should have the LF $\lambda z.(\exists p)program(p)\&wrote(z,p)$. Recall that the LFs for "wrote" and for "a program" are, respectively, $\lambda x.\lambda y.wrote(y,x)$ and $\lambda q.(\exists p)program(p)\&q(p)$. Thus we want the VP's LF to be $\lambda z.NP'(TV'(z))$.

Exercise 4.3 *Check that this lambda expression is the appropriate one for NP' and TV' as in the example above.*

In Prolog, we have:

```
vp(Z^S) -->
    tv(TV), np(NP),
    {reduce(TV,Z,IV),
     reduce(NP,IV,S)}.
```

which through partial execution is equivalent to

```
vp(Z^S) --> tv(Z^IV), np(IV^S).
```

The full fragment of Program 3.12, augmented so as to produce logical forms, is given below.

Program 4.2

```
:- op(500,xfy,&).
:- op(510,xfy,=>).

s(S) --> np(VP^S), vp(VP).

np(NP) -->
    det(N2^NP), n(N1), optrel(N1^N2).
np((E^S)^S) --> pn(E).

vp(X^S) --> tv(X^IV), np(IV^S).
vp(IV) --> iv(IV).

optrel((X^S1)^(X^(S1 & S2))) --> [that], vp(X^S2).
optrel(N^N) --> [].

det(LF) --> [D], {det(D, LF)}.
det( every, (X^S1)^(X^S2)^all(X,(S1=>S2)) ).
det( a,     (X^S1)^(X^S2)^exists(X,S1&S2) ).

n(LF)    --> [N], {n(N, LF)}.
n( program, X^program(X) ).
n( student, X^student(X) ).

pn(E) --> [PN], {pn(PN, E)}.
pn( terry,  terry  ).
pn( shrdlu, shrdlu ).

tv(LF) --> [TV], {tv(TV, LF)}.
tv( wrote, X^Y^wrote(X,Y) ).
```

```
iv(LF) --> [IV], {iv(IV, LF)}.
iv( halts, X^halts(X) ).
```

Exercise 4.4 *Check that the grammar as augmented now allows the following parses, and give their proof trees:*

```
?- s(LF, [terry, wrote, shrdlu], []).
LF = wrote(terry, shrdlu)
yes

?- s(LF, [every, program, halts], []).
LF = all(P,program(P)=>halts(P))
yes

?- s(LF, [every, student, wrote, a, program], []).
LF = all(S,student(S)=>
            exists(P,program(P)&
                    wrote(S,P)))
yes
```

Exercise 4.5 *How does this grammar handle the semantics of relative clauses?*

The role of unification and the logical variable in incrementally building complex representations is clearly evident in DCGs that describe the relation between natural-language sentences and their logical meaning representations.

We can illustrate the order in which a logical form is built during parsing by the analysis trace of the sentence "Every program halts". The trace has been simplified by replacing variables referring to string positions with ? and by omitting uninteresting subgoals. String positions were changed from lists to integers for readability.

```
?- s(LF, 0, 3).
    (1) 0 Call: s(S_1,0,3)
    (2) 1 Call:   np(VP_2^S_1,0,?)
    (3) 2 Call:     det(N2_3^VP_2^S_1,0,?)
    (5) 3 Call:       det(every,N2_3^VP_2^S_1)
    (5) 3 Exit:       det(every,(X_5^S1_5)^
                                 (X_5^S2_5)^
                                 all(X_5,S1_5=>S2_5))
```

```
  (3) 2 Exit:      det((X_5^S1_5)^
                       (X_5^S2_5)^
                       all(X_5,S1_5=>S2_5),0,1)
  (6) 2 Call:      n(N1_6,1,?)
  (8) 3 Call:       n(program,N1_6)
  (8) 3 Exit:       n(program,X_8^program(X_8))
  (6) 2 Exit:      n(X_8^program(X_8),1,2)
  (9) 2 Call:      optrel((X_8^program(X_8))^
                       X_5^S1_5,2,?)
  (9) 2 Exit:      optrel((X_5^program(X_5))^
                       X_5^program(X_5),2,2)
  (2) 1 Exit:      np((X_5^S2_5)^
                       all(X_5,program(X_5)=>S2_5),0,2)
 (11) 1 Call:      vp(X_5^S2_5,2,3)
 (12) 2 Call:       tv(X_5^IV_12,2,?)
 (14) 3 Call:        tv(halts,X_5^IV_12)
 (14) 3 Fail:        tv(halts,X_5^IV_12)
 (12) 2 Fail:       tv(X_5^IV_12,2,?)
 (15) 2 Call:       iv(X_5^S2_5,2,3)
 (17) 3 Call:        iv(halts,X_5^S2_5)
 (17) 3 Exit:        iv(halts,X_5^halts(X_5))
 (15) 2 Exit:       iv(X_5^halts(X_5),2,3)
 (11) 1 Exit:      vp(X_5^halts(X_5),2,3)
  (1) 0 Exit: s(all(X_5,program(X_5)=>
                       halts(X_5)),0,3)

LF = all(X_5,program(X_5)=>halts(X_5))
yes
```

During the DCG execution by Prolog, the np in the s rule is executed first, even though part of its argument VP will be fully determined only when the vp literal is executed. This pattern of operation pervades the grammar, and shows how the logical variable helps put together a complex expression without having to know beforehand the full specification of its parts.

4.1.6   Quantifier Scope

The DCG of Program 4.2 and those of Problems 4.6 and 4.7 have a serious deficiency in their handling of *quantifier scope*. For a sentence like

Every professor wrote a book.

the grammar assigns the single interpretation

```
all(P, professor(P) =>
        exists(B, book(B) & wrote(P, B)))    ;
```

that is, for every professor there is a book that he or she wrote. Now, this *wide scope* interpretation of "every" might agree with our common sense, but it is not the only *combinatorially possible* one. In the other, less intuitive interpretation, there is a single book that every professor wrote:

```
exists(B, book(B) &
        all(P, professor(P) => wrote(P,B)))
```

This *narrow scope* interpretation for "every" is in fact the more intuitive one in sentences like

> Every student ran a program that the professor wrote for his dissertation.

It is clear that decisions on the likelihood of differently scoped logical forms for a sentence depend on many sources of information, such as empirical knowledge about the kind of situation being described and the actual order of words in the sentence. In any case, scope decisions are too subtle to be determined purely by the syntactic structure of sentences, as they are in the grammar of Program 4.2.

The overall issue of scope *determination* is therefore a very difficult open research question (Woods, 1977; Vanlehn, 1978; F. C. N. Pereira, 1982). Here, we will address the simpler question of *scope generation*: how to generate logical forms for a sentence with all combinatorially possible quantifier scopings. Such a generator could then be used to propose alternative scopings to *scope critics* that would use syntactic and empirical information to choose likely scopings.

A scope generator has to satisfy two major constraints:

o *Soundness:* Every formula generated must be a closed well-formed formula (that is, without free variables) corresponding to a correct scoping of the sentence.

o *Completeness:* Every combinatorially possible scoping will be generated.

A basic observation we need is that the meaning of a determiner is a function of a noun meaning and an intransitive verb phrase meaning, the *range* and *scope* respectively. Alternative quantifier scopings in the logical form correspond to alternative choices of range and scope for the quantifiers

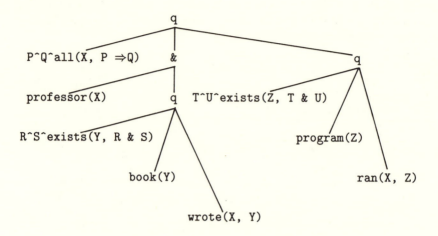

Figure 4.2. Quantifier tree

in the sentence meaning. The job of the scope generator is thus to consider the determiners in a sentence and generate all possible choices of range and scope for the corresponding quantifiers.

The method we will use here for scope generation relies on building an intermediate representation, a *quantifier tree*, whose nonleaf nodes correspond to determiner meanings (*quantifier* nodes) or logical connectives (*connective* nodes) and whose leaf or *predication* nodes correspond to the translations of nouns, verbs and other content words in the input sentence. The daughters of a quantifier node include a determiner meaning and two subtrees from which the determiner meaning at the node will get its range and scope. The quantifier nodes thus represent *delayed* decisions as to the range and scope of their quantifiers. For example, the quantifier tree for

Every professor that wrote a book ran a program.

is shown in Figure 4.2.

In practice, we will represent a quantifier node by a term of the form q(D, R, S), where D is the expression representing the determiner meaning and R and S are the subtrees from which Ds range and scope will be obtained. A connective node is represented by the connective itself applied to its arguments, and a predication node with contents P will be represented by 'P. The backquote (" ' ") is used as a prefix operator to syntactically distinguish predications that have not been scoped both from predications that have been scoped and from the quantifier and connective nodes. The use of the operator allows a simple check of the main functor to distinguish among the various cases.

The following grammar is a simple modification of that of Program 4.2 that builds a quantifier tree rather than a logical form directly.

Program 4.3

```
:- op(500,xfy,&).
:- op(510,xfy,=>).
:- op(100,fx,').

s(T) --> np(VP^S), vp(VP), {pull(S, T)}.

np(NP) -->
    det(N2^NP), n(N1), optrel(N1^N2).
np((E^S)^S) --> pn(E).

vp(X^S) --> tv(X^IV), np(IV^S).
vp(IV) --> iv(IV).

optrel((X^S1)^(X^(S1 & S2))) --> [that], vp(X^S2).
optrel(N^N) --> [].

det(LF) --> [D], {det(D, LF)}.
det( every, (X^S1)^(X^S2)^
                q(P^Q^all(X,P=>Q),S1,S2) ).
det( a,     (X^S1)^(X^S2)^
                q(P^Q^exists(X,P&Q),S1,S2) ).

n(LF)    --> [N], {n(N, LF)}.
n( book,      X^('book(X))        ).
n( professor, X^('professor(X)) ).
n( program,   X^('program(X))   ).
n( student,   X^('student(X))   ).

pn(E) --> [PN], {pn(PN, E)}.
pn( terry,  terry ).
pn( shrdlu, shrdlu ).

tv(LF) --> [TV], {tv(TV, LF)}.
tv( ran,   X^Y^('ran(X,Y))   ).
tv( wrote, X^Y^('wrote(X,Y)) ).
```

```
iv(LF) --> [IV], {iv(IV, LF)}.
iv( halts, X^('halts(X)) ).
```

This grammar generates the following quantifier tree for the sample sentence above.

```
q(P^Q^all(X,P=>Q),
  'professor(X)&q(R^S^exists(Y,R&S),
                  'book(Y),
                  'wrote(X,Y)),
  q(T^U^exists(Z,T&U),
    'program(Z),
    'ran(X,Z)))
```

This is just the term encoding of the tree of Figure 4.2.

In the first sentence rule, the extra condition `pull(S, T)` invokes the `pull` predicate that defines the translation relation between quantifier trees and first-order formulas. Thus the quantifier tree is translated into FOL to provide a logical form for the whole sentence.

The binary predicate `pull` is itself defined in terms of a ternary predicate, also called `pull`, which defines the relation between a quantifier tree, a *matrix*, and a *store* of quantifiers. The matrix is a formula with free variables, and the store is a list of quantifiers whose ranges have been determined, but not their scopes. The name "pull" suggests the idea of "pulling" quantifiers out of storage and applying them to a matrix to produce a closed formula. The quantifiers in storage are represented by λ-expression encodings. For example, the stored element for the noun phrase "every student" is the term `P^all(S, student(S) => P)`. Applying a quantifier to a matrix is thus simple function application with reduction.

The order of quantifiers in a store list indicates their relative scopes in the final result. The quantifiers that appear earlier in the list, i.e., farther towards the front, have been chosen to have wide scope over those at the back of the list.

The nondeterminism in the definition which produces alternative scopings comes from the uses of the predicates `shuffle` and `conc` to operate on storage lists. These predicates were defined previously as Programs 3.3 and 3.4 in Section 3.4.1, where we noted that `shuffle` was nondeterministic, as was `conc` when used in its "reverse" mode.

The ternary `pull` predicate turns a simple predication node into a matrix with empty store.

```
pull('Predication, Predication, []).
```

A node with the conjunction connective & is treated as follows. Each conjunct is separately pulled, thereby obtaining a matrix and store for both the left and the right conjunct. Now, we want to apply some of the remaining quantifiers in each of the stores, passing some on for application at a higher level. The conc predicate is used "backwards" to break each store list into a front and a back, the back to be applied to the corresponding conjunct matrix and the front to be passed as part of the store of the whole conjunction. Note that since we apply the back part only, we maintain the condition that things earlier in the store have wider scope. After applying quantifiers to each of the conjuncts, we shuffle the remaining quantifiers (the fronts of the lists for both conjuncts) to form the store list for the whole conjunction.

```
pull(QuantTree1 & QuantTree2,
    Formula1 & Formula2, Store) :-
    pull(QuantTree1, Matrix1, Store1),
    pull(QuantTree2, Matrix2, Store2),
    conc(Pass1, Apply1, Store1),
    conc(Pass2, Apply2, Store2),
    apply_quants(Apply1, Matrix1, Formula1),
    apply_quants(Apply2, Matrix2, Formula2),
    shuffle(Pass1, Pass2, Store).
```

Finally, a quantifier node with quantifier Q is similar in its handling to a connective node except that instead of two conjuncts, we have the range and scope of the quantifier to scope recursively. Recursive calls to pull deliver a matrix and a store for both the range and the scope trees of the quantifier. The range store list is split by conc into a front and a back, the front quantifiers outscoping Q and the back quantifiers to be applied to the range matrix to form the range of Q. Then, the front quantifiers are concatenated with the singleton list [Q], because they have been chosen to have wider scope than Q. Finally, the result is shuffled with the scope store to make the store for the whole node. Note that it is not necessary to split the store associated with the scope subtree, because the shuffle determines the position of Q in the overall store.

```
pull(q(Quantifier, RangeTree, ScopeTree),
    Matrix, Store) :-
    pull(RangeTree, RangeMatrix, RangeStore),
    pull(ScopeTree, Matrix, ScopeStore),
```

```
conc(RangePass, RangeApply, RangeStore),
apply_quants(RangeApply, RangeMatrix, Range),
reduce(Quantifier, Range, StoreElement),
conc(RangePass, [StoreElement], Pass),
shuffle(Pass, ScopeStore, Store).
```

The predicate `apply_quants` takes a store list and applies all its quantifiers in order to a matrix to produce a new matrix.

```
apply_quants([], Formula, Formula).
apply_quants([StoreElement|Elements],
             Matrix, Formula) :-
    apply_quants(Elements, Matrix, SubFormula),
    reduce(StoreElement, SubFormula, Formula).
```

The binary `pull` predicate itself merely scopes its quantifier-tree argument, yielding a matrix and a store, and then uses `apply_quants` to apply all the outstanding quantifiers to the matrix, resulting in a closed formula.

```
pull(QuantTree, Formula) :-
    pull(QuantTree, Matrix, Store),
    apply_quants(Store, Matrix, Formula).
```

As an example of the operation of `pull`, we will consider the possible scopings of the quantifier tree for the sample sentence

Every professor that wrote a book ran a program.

The binary predicate `pull` first generates a matrix and a store from the tree by applying some quantifiers in the tree and storing the rest. The outermost quantifier corresponding to "every professor..." is dealt with by recursively pulling its range and scope. We consider each of these recursive calls in order.

The range

```
'professor(X)&q(R^S^exists(Y,R&S),
              'book(Y),
              'wrote(X,Y))
```

might be decomposed into matrix and store by placing the single quantifier into storage, yielding the matrix

```
professor(X) & wrote(X,Y)
```

with store

```
[S^exists(Y, book(Y) & S)]      ,
```

thereby leading to the wide-scope reading for the existential. Alternatively, the quantifier might be applied directly, rather than stored, leading to the matrix

```
professor(X) & exists(Y, book(Y) & wrote(X,Y))
```

with empty store. We will pursue the former possibility here to demonstrate how the wide-scope reading is achieved.

Once the range is pulled, the scope must be as well. Again, let us suppose that the quantifier in the scope is placed in storage, so that the matrix

```
ran(X,Z)
```

is associated with the store

```
[U^exists(Z, program(Z) & U)]      .
```

Now, to form the matrix for the whole tree (recall that the main quantifier we are trying to scope is the universal for "every professor"), we take the store of the range and decide which quantifiers should be applied to the range matrix (thereby taking narrow scope relative to the universal) and which should take wide scope. Again, let us suppose the single element in the range store is to take wide scope. Then the formula that serves as the range of the main quantifier is

```
professor(X) & wrote(X,Y)
```

and, applying the range to the quantifier, the appropriate store element corresponding to the quantifier is

```
Q^all(X, (professor(X) & wrote(X,Y)) => Q)      .
```

We now place this element in the store after the range quantifier we are passing on, yielding the Pass store

```
[S^exists(Y, book(Y) & S),
 Q^all(X, (professor(X) & wrote(X,Y)) => Q)]      .
```

This is shuffled with the store from the scope. The one element in the scope store can be placed in any of three places in the combined store corresponding to its possible scopings relative to the other two quantifiers in the sentence. We will choose the placement of the scope store at the front of the list giving it widest scope. The full store is then

```
[U^exists(Z, program(Z) & U),
 S^exists(Y, book(Y) & S),
 Q^all(X, (professor(X) & wrote(X,Y)) => Q)]
```

and the matrix, recall, is

```
ran(X, Z)      .
```

This decomposition of the quantifier tree into range and scope is only one of seven nondeterministic possibilities. The binary `pull` predicate successively applies the three quantifiers remaining in store to the matrix, the last getting narrowest scope as it is applied first. This first application yields the formula

```
all(X, (professor(X) & wrote(X,Y)) =>
        ran(X,Z))        .
```

The next derives

```
exists(Y, book(Y) &
          all(X, (professor(X) & wrote(X,Y)) =>
                  ran(X,Z)))       .
```

Finally, the last quantifier is applied, giving the fully scoped form

```
exists(Z, program(Z) &
          exists(Y, book(Y) &
                    all(X, (professor(X) &
                            wrote(X,Y)) =>
                        ran(X,Z))))      .
```

In all, seven fully scoped forms can be generated for this sentence—corresponding to the seven decompositions of the quantifier tree into matrix and store—as can be seen by backtracking through the solutions.

```
?- s(LF, [every,professor,that,wrote,a,book,
          ran,a,program], []).

LF = exists(Z,program(Z)&
            all(X,professor(X)&
```

```
                    exists(Y,book(Y)&
                              wrote(X,Y))=>
                    ran(X,Z))) ;

LF = all(X,professor(X)&
            exists(Y,book(Y)&
                      wrote(X,Y))=>
            exists(Z,program(Z)&
                      ran(X,Z))) ;

LF = exists(Z,program(Z)&
            all(X,exists(Y,book(Y)&
                              professor(X)&
                              wrote(X,Y))=>
                    ran(X,Z))) ;

LF = all(X,exists(Y,book(Y)&
                      professor(X)&
                      wrote(X,Y))=>
            exists(Z,program(Z)&
                      ran(X,Z))) ;

LF = exists(Z,program(Z)&
            exists(Y,book(Y)&
                      all(X,professor(X)&
                              wrote(X,Y)=>
                              ran(X,Z)))) ;

LF = exists(Y,book(Y)&
            exists(Z,program(Z)&
                      all(X,professor(X)&
                              wrote(X,Y)=>
                              ran(X,Z)))) ;

LF = exists(Y,book(Y)&
            all(X,professor(X)&
                    wrote(X,Y)=>
                    exists(Z,program(Z)&
                              ran(X,Z)))) ;
```

no

The solution illustrated above is the fifth of the seven as listed in this query.

The quantifier scoping method outlined here is sound with respect to the quantifier trees that are the output of the presented grammar. However, certain quantifier trees involving nested quantifiers are not correctly handled by the algorithm; ill-formed scopings are generated in which quantifiers do not outscope all variable occurrences they were intended to bind. Such quantifier trees do not arise with the particular grammar given here, although more complete grammars including both relative clause and PP modifiers for nouns would exhibit the problem. Thus, the presented algorithm is only an approximation to a fully general sound scoping mechanism. For a full discussion of this issue and a particular solution (including a Prolog implementation), see (Hobbs and Shieber, 1987).

4.2   Extending the Syntactic Coverage

In this section, we discuss several changes to the grammar we have been developing that expand its coverage to include auxiliary verbs, full relative clauses, and various types of questions.

4.2.1   Auxiliary Verbs

None of the grammars dealt with so far allow for auxiliary verbs like *could, have,* and *been* in the sentence "Bill could have been writing a program". In this problem we extend the grammar to allow for this subclass of verbs. The simple analysis of English auxiliaries which we will use is the following: a verb phrase can always have an auxiliary prefixed to it if a certain condition holds, namely, that the *form* of the verb phrase that follows the auxiliary is the form that the auxiliary *requires.*

This analysis depends on the fact that verbs come in different forms: finite, nonfinite,[5] infinitival, and so forth. Every main verb (i.e., nonauxiliary) is of one of these forms, as is every auxiliary verb. Furthermore, each auxiliary verb specifies a form for the verb phrase it is attached to. Below are listed some examples of the forms of verb phrases.

form	*examples*
finite	halts, halted, writes a program, is halting, has been halting
present participle	halting, writing a program
past participle	halted, written a program, been halting
nonfinite	halt, write a program, be halting
infinitival	to halt, to write a program, to have been halting

Now the auxiliary verb *be* requires that the verb phrase following it be of

---

[5]The class of verbs we call "nonfinite" is not the class of all verbs except for the finite ones. Rather it consists of the base or stem forms of verbs only.

present participle form. Thus "be halting" is a grammatical verb phrase, but "*be halts" and "*be halt" are not. The auxiliary verb *have* requires that the verb phrase following it be of past participle form, as in "have been halting" or "have halted" but not "*have halting".

We can even treat the word "to" (when used to introduce a verb phrase) as an auxiliary verb, rather than a preposition. As an auxiliary verb, "to" requires a nonfinite verb phrase, and is itself infinitival.

We will encode verb form information as an argument to the nonter-minal in a DCG grammar. For main verbs, this argument will contain one of the constants `nonfinite`, `infinitival`, etc. For auxiliary verbs, the argument will contain a term of the form `Form/Requires`, where `Form` is the form of the auxiliary and `Requires` is the form that the auxiliary requires the following verb phrase to be.[6] We can think of the auxiliary as converting a `Requires` type of verb phrase into a `Form` type. Thus we will have main verb entries like

```
iv(Form) --> [IV], {iv(IV, Form)}.

iv( halts,    finite            ).
iv( halt,     nonfinite         ).
iv( halting,  present_participle ).
iv( halted,   past_participle   ).
...
```

and auxiliary verb entries such as

```
aux(Form) --> [Aux], {aux(Aux, Form)}.

aux( could, finite          / nonfinite          ).
aux( have,  nonfinite       / past_participle    ).
aux( has,   finite          / past_participle    ).
aux( been,  past_participle / present_participle ).
aux( be,    nonfinite       / present_participle ).
...
```

The form of a simple verb phrase composed of a main verb and its various complements is the form of the main verb itself. We can modify the VP rules to reflect this as follows:

```
vp(Form) --> iv(Form).
vp(Form) --> tv(Form), np.
```

---

[6]The use of "/" in this context is inspired by categorial grammar (Section 4.3.4).

To combine an auxiliary verb with a verb phrase, it is only necessary that the verb phrase be of the required form. The combined phrase will be of the form that the auxiliary is.

```
vp(Form) --> aux(Form/Require), vp(Require).
```

This augmented grammar will allow "could have been halting" as a VP because "halting" is a present participle intransitive verb, hence a present participle VP which satisfies the requirement of the verb "been". Thus "been halting" is a well-formed VP whose form is the form of "been", namely past participle. "Have" requires a past participle VP forming the nonfinite VP "have been halting", which combines with "could" to form the finite VP "could have been halting".

The rule for forming sentences

```
s --> np, vp.
```

must be modified to account for the fact that VPs now have verb form information. In deciding on the form of the VP in sentences, we note that the following NP-VP combinations are not grammatical English:

* Bertrand write a book.
* The program been halting.
* Bill writing every program.

The pertinent restriction is that full-fledged sentences always incorporate a finite VP. Thus the sentence formation rule should be

```
s --> np, vp(finite).
```

4.2.2   Yes-No Questions

Yes-no questions are formed in English exactly like declarative sentences, except for two differences.

o Yes-no questions always have at least one auxiliary verb.

o The leftmost auxiliary verb occurs before, rather than after, the subject NP.

This switching of the placement of the leftmost auxiliary verb and the subject is called *subject-aux inversion*. We will allow such inverted sentences with the following rule for the new nonterminal `sinv`:

```
sinv --> aux(finite/Required), np, vp(Required).
```

This rule allows finite subject-aux-inverted sentences like

> Could Bertrand write a book?
> Has the program been halting?
> Is Bill writing every program?

all of which are typical examples of English yes-no questions. We can state this in a rule for forming questions from inverted sentences:

```
q --> sinv.
```

But, as we will see in Section 4.2.5, inverted sentences play a role in the formation of WH-questions as well as yes-no questions.

4.2.3   Filler-Gap Dependencies

The grammars that have been presented heretofore have included a very simple analysis of relative clauses as verb phrases preceded by the word *that*. This analysis vastly oversimplifies the variety of relative clauses possible in English. For instance, relative clauses such as "that Bertrand wrote" (as in the NP "every book that Bertrand wrote") are not the concatenation of "that" and a VP; instead of a VP, a sentence missing its object is substituted. Intuitively, the head of the noun phrase, i.e., "every book" fills the role of the missing object, the thing(s) that Bertrand wrote. For this reason, the phenomenon has been called a *filler-gap dependency*.

In general, a filler-gap dependency occurs in a natural-language sentence when a subpart of some phrase (the *gap* or *trace*) is missing from its normal location and another phrase (sometimes called the *filler*), outside of the incomplete one, stands for the missing phrase. The occurrence of a gap is said to be *licensed* by the previous occurrence of the filler, and we have a dependency between the gap and the filler because the gap can only occur (i.e., the corresponding phrase be missing) when the appropriate filler occurs.

The canonical instances of filler-gap dependency constructions in English are relative clauses and WH-questions. For example, in the sentence

> Terry read every book that Bertrand wrote.

we have seen that there is a filler-gap dependency between the relative pronoun "that" (the filler)[7] and the missing direct object (the gap). The

---

[7]Analyses differ as to whether the filler is the relative pronoun or the head of the NP as first mentioned. Although the latter may be more intuitive, other factors lead us to the former, not the least of which is ease of semantic interpretation.

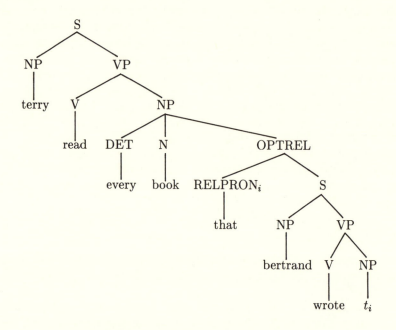

Figure 4.3. Parse tree including filler-gap dependency

parse tree for the sentence, given in Figure 4.3, indicates the trace by the pseudo-terminal t_i. The subscript i on the trace and filler is intended to indicate the dependency between the two.

Filler-gap dependencies are a subclass of *long-distance* or *unbounded dependencies*, so-called because the amount of material between the dependent phrases—the gap and the filler in this case—can be arbitrarily large, and the path in the analysis tree from the filler to the gap can in principle cross an arbitrary number of phrase boundaries (but only for some kinds of phrases). The long-distance behavior of filler-gap dependencies is exemplified in such sentences as

> Terry read every book that Bertrand told a student to write.
> Terry read every book that Bertrand told a student to ask a
>   professor to write.

and so forth.

The obvious way of representing long-distance dependencies in a DCG is to use a nonterminal argument to indicate the presence or absence of a gap within the phrase covered by the nonterminal. If there is a gap, we must also indicate the syntactic category (nonterminal) of the gap. Although the grammar we develop below does not require this information (as only noun phrase gaps are allowed), the ability to extend the coverage by including, for instance, prepositional phrase gaps, motivates this requirement. We will use the constant `nogap` as the value for the gap information argument to indicate the absence of a gap, and the term `gap(T)` to indicate the presence of a gap with category T. For instance, the sentence "Bertrand wrote a book" would be covered by the nonterminal `s(nogap)`, whereas the incomplete sentence "Bertrand wrote" (as in "the book that Bertrand wrote") would be covered by the nonterminal `s(gap(np))`.

To allow noun phrase gaps in the grammar, we add a special rule which introduces an NP covering no string.

```
np(gap(np)) --> [].
```

This rule states that a noun phrase containing a noun phrase gap can cover the empty string; that is, a noun phrase gap can be realized by omitting a noun phrase.

Now the information about the presence of a gap must be appropriately distributed throughout the grammar so that "Bertrand wrote", but not "Bertrand wrote a book", is associated with `gap(np)`. For instance, the transitive VP rule must be modified so that the VP is associated with the same gap information as its object. (We ignore verb form information in this section and the next. The grammar in Appendix A contains both verb form and filler-gap information in the nonterminals.)

```
vp(GapInfo) --> tv, np(GapInfo).
```

Similarly, the S rule must force the S and VP to share gap information.

```
s(GapInfo) --> np(nogap), vp(GapInfo).
```

In addition, the rule disallows subject NPs that contain gaps bound outside of them, thereby embodying a so-called *island constraint* that linguists have proposed as accounting for the ungrammaticality of noun phrases like

* the book that the author of wrote *Principia*

as compared with

the book that the author of *Principia* wrote   .

Island constraints are so-called because they constrain certain constituents, e.g., subject noun phrases, to act as if surrounded by a boundary which allows no filler-gap dependencies to cross.

There is considerable debate in the linguistics literature of the status of island constraints such as these. Certainly, some phrases with gaps within subjects seem quite grammatical, e.g.,

> the professor who a picture of has appeared in every newspaper
> in the country   .

Furthermore, certain constructions can license the existence of a gap within an island. For instance, the *parasitic gap* construction allows sentences with multiple gaps bound by the same filler, even when one of the gaps is within an island.

> the book that the author of wrote a letter about

We have merely represented here one traditional analysis of the phenomenon. Other analyses, including ones in which filler-gap dependencies which cross a subject NP boundary were allowed, could easily be designed.

4.2.4   Relative Clauses

Relative clauses can be formed by concatenating a relative pronoun filler with a sentence that contains the corresponding gap.

```
rel --> relpron, s(gap(np)).
```

This rule then embodies the actual filler-gap dependency and allows relative clauses such as "the book that Bertrand wrote". Unfortunately, because of the island constraint disallowing gaps in subjects of sentences, this rule will admit only *complement relatives*, i.e., relative clauses in which a complement of a verb is gapped. *Subject relatives*, in which the entire subject is gapped, as in "the professor who wrote *Principia*" are not allowed by this rule. To remedy this problem, we introduce a special rule for subject relatives, akin to the relative clause rule of Program 3.12.

```
rel --> relpron, vp(nogap).
```

In summary, here is the grammar of Program 3.12 augmented to handle both subject- and complement- relative clauses.

Program 4.4
```
s --> s(nogap).
s(Gap) --> np(nogap), vp(Gap).
```

```
np(Gap) --> det, n, optrel.
np(nogap) --> pn.
np(gap(np)) --> [].

vp(Gap) --> tv, np(Gap).
vp(nogap) --> iv.

optrel --> [].
optrel --> relpron, vp(nogap).
optrel --> relpron, s(gap(np)).

det --> [Det], {det(Det)}.
det(a).      det(every).
det(some).   det(the).

n --> [N], {n(N)}.
n(author).       n(book).
n(professor).    n(program).
n(programmer).   n(student).

pn --> [PN], {pn(PN)}.
pn(begriffsschrift).  pn(bertrand).
pn(bill).             pn(gottlob).
pn(lunar).            pn(principia).
pn(shrdlu).           pn(terry).

tv --> [TV], {tv(TV)}.
tv(concerns).  tv(met).
tv(ran).       tv(wrote).

iv --> [IV], {iv(IV)}.
iv(halted).

relpron --> [RelPron], {relpron(RelPron)}.
relpron(that).   relpron(who).
relpron(whom).
```

4.2.5   WH-Questions

WH-questions, that is, questions introduced by a word starting with "wh",
as in

Who wrote *Principia*?
What did Bertrand write?
Who did Alfred tell Bertrand to write a book about?

and so forth, also exhibit a filler-gap dependency. The filler this time is the WH word; the gap, as usual, can be arbitrarily deep in the adjacent sentence. We will use a technique similar to that for relative clauses to handle WH-questions. Just as subject relatives and complement relatives must be distinguished, we will distinguish subject and complement questions.

Subject questions, such as

Who loves Mary?

are constructed from a WH pronoun and a finite VP.

```
q --> whpron, vp(nogap).
```

Complement questions, for instance,

Who does Mary love?

are formed from a WH pronoun acting as a filler for a gap in a subject-aux-inverted sentence.

```
q --> whpron, sinv(gap(np)).
```

Of course, the sinv rule must be modified to allow gaps.

```
sinv(GapInfo) --> aux, np(nogap), vp(GapInfo).
```

4.2.6   Semantics of Filler-Gap Dependencies

A treatment of semantics of relative clauses is possible by combining the syntactic analysis of Program 4.4 with the semantic analysis of Program 4.2. The basic idea is that a gap is analyzed very much like a proper noun, except that instead of supplying a constant term to the logical form it supplies a variable which is carried as the second argument of the gap information term gap(T,v).

```
np((X^S)^S, gap(np, X)) --> [].
```

A relative clause meaning is like an intransitive verb meaning, namely, a property. However, relative clause meanings will be conjoined with a noun meaning to make a complex property such as

```
M^(professor(M) & wrote(M, principia))
```

for "professor who wrote *Principia*". In the case of a subject relative the meaning comes directly, because the clause is itself a verb phrase.

```
optrel((X^S1)^(X^(S1&S2))) -->
    relpron, vp(X^S2, nogap).
```

For complement relative clauses, the meaning representation is of the form $X^{\wedge}S$ where X is the variable associated to the argument position filled by the gap, and S is the encoding of the meaning of the sentence in the relative clause, in which X is a free variable.

```
optrel((X^S1)^(X^(S1&S2))) -->
    relpron, s(S2, gap(np, X)).
```

Thus, for the relative clause "that Bertrand wrote" we will have $S =$ wrote(bertrand,B), $X =$ B, and the gap argument will have the form gap(np,B).

We interpret a question as a property which is to be true of the answers to the question. For subject WH-questions, the property is that given by the VP. For complement questions, it is the property that the S predicates of the gap.

```
q(VP) --> whpron, vp(VP, nogap).
q(X^S) --> whpron, sinv(S, gap(np, X)).
```

For yes-no questions, the property we want of the answers to the question is that the answer be "yes" if the condition given by the inverted sentence holds.

```
q(yes^S) --> sinv(S, nogap).
```

For the time being, we ignore the contribution of the auxiliary to the meaning of the inverted sentence.[8] Thus the rule for sinv, including semantics, is

```
sinv(S, GapInfo) -->
    aux, np(VP^S, nogap), vp(VP, GapInfo).
```

---

[8]The talk program described in Chapter 5 can handle the semantics of simple auxiliaries, although the logical forms provided lexically for auxiliaries do not happen to modify their VP arguments.

A slightly different approach to the semantics of questions will be used in the `talk` program developed in Chapter 5, in which the meaning of a question is an implication of the form: If some condition holds of x then x is an answer.

Summarizing, the grammar for relative clauses and questions we have developed in this chapter is the following:

Program 4.5

```
q(VP) --> whpron, vp(VP, nogap).
q(X^S) --> whpron, sinv(S, gap(np, X)).
q(yes^S) --> sinv(S, nogap).

s(S) --> s(S, nogap).
s(S, Gap) --> np(VP^S, nogap), vp(VP, Gap).

sinv(S, GapInfo) -->
    aux, np(VP^S, nogap), vp(VP, GapInfo).

np(NP, nogap) --> det(N2^NP), n(N1), optrel(N1, N2).
np((E^S)^S, nogap) --> pn(E).
np((X^S)^S, gap(np, X)) --> [].

vp(X^S, Gap) --> tv(X^VP), np(VP^S, Gap).
vp(VP, nogap) --> iv(VP).

optrel(N^N) --> [].
optrel((X^S1)^(X^(S1&S2))) -->
    relpron, vp(X^S2, nogap).
optrel((X^S1)^(X^(S1&S2))) -->
    relpron, s(S2, gap(np, X)).

det(LF) --> [D], {det(D, LF)}.
det( every, (X^S1)^(X^S2)^all(X,(S1=>S2)) ).
det( a,     (X^S1)^(X^S2)^exists(X,S1&S2) ).

n(LF)   --> [N], {n(N, LF)}.
n( program, X^program(X) ).
n( student, X^student(X) ).

pn(E) --> [PN], {pn(PN, E)}.
pn( terry,  terry ).
pn( shrdlu, shrdlu ).
```

```
tv(LF) --> [TV], {tv(TV, LF)}.
tv( wrote, X^Y^wrote(X,Y) ).

iv(LF) --> [IV], {iv(IV, LF)}.
iv( halts, X^halts(X) ).

relpron --> [RelPron], {relpron(Relpron)}.
relpron(that).   relpron(who).
relpron(whom).
```

4.2.7   Gap Threading

The technique used for passing gap information among the nonterminals in grammar rules outlined in the previous section has two problems:

1. Several versions of each rule, differing only in which constituent(s) the gap information is passed to, may be needed. For instance, a rule for building dative verb phrases

   ```
   vp --> datv, np, pp.
   ```

   would need two versions

   ```
   vp(GapInfo) -->
       datv, np(GapInfo), pp(nogap).
   vp(GapInfo) -->
       datv, np(nogap), pp(GapInfo).
   ```

   so as to allow a gap to occur in either the NP or PP, as in the sentences

   > What did Alfred give to Bertrand?
   > Who did Alfred give a book to?

2. Because of the multiple versions of rules, sentences with no gaps will receive multiple parses. For instance, the sentence

   > Alfred gave a book to Bertrand.

   would receive one parse using the first dative VP rule (with `GapInfo` bound to `nogap`) and another with the second dative VP rule.

An alternative method for passing gap information, sometimes referred to as *gap threading*, has been used extensively in the logic programming literature. It is based on data structures called *difference lists*.

Difference Lists

The encoding of sequences of terms as lists using the . operator and [] is so natural that it seems unlikely that alternatives would be useful. However, in certain cases, sequences may be better encoded with a data structure known as a *difference list*. A difference list is constructed from a pair of list structures one of which is a *suffix* of the other. Every list is a suffix of itself. Also, if the list is of the form [Head|Tail] then every suffix of Tail is a suffix of the whole list. Thus the relation between lists and their suffixes is the reflexive transitive closure of the relation between list and their tails. We will use the binary infix operator "-" to construct a difference list from the two component lists. A difference list List-Suffix encodes the sequence of elements in List up to but not including those in Suffix. Thus the elements in List-Suffix are the list *difference* of the elements in List and the elements in Suffix. For instance, the sequence of elements ⟨1, 2, 3⟩ might be encoded as the list [1,2,3] or as any of the difference lists [1,2,3,4]-[4], [1,2,3]-[], [1,2,3|X]-X.

We will be especially concerned with the *most general* difference-list encoding of a sequence, that is, the encoding in which the suffix is a variable. The final example of a difference-list encoding of the sequence ⟨1, 2, 3⟩ is of this form. Any other difference-list encoding of the sequence is an instance of [1,2,3|X]-X. Henceforth, the term "difference list" will mean a most general difference list. We will also use the terms *front* and *back* for the two components of a difference list. Note that the empty difference list is X-X.

The difference-list encoding of sequences has one key advantage over the standard list encoding. Concatenation of difference lists is far simpler, requiring only a single unit clause.

Program 4.6
```
conc_dl(Front-Back1, Back1-Back2, Front-Back2).
```

The predicate conc_dl performs concatenation of difference lists by simply unifying the back of the first list with the front of the second. This engenders the following behavior:

```
?- conc_dl([1,2,3|X]-X, [4,5|Y]-Y, Result).
Result = [1,2,3,4,5|Y]-Y
yes
```

Actually, we have seen difference lists before. The use of pairs of string positions encoded as lists to encode the list between the positions is an instance of a difference list encoding. We can see this more clearly by taking the encoding of grammar rules using explicit concatenation, as briefly mentioned in Chapter 1, and substituting difference-list concatenation. Using explicit concatenation, the rule

$$S \rightarrow NP\ VP$$

would be axiomatized (as in Chapter 1) as

$$(\forall u, v, w) NP(u) \wedge VP(v) \wedge conc(u, v, w) \Rightarrow S(w)$$

or in Prolog,

```
s(W) :- np(U), vp(V), conc(U, V, W).
```

Substituting difference-list concatenation, we have

```
s(W) :- np(U), vp(V), conc_dl(U, V, W).
```

and partially executing this clause with respect to the `conc_dl` predicate in order to remove the final literal, we get the following clause (with variable names chosen for obvious reasons):

```
s(P0-P) :- np(P0-P1), vp(P1-P).
```

Thus, we have been using a difference list encoding for sequences of words implicitly throughout our discussion of DCGs.

Difference Lists for Filler-Gap Processing

We now turn to the use of difference lists in filler-gap processing. First, think of the gap information associated with each node as providing the list of gaps covered by the node whose corresponding fillers are not covered by it. Alternatively, this cn be viewed as the list of gaps whose filler-gap dependency passes through the given node. We will call this list the *filler list* of the node. For the most part the filler list of each constituent is the concatenation of the filler lists of its subconstituents. For instance, for the dative VP rule, we have

```
vp(FL) --> datv, np(FL1), pp(FL2),
           {conc_dl(FL1, FL2, FL)}.
```

We include only those constituents which might potentially include a gap in the concatenation. Again, we remove the explicit concatenations by partial execution yielding

```
vp(F0-F) --> datv, np(F0-F1), pp(F1-F).
```

Similarly, other rules will display this same pattern.

```
s(F0-F) --> np(F0-F1), vp(F1-F).
vp(F0-F) --> tv, np(F0-F).
vp(F0-F0) --> iv.
   ...
```

We turn now to constituents in which a new filler or a new gap is introduced. For instance, the complement relative clause rule requires that a gap be contained in the S which is a sibling of the filler. It therefore states that the filler list of the S contains a single NP.

```
optrel(F-F) --> relpron, s([gap(np)|F]-F).
```

The rule introducing NP gaps includes a single NP filler marker on the S, thereby declaring that the S covers a single NP gap.

```
np([gap(np)|F]-F) --> [].
```

Island constraints can be added to a grammar using this encoding of filler-gap dependencies in two ways. First, we can leave out filler information for certain constituents, as we did for verbs and relative pronouns. More generally, however, we can mandate that a constituent not contain any gaps bound outside the constituent by making its filler list the empty list (i.e., F-F). For instance, the sentence formation rule above can be modified to make the subject of the sentence an island merely by unifying the two parts of its filler list.

```
s(F0-F) --> np(F0-F0), vp(F0-F).
```

The gap-threading technique for encoding filler-gap dependencies solves many of the problems of the more redundant gap-passing method described earlier. Each unthreaded rule generates only one rule with appropriate gap information. The filler-list information is added in a quite regular pattern. Fillers, islands, and gaps are all given a simple treatment. All of these properties make the gap-threading technique conducive to automatic interpretation as we will do in Section 6.3.3.

However, several problems with the gap-threading technique are known, most showing up only in rather esoteric constructions such as parasitic gap constructions, multiple gaps, crossing filler-gap dependencies, and so forth. Many of these problems can be handled by using more complex combinations of filler lists rather than simple concatenation. For instance, crossing dependencies can be handled by shuffling the filler lists of subconstituents to yield the filler list of the full constituent. Of course, this defeats the simple elegant pattern of variable sharing that difference-list concatenation engenders.

4.3   Problem Section: Grammar Extensions

These problems concern the extension of Program 4.2 to accept a few other English constructions, namely some simple cases of *noun complements* and *postmodifiers* and the corresponding gapped constructions. Since these examples require prepositional phrases in the grammar, you may want to refer to Problem 3.20 for background. In addition, we will discuss a system of grammar writing used by Montague himself for his semantic work. This system, *categorial grammar*, is quite different from the phrase-structure-based methods we have been using previously.

4.3.1   Noun Complements

A noun phrase complement plays a similar role to that of an argument of a predicate. For example, in the noun phrase "an author of every book" the noun *author* has as its complement the prepositional phrase "of every book". For the purposes of this section, we will assume that nouns that take a complement are interpreted as binary predicates. For example, the sentence

An author of every book wrote a program.

might have the logical form

```
all(B, book(B) =>
        exists(A, author_of(A,B) &
                    exists(P, program(P) &
                                wrote(A,P))))
```

Notice that *author* is here translated by the binary predicate `author_of`. Note also that the quantifier `all` that translates the determiner *every* in the complement of *author* is given a wider scope than the quantifier `exists` that translates the determiner *an* of the phrase "an author ...". This is not the only possible reading for the English sentence, but for the time being we will assume that the quantifiers from noun complements always outscope the quantifier for the determiner preceding the noun that has the complement. To achieve this effect in a DCG, the translation of "an author" must somewhow be given as an argument to the translation of the complement "of every book", in a way similar to the passing of an intransitive verb phrase meaning into a noun phrase meaning to make a sentence meaning in the first rule in the DCG of Program 4.2.

Problem 4.6 *Add one or more DCG rules to the grammar in Program 4.2 to analyze and translate noun complements. We will assume that there is a separate lexical category* n2 *for nouns that take a prepositional phrase as a complement. To simplify the problem, we will also assume that all complements are prepositional phrases (see Problem 3.20) introduced by the preposition* of. *Your DCG should be able to analyze the sample sentence above and assign to it the given logical form. You need not handle noun phrases with both a relative clause and a complement prepositional phrase.*

4.3.2   Noun Postmodifiers

A prepositional phrase can also appear as a noun postmodifier, where it does not supply an argument to the noun but instead it further restricts the range of objects described by the noun. In this case, such a postmodifier operates like a restrictive relative clause. For example, the prepositional phrase "about Gottlob" in the sentence

Bertrand wrote a book about Gottlob.

is a postmodifier of *book* that further restricts the book in question to be about Gottlob. We may in this case interpret the preposition *about* very much like a transitive verb, and give the sentence the translation

```
exists(B, (book(B) & about(B,gottlob)) &
           wrote(bertrand,B))      .
```

We will assume that the quantifiers in the translation of the postmodifier have smaller scope than that of the quantifier for the determiner preceding the modified noun. As mentioned in the previous problem, such assumptions are overly restrictive, and we will discuss how to do better in Section 4.1.6.

Problem 4.7 *By adding appropriate lexical items and rules (or modifying existing ones), change the DCG of Program 4.2 to handle prepositional phrases as noun postmodifiers. The new rules for postmodifiers may be modeled closely on those for optional relative clauses, and the resulting grammar should be tested on sentences like the one above. Make sure that quantifiers from the postmodifier are properly scoped.*

4.3.3   More Filler-Gap Constructions

Many other filler-gap constructions occur in English. In the next two problems we will discuss gaps in the constructions introduced in the previous two problems. Later, in Problem 6.15, we will see two more English filler-gap constructions.

Problem 4.8 *Extend your solution to Problems 4.6 and 4.7 so that gaps are allowed in prepositional phrases used as NP modifiers and complements and as adverbials. The solution should allow sentences like*

> *What did Bertrand write a book about?*
> *Who did Terry meet a student of?*
> *What did Terry write a program with?*
> *The professor that Terry met a student of wrote a program.*

Problem 4.9 *Extend the solution to Problem 4.8 so that it can handle questions where the filler is a prepositional phrase and the PP gap is playing an adverbial role, e.g., questions like*

> *With what did Terry write a program?*

Note that the grammaticality status of PP gaps used as NP modifiers or complements in English is unclear. Sentences containing such constructions often seem ungrammatical.

> *? About what did Terry write a program?
> *? Of whom did Terry meet a student?

However, the data are unclear, and the correct analysis is certainly not a foregone conclusion.

4.3.4   Categorial Grammars

A *categorial grammar* (CG) specifies a language by describing the combinatorial possibilities of its lexical items directly, without the mediation of phrase-structure rules (like CFG or DCG rules). Consequently, two grammars in the same categorial grammar system differ only in the lexicon.

The ways in which a phrase can combine with other phrases are encoded in a *category* associated with the phrase. The set of categories is defined inductively as follows:

o A primitive category is a category. For the purposes of this problem, the primitive categories are *S* and *NP*.

- If A and B are categories then A/B and $A\backslash B$ are categories. These are called *compound* or *functor* categories.

- Nothing else is a category.

Combination of phrases is sanctioned by their categories according to two rules:

- **Forward application (FA):** A phrase p_f of category A/B can be combined with a phrase p_a of category B to form a phrase $p_f p_a$ of category A.

- **Backward application (BA):** A phrase p_f of category $A\backslash B$ can be combined with a phrase p_a of category B to form a phrase $p_a p_f$ of category A.

Notice that the direction of the slash ("/" or "\") determines which side of the functor phrase its argument will be found on (right or left, respectively).

As an example of a categorial grammar, we might associate lexical items with categories as follows:

type of word	*examples*	*category*
proper nouns	Terry	NP
	Bertrand	
	Principia	
intransitive verbs	halts	$S\backslash NP$
transitive verbs	wrote	$(S\backslash NP)/NP$
	met	

Then combining "wrote" and "*Principia*" by FA, we conclude that "wrote *Principia*" is of category $S\backslash NP$. Combining this with "Bertrand", we have that "Bertrand wrote *Principia*" is an S. As usual, we can summarize the derivation in a parse tree as in Figure 4.4

Problem 4.10 *Write a Prolog program (including DCG rules) to implement a categorial grammar system. Lexical entries can be encoded as unit clauses of the form*

```
lex( bertrand, NP        ).
lex( halts,    S\NP      ).
lex( wrote,    (S\NP)/NP ).
...
```

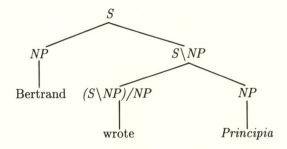

Figure 4.4. Parse tree for categorial grammar derivation

Given a lexicon encoded as above, the program should be able to parse sentences containing those lexical items.

Categorial grammars have been widely used in linguistic research concerning semantics of natural language. The close relation between CG and semantic interpretation follows from the observation that forward or backward syntactic application of a functor category to its argument corresponds to the semantic applications of the corresponding logical forms. Thus, the application rules can be used to control semantic application as well as syntactic combinatorics. We merely make sure that lexical items are associated with semantic functions which correspond to the syntactic functions implicit in their categories. For instance, a phrase of category S/NP must semantically be a function from NP-type items to S-type items. In terms of logical forms, it must be associated with a lambda expression of the form $\lambda x.\phi$ for ϕ a formula. (This relationship can be made more rigorous by defining a notion of *type* and using a typed lambda-calculus for the logical forms, as Montague in fact did.)

The logical forms of Section 4.1.2 are appropriate for the category assignments above. Given these logical forms, we can determine the logical form for the entire sentence by performing the applications according to the syntactic structure of the sentence. For instance, since "wrote" is associated with a functor category applying (by FA) to "*Principia*", we apply its logical form $\lambda x.\lambda y.wrote(y,x)$ to that of its argument *principia* yielding $\lambda y.wrote(y,principia)$. Similarly, by BA, we will associate the whole sentence with the logical form $wrote(bertrand,principia)$. The beauty of this system is that the semantic constraints are universal, as opposed to the types of grammars seen previously in which semantic constraints are stated on a rule-by-rule basis. Merely augmenting the lexicon with primitive LFs determines LFs for all the possible sentences admitted by the grammar.

Problem 4.11 *Augment your solution to the previous problem so that logical forms are built during parsing.*

Problem 4.12 *Using the solution to Problem 4.11 write a categorial grammar which handles quantified NPs as in Section 4.1.5 and builds logical forms. You should need to change only the lexicon. Take IV, N, and S to be the primitive categories.*

As a side note to the discussion of categorial grammar, note that since the matching of the argument category to the requirement of the functor category proceeds by unification, we can use full terms instead of atoms as the primitive categories and thereby pass information among the categories in ways reminiscent of DCGs. In fact, this extension to categorial grammar which we get "for free" is the correlate of the DCG extension to CFGs. Systems that use unification for matching in categorial grammars have come to be known as *categorial unification grammars* and are the subject of active research.

4.4   Bibliographic Notes

Our discussion of semantic interpretation (Section 4.1) is loosely based on some of the ideas of Montague grammar, although our goals are radically more modest than Montague's. Basically, we take from Montague the idea of using some form of the lambda calculus to represent the meanings of phrases and function application as the means of combining the meanings of subphrases into the meaning of a phrase. The simplifications in our presentation are made clear by observing that the fully reduced form for the meaning of a sentence is given by a first-order sentence. In contrast, sentence meanings in Montague have to be represented by sentences in the much richer system of *intensional logic* (IL), because the English fragment under consideration includes semantic phenomena such as intensional contexts (as in "John seeks a unicorn").

Montague introduced his approach to the relation between syntax and semantics of natural language in the articles "English as a Formal Language," "Universal Grammar," and "The Proper Treatment of Quantification in Ordinary English" which have been reprinted in the volume of his selected works edited by Thomason (1974). The textbook by Dowty, Wall, and Peters (1981) gives a full account of Montague's theory and of all the required background material, which is omitted in Montague's extremely concise papers. For further details on the lambda calculus (Section 4.1.1), and in particular its logical and computational properties, we refer the reader to the book by Hindley and Seldin (1986) for the untyped lambda calculus, and the book by Andrews (1986) for the typed lambda calculus (Church's simple theory of types).

Our Prolog encoding of semantic interpretation rules, and in particular the encoding of β-reduction as unification, was implicit in the early work on logic grammars (Colmerauer, 1982; Dahl, 1981; Pereira and Warren, 1980). Our presentation tries to make clear the connection between the logic grammar techniques and the techniques of compositional semantics. Some of our semantic rules are clearly too simplistic, and were shown mainly to illustrate the power of the logical variable for incrementally building complex descriptions. More sophisticated examples can be found in the Prolog natural-language analysis literature (McCord, 1982; F. C. N. Pereira, 1982; Dahl and McCord, 1983). Compositional semantics based on Montague grammar has also been used in natural-language processing systems not based on logic programming (Rosenschein and Shieber, 1982; Warren and Friedman, 1982; Schubert and Pelletier, 1982). Moore (1981) surveys some of the main difficulties involved in constructing logical representations for the meanings of a wider class of natural-language constructions. Last but not least, it should be noted that the above work on computing logical forms for natural-language derives many of its analyses and techniques from Woods's early and influential research (1977).

As we noted, the encoding of β-reduction in unification has to be used very carefully because of the lack of a full reduction mechanism for λ-terms within Prolog. This question has been discussed in detail by D. S. Warren (1983), and a general solution in the framework of a Prolog extension based on Church's simple theory of types was given by Miller and Nadathur (1986).

Partial execution has long been in the folklore of logic programming. The notion is implicit in Kowalski's connection-graph resolution proof procedure (1975; Eisinger, 1986). A related notion in functional programming is Burstall and Darlington's *unfolding* rule for program transformation (1977). Their techniques were extended to logic programs by Clark and Sickel (1977) and Tamaki and Sato (1984), among others. Further techniques involving deductive derivations of programs are discussed by Clark and Tärnlund (1977) and Hogger (1981).

The discussion of quantifier scope in Section 4.1.6 presents a simplified version of some of the concepts developed independently by Woods in a computational framework (1977) and by Cooper in a compositional semantics setting (1983). In particular, the explicit notion of quantifier storage is due to Cooper. Hobbs and Shieber (1987) give a precise account of an algorithm for generating scope alternatives and prove some important properties relative to its soundness and completeness. Reliable criteria for choosing among scoping alternatives are notoriously hard to come by.

Vanlehn (1978) gives a comprehensive account of the difficulties. Various partial engineering solutions for the problem have nevertheless been proposed (Woods, 1977; F. C. N. Pereira, 1982; Grosz et al., 1987).

Our treatment of the English auxiliary system in Section 4.2.1 is based on that by Gazdar et al. (1982).

The treatment of long-distance dependencies and, in particular, filler-gap dependencies given in Section 4.2.3 is rather idealized, its goal being just to outline a few basic techniques. For a linguistically sophisticated treatment of the problem covering a much broader subset of English, see for example the book by Gazdar et al. (1985). The analysis of subject relatives as being composed from VPs and not Ss follows Gazdar (1981). Island constraints were originally proposed by Ross (1974).

As far as we know, the idea of gap threading appeared first, in form somewhat different from the one used in Section 4.2.7, as part of the extraposition grammar formalism (Pereira, 1981). It has been reinvented numerous times.

Categorial grammars as formal systems originated with the work of the Polish logicians Leśniewski and Adjukiewicz in the 1930s, but it was Bar-Hillel (1964) who considered their application to natural-language syntax. With Gaifman and Shamir, Bar-Hillel proved that the basic categorial grammars have the same weak generative capacity as context-free grammars. Lambek (1961) provided important early research in the area. Since this work, many different categorial accounts of the syntax and semantics of natural languages have been developed, including those by Lewis (1972) and by Cresswell (1973) from a philosophical perspective and that of Ades and Steedman (1982) from a linguistic one. Van Benthem (1986) provides a recent survey of logical and semantic issues in categorial grammar. For discussion of categorial unification grammars, see the papers by Karttunen (1986) and Uszkoreit (1986) and works cited therein.

5

Full Prolog and a
Simple Dialogue Program

The subset of Prolog used up to this point has been pure in the sense that a Prolog system can be viewed as a sound (though incomplete) inference engine for a particular logic. However, the Prolog language includes several extralogical facilities which have been found to be of considerable utility in writing large programs. Some of these facilities are referred to as "metalogical" because their semantic domain is the domain of logical expressions and proofs. This section introduces some of the most important extralogical mechanisms in Prolog by means of an example of a simple natural-language dialogue program, `talk`.

5.1   Metalogical Facilities

5.1.1   The `call` predicate

The first metalogical predicate exemplifies the level-crossing involved in interpreting Prolog terms as encoding Prolog clauses and goals. The `call` predicate takes a single term argument which encodes a Prolog goal. The argument of `call` is executed by reinterpreting it as the goal which the term encodes. Thus, execution of `call(conc([a,b],[c,d],A))` is equivalent to execution of the goal `conc([a,b],[c,d],A)` directly. The utility of `call` comes about because the goal to be executed can be a variable in the program, *as long as it is instantiated to an appropriate term by execution time.* Since `call` depends on the instantiation of its arguments and reinterprets terms as literals, it is clearly a metalogical predicate. Note that the argument to call can represent not only single literal goals but any clause body, including conjunctions, disjunctions and so forth.

The `call` predicate can be used to implement a simple Prolog interpreter, a unary predicate which holds of its argument if Prolog would prove the argument when interpreted as a goal. The definition is trivial.

Program 5.1
```
prove(G) :- call(G).
```

We will see other more interesting examples of predicates that act like interpreters in Chapter 6.

5.1.2   The cut command

The behavior of a Prolog program is based on the depth-first, backtracking control regime that the Prolog system follows. The Prolog interpreter will explore the entire space of backtracking alternatives in search of a solution to a goal. This behavior, although simple and (in the limit) complete, sometimes has undesirable consequences. In this section we present a metalogical facility that changes the control regime of a Prolog program and that can be used for several purposes including increasing efficiency, eliminating redundancy, and encoding conditionals.

The cut command, notated by an exclamation mark "!", is used to eliminate branches of the search space. We refer to cut as a command, rather than a predicate or operator, to emphasize that it does not fit smoothly into the logical view of Prolog, and cannot be felicitously thought of as a predicate which holds or does not hold of arguments.

The clauses for a predicate give alternative ways of proving instances of that predicate. In proving a goal, Prolog chooses each alternative in turn until one leads to a proof of the goal. The cut command always succeeds, but as a side effect it makes some of the current clause choices permanent for the duration of the proof. Specifically, if a clause

$$p \; :\text{-} \; g_1,\ldots,g_i,!,\ldots,g_n.$$

is being used to prove an instance of p and the cut is reached, then the choice of this clause to prove that instance of p, as well as *all* choices of clauses in proving g_1 through g_i, are made permanent for the duration of the overall proof of which the proof of p is a part.

Another way of looking at the action of the cut command is as the converse of the previous statements, that is, by examining which proofs the cut eliminates. When Prolog backtracks to find an alternative proof of an occurrence of cut, not only is no other proof found for the cut instance but also the whole goal that invoked the clause with this cut instance is taken to have no proof (even if other clause alternatives might lead to such proof in the absence of the cut).

The cut command can be used in several ways. If we have a series of clauses for a particular predicate which we happen to know are all mutually exclusive, then once one of the clauses has succeeded, there is no use in attempting to find other solutions; all other branches in the search space will ultimately fail. We can eliminate the inefficiency engendered by searching these blind alleys by using cut to force the clause choice.

For instance, consider the definition of a `max_valued` predicate which holds of a nonempty list of terms and the term in the list with highest valuation according to a binary comparison predicate `higher_valued`. (We assume that all objects in the list have distinct valuations; there must be no "ties".) Such a predicate might be used, for instance, in implementing a priority system on terms. In the case where `higher_valued` is simple arithmetic comparison of numbers, `max_valued` computes the maximum number in a list.

The maximum-valued term of a nonempty list is the higher valued of the head of the list and the maximum valued term of the tail of the list. We will use a ternary `max_valued` predicate to capture this latter relationship between a list, a term, and the maximum-valued element in the entire bunch.

```
max_valued([Head|Tail], Max) :-
    max_valued(Tail, Head, Max).
```

The ternary predicate is easily implemented. If the list is empty, then the lone term is the highest valued. Otherwise, we pick the highest valued of the head of the list, the lone term, and the tail of the list, by using the ternary `max_valued` predicate recursively.

```
max_valued([], Term, Term).
max_valued([Head|Tail], Term, Max) :-
    higher_valued(Head, Term),
    max_valued(Tail, Head, Max).
max_valued([Head|Tail], Term, Max) :-
    higher_valued(Term, Head),
    max_valued(Tail, Term, Max).
```

The clauses in the definition of ternary `max_valued` are mutually exclusive. In particular, the last two require different relative magnitudes of `Head` and `Term`. However, if the second clause is used and later failure causes backtracking, the third clause will then be tried. The complete recomputation of `higher_valued(Term, Head)` will be performed which, by virtue of the asymmetry of the notion "higher valued", will fail. However, arbitrary computation may have to be performed before this mutual exclusivity of the two clauses is manifested, because the computation of `higher_valued(Term, Head)` may be arbitrarily complex.

We can increase the efficiency of `max_valued` by making this exclusivity explicit so that if the second clause is chosen, the third clause will never be backtracked into. The following redefinition suffices:

```
max_valued([Head|Tail], Max) :-
    max_valued(Tail, Head, Max).

max_valued([], Term, Term).
max_valued([Head|Tail], Term, Max) :-
    higher_valued(Head, Term),
    !,
    max_valued(Tail, Head, Max).
max_valued([Head|Tail], Term, Max) :-
    higher_valued(Term, Head),
    max_valued(Tail, Term, Max).
```

In this version of the program, as soon as we have ascertained that `Head` is higher than `Term` in value, we will eliminate the possibility of using the third clause, since we know that its first literal is doomed to failure anyway.

This cut maintains the semantics of the program only for certain modes of execution of the program. In particular, if the mode is `max_valued(-,?)`, then the cut version may return fewer solutions than the uncut. However, use of `max_valued` in this way will in any case generate instantiation errors if the arithmetic operators are used within `higher_valued`.

In summary, using cuts in this way without changing the meaning of the program can in some cases improve performance significantly. Nonetheless, this trick (and trick it is) should only be used when *necessary*, not when *possible*.

A second use of cuts is for eliminating redundancy in a program. Consider the alternate `shuffle` predicate defined by the following clauses:

```
shuffle(A, [], A).
shuffle([], B, B).
shuffle([A|RestA], B, [A|Shuffled]) :-
    shuffle(RestA, B, Shuffled).
shuffle(A, [B|RestB], [B|Shuffled]) :-
    shuffle(A, RestB, Shuffled).
```

This `shuffle` program correctly implements the *shuffle* relation. However, the predicate allows redundant solutions; we can see this by backtracking through the solutions it allows.

```
?- shuffle([a,b],[1],Shuffled).
Shuffled = [a,b,1] ;
Shuffled = [a,b,1] ;
Shuffled = [a,b,1] ;
Shuffled = [a,1,b] ;
Shuffled = [a,1,b] ;
Shuffled = [a,1,b] ;
Shuffled = [1,a,b] ;
Shuffled = [1,a,b] ;
Shuffled = [1,a,b] ;
Shuffled = [1,a,b] ;
no
```

The problem is that if one of the lists is empty, the program has the choice either of using one of the first two clauses to immediately determine the answer, or of traversing the nonempty list using one of the last two clauses. In either case, the solution is the same. One way to fix the predicate is to guarantee that the clauses are mutually exclusive.

```
shuffle([], [], []).
shuffle([A|RestA], B, [A|Shuffled]) :-
    shuffle(RestA, B, Shuffled).
shuffle(A, [B|RestB], [B|Shuffled]) :-
    shuffle(A, RestB, Shuffled).
```

However, this solution might be seen as inefficient, since in the case that one of the lists is empty, the other list is still entirely traversed. An alternative is to place cuts after the first two clauses so that if one of the lists is empty, the use of one of the first two clauses will cut away the possibility of using the later clauses to traverse the nonempty list.

```
shuffle(A, [], A) :- !.
shuffle([], B, B) :- !.
shuffle([A|RestA], B, [A|Shuffled]) :-
    shuffle(RestA, B, Shuffled).
shuffle(A, [B|RestB], [B|Shuffled]) :-
    shuffle(A, RestB, Shuffled).
```

As a matter of style, we prefer the nonredundant solution with no cuts to this final one. The example was introduced merely as an illustration of the general technique of removing redundancy.

The third use of cut we will discuss here is a technique for implementing conditionals. Unlike the previous two uses, in which the declarative interpretation of the programs was the same whether or not the cuts were inserted, this use of cut actually changes both the procedural *and* the declarative interpretations. Such uses of cut are often referred to as "red" cuts, to distinguish them from the less dangerous "green" cuts we first discussed.

A conditional definition of a predicate *p* of the form "if *condition* then *truecase* else *falsecase*" can be represented in Prolog using cuts as follows:

```
p :-   condition, !,  truecase.
p :-   falsecase.
```

If the condition holds, the cut will prevent backtracking into the *falsecase*. On the other hand, if the condition fails, the *truecase* will, of course, not be executed. Thus the cases are executed just according to the normal notion of the conditional.

As an application of such a conditional, consider the merge function introduced in Section 3.4.1.

```
merge(A, [], A).
merge([], B, B).
merge([A|RestAs], [B|RestBs], [A|Merged]) :-
    A < B,
    merge(RestAs, [B|RestBs], Merged).
merge([A|RestAs], [B|RestBs], [B|Merged]) :-
    B =< A,
    merge([A|RestAs], RestBs, Merged).
```

The last two clauses can be thought of as saying: "if *A* < *B* then pick *A* else pick *B*." The predicate can be reimplemented using cut to reflect this conditional:

```
merge(A, [], A).
merge([], B, B).
merge([A|RestAs], [B|RestBs], [A|Merged]) :- !,
    A < B,
    merge(RestAs, [B|RestBs], Merged).
merge([A|RestAs], [B|RestBs], [B|Merged]) :-
    merge([A|RestAs], RestBs, Merged).
```

Certain versions of Prolog include a notation for conditionals which generalizes those built with cuts in this way. The goal

```
condition -> truecase ; falsecase
```

is used for this purpose. Use of the explicit conditional is preferred to implicit conditionals built with cut. With this notation, the `merge` example can be rewritten as

```
merge(A, [], A).
merge([], B, B).
merge([A|RestAs], [B|RestBs], [C|Merged]) :-
    A < B
      -> (merge(RestAs, [B|RestBs], Merged),
          C = A)
      ; (merge([A|RestAs], RestBs, Merged),
          C = B).
```

Note the use of the = operator defined in Program 3.2.

5.1.3   The Negation-as-Failure Operator

In pure Horn clauses, it is possible to prove only positive conclusions; Prolog can prove that something *is* the case, but never that something is *not*. However, some situations intuitively have the same character as reaching a negative conclusion, namely those in which Prolog fails to prove a goal. We might assume that if Prolog cannot prove something true, then it must be false. Implicit in this assumption is the idea that the Prolog program from which Prolog could not prove the given goal has complete information about its intended domain of interpretation. This "complete information" interpretation (or *closed world assumption* as it is called) is so natural that we use it all the time without noticing. For example, if a string cannot be analyzed as a sentence for some grammar, we may conclude that the string is not grammatical. If two people are not related by the `ancestor` relation in our family database, we may conclude that neither is an ancestor of the other. Concluding the negation of a statement from failure to prove it has become known in logic programming as *negation as failure* (Clark, 1978).

Negation as failure is a reasonable interpretation of proof failure under the closed world assumption because Prolog provides a *complete* proof procedure; that is, Prolog will not conclude there is no proof of a goal when there is one. However, things are more subtle than the foregoing discussion implies. Since any Turing machine can be represented by a pure Prolog program (Tärnlund, 1977), the recursive unsolvability of the Turing-machine halting problem implies that the determination of whether a goal is provable is in general an undecidable question. If a goal is unprovable, Prolog may terminate with a failure answer, or it may loop forever (ignoring resource limitations!). Because of its leftmost-literal selection rule, Prolog might in fact loop even for goals for which a proof procedure with a different selection rule would terminate with failure. In general, a goal is *finitely failed* (with respect to a program) if the proof procedure terminates with failure for the goal.

All versions of Prolog provide some form of negation-as-failure operator. We will here assume the Edinburgh \+ operator. A goal \+G succeeds if and only if Prolog (finitely) fails to prove G. It turns out that \+ behaves exactly as if defined by the program

```
\+ Goal :- call(Goal) -> fail ; true.
```

This program has no reasonable declarative interpretation. Procedurally, \+ tries to execute its argument `Goal` in the first clause. If `Goal` succeeds, the `fail` causes the whole call to \+ to fail. Otherwise, \+ `Goal` succeeds trivially in the second branch of the conditional.

An important limitation of the above operator is that it does not achieve its intended interpretation if its argument contains unbound variables. This is shown by the different behaviors of the queries

```
?- \+ p(X), X = a.
```

and

```
?- X = a, \+ p(X).
```

with the program

```
p(b).
```

Tracing the execution of \+ in both queries, we see that the first query fails while the second one succeeds, even though the two queries have the same logical interpretation.

The problem here is that the implementation of \+G behaves as if any unbound variables in G were existentially quantified *inside* the operator, whereas, to be consistent with the variable scoping conventions Prolog uses (as discussed in Section 2.3), the variables should be treated as quantified at the outermost level in the enclosing query or clause. In other words, a goal such as

```
:- \+ p(X).
```

is executed as if it meant :- \+$((\exists X)p(X))$, while in fact it should mean $(\forall X)$:- \+p(X). As a consequence, \+ can be interpreted declaratively as negation-as-failure only if its argument has no unbound variables. Some versions of Prolog, for instance MU-Prolog (Naish, 1986), have a sound negation-as-failure operator, which basically delays the execution of the negated goal until all of its variables have been sufficiently instantiated. (What "sufficiently" means here is beyond the scope of this book.)

5.1.4   The setof predicate

The control regime of Prolog generates alternative solutions for a goal only through backtracking. Unless some literal fails, an alternate solution to an earlier goal will never be generated. On occasion, however, we may be interested not in *some* solution to a goal, but in *all* solutions. The setof predicate allows execution of a goal—like call—but in such a way that a list of all solutions is generated.

A literal of the form setof(T, G, S), where T is some term (usually a variable) and G is a goal (usually containing the variable), will hold just in case S is a list representing the instantiations of T under all assignments generated as solutions to the goal G. This goal can be read "the set of Ts such that G holds of each one is S". For instance, the query

```
?- setof(T, shuffle([a,b],[1],T), S).
S = [[1,a,b],[a,1,b],[a,b,1]],
T = _ ;
no
```

computes the set of shuffles of [a,b] and [1], encoded as a list.

An important issue concerns variables in the goal G other than those in T. For instance, consider the goal setof(T, conc(T, U, [1,2,3]), S). We must distinguish between variables that are interpreted as bound by an existential quantifier within the scope of a setof literal and variables that are bound outside the scope of the setof, or, in other words, to distinguish between "the set of Ts such that there is a U ..." and "for some U, the set of Ts such that...". As seen in the following query, variables occurring in G that are not in T are in general treated as being outside of the scope of the setof.

```
?- setof(T, conc(T, U, [1,2,3]), S).

T = _,
U = [],
S = [[1,2,3]] ;

T = _,
U = [1,2,3],
S = [[]] ;
```

```
T = _,
U = [2,3],
S = [[1]] ;

T = _,
U = [3],
S = [[1,2]] ;

no
```

To obtain behavior reflecting the narrow scope for binding of such variables, the setof predicate allows "existentially quantified" variables to be prefixed to the goal G with the infix operator "^".[1]

```
?- setof(T, U^conc(T, U, [1,2,3]), S).
T = _,
U = _,
S = [[],[1],[1,2],[1,2,3]] ;
no
```

Note that a setof literal fails (rather than succeeding with S the empty list) if the goal G has no solutions.

A related predicate, bagof, differs from setof only in that redundant solutions are not removed.

```
?- setof(T, member(T, [1,1,2]), S).
T = _,
S = [1,2]
yes

?- bagof(T, member(T, [1,1,2]), S).
T = _,
S = [1,1,2]
yes
```

5.1.5   The assert command

Interaction with Prolog as discussed so far consists of presenting queries to be executed against a static database of Horn clauses. The assert command (and related commands like retract) allow a program to alter the clause database dynamically; the program can "rewrite itself" as execu-

---

[1]This use of ^ is unrelated to and should not be confused with its use in lambda-expression encodings.

tion progresses. The idea of a program changing itself while executing is both powerful and dangerous. The use of facilities to perform such actions is therefore tendentious. Overuse of these facilities is one of the most common errors of beginning Prolog programming.

A clause can be added to the database by calling `assert` with the clause as argument. For example, the clause

```
remembered([shrdlu, halts],
           s(np(shrdlu),vp(iv(halts)))).
```

can be added to the database by execution of the following goal:

```
assert(remembered([shrdlu, halts],
                  s(np(shrdlu),vp(iv(halts))))))
```

Here again Prolog relies on the trick of representing object-level variables by metalevel variables.

The following program, for instance, will compute the parse tree for a sentence (assuming a DCG like that in Program 3.11). Furthermore, once the parse tree has been computed, it is "remembered" by asserting a unit clause into the database. If the parse tree for the sentence is ever again requested, the computation using the grammar will not be done; instead, the appropriate unit clause will be used. The cut in the program guarantees that even on backtracking, no recomputation of the parse tree is performed.

```
remember(Sentence, Parse) :-
    remembered(Sentence, Parse), !.

remember(Sentence, Parse) :-
    s(Parse, Sentence, []),
    assert(remembered(Sentence, Parse)).
```

This program can be understood only procedurally. It makes sense only under certain execution modes and calling conventions. In particular, if the grammar was ambiguous for a particular sentence, this ambiguity will never be manifested, since on backtracking after the first call the cut eliminates further possibilities. We will see a more coherent, useful application for `assert` as a tool for remembering lemmas (that is, previously proven results) in Section 6.6.3.

5.1.6   Other Extralogical Predicates

We conclude our discussion of extralogical features of Prolog with a grab bag of built-in Prolog predicates that we will find useful in later examples.

Of course, since these predicates fall outside the pure subset of Prolog they should be used sparingly and with appropriate trepidation.

Perhaps the canonical metalogical predicate is `var`, which holds if its single argument is a variable at the time the literal is executed. Similarly, `atomic` holds of a term if it is a constant (i.e., a number or atom) at execution time. Note that procedural issues like literal ordering are crucial in determining the behavior of these predicates. For instance, compare the two queries

```
?- var(X), X = a.
X = a
yes

?- atomic(X), X = a.
no
```

to the queries with literals reversed.

```
?- X = a, var(X).
no

?- X = a, atomic(X).
X = a
yes
```

A useful device for composing and decomposing terms is the binary infix operator =.., which holds of two arguments `Term` and `List` if `Term` is a term with functor of arity k and `List` is a list of length $k+1$ whose first element is the functor name of `Term` and whose last k elements are the k arguments of `Term`. For example, we have

```
?- T =.. [f, a, X, g(X)].
T = f(a,X,g(X))
yes

?- f(a,X,g(X)) =.. L.
L = [f, a, X, g(X)]
yes
```

This predicate, like the arithmetic predicates of Section 3.4.1, is not so much extralogical as incompletely implemented, in that execution of the predicate with improper instantiation of its arguments results in an instantiation error rather than a failure of the call. In particular, it must be called with either one or the other of its arguments instantiated. Furthermore, if the first argument is uninstantiated, the second must be a list whose first element is a constant. These restrictions follow from the requirement that appropriate solutions for variables must be determinable at the execution time of the predicate.[2]

5.2   A Simple Dialogue Program

We now turn to the design of the `talk` program, a simple natural-language question-answering system which demonstrates some of the metalogical facilities just described. Here is a typical dialogue that could be handled by `talk`.

```
?- main_loop.
>> principia is a book
Asserted "book(principia)."
>> bertrand wrote every book
Asserted "wrote(bertrand,B) :- book(B)."
>> which of the books did bertrand write
Error: too difficult.
>> what did bertrand write
principia.
>> every professor that wrote a program met bertrand
Asserted "met(P,bertrand) :-
            professor(P), program(R), wrote(P,R)."
```

Notice that `talk` can give only *extensional* answers to questions; for example, to the question "What did Bertrand write?" it can answer only with specific entities that it can prove Bertrand wrote, and not with general answers such as "every book." In fact, the best way of understanding `talk` input is as convenient notation for Prolog clauses to be added to the knowledge base and for Prolog goals to be proved.

`talk` is also limited in that it works with a predefined vocabulary, specified in the grammar. It would not be difficult to add a simple mechanism to allow the user to define new words, but such a mechanism would be usable only because of the small grammatical and semantic capabilities of `talk`. The more general problem of vocabulary acquisition for large natural-language processing systems is a separate research topic (Grosz et al., 1987).

---

[2]Often the use of `=..` can be replaced by the more efficient built-in predicates `functor(Term, Name, Arity)`, which holds when `Term` has main functor with name `Name` and arity `Arity`, and `arg(Number, Term, Arg)`, which holds when the argument of `Term` in position `Number` is `Arg`. In the cases we will consider, the `=..` operator is more readable.

The `talk` program works by

1. Parsing a sentence, simultaneously building a representation of its logical form.

2. Converting the logical form to a Horn clause (if possible).

3. Either adding the clause to the Prolog database (if the sentence was declarative) or interpreting the clause as a query and retrieving the answers to the query.

To perform these tasks, the program makes use of the metalogical facilities just described. The cut command is used to encode conditionals. The `assert` command is used to modify the Prolog database incrementally while the program is running. The `setof` predicate is used to find all answers to a query.

5.2.1 Overall Operation

The main predicate is `talk` which when executed performs the three phases of computation just described.

```
talk(Sentence, Reply) :-
    parse(Sentence, LF, Type),
    clausify(LF, Clause, FreeVars), !,
    reply(Type, FreeVars, Clause, Reply).
talk(Sentence, error('too difficult')).
```

Note the use of cut. If the sentence cannot be parsed or if its logical form cannot be converted to a Horn clause, the reply will be `error('too difficult')`. The cut encodes the conditional "if the sentence can be parsed and clausified then reply appropriately else the sentence is too difficult".

5.2.2 Parsing

The sentence is parsed by the `parse` predicate instantiating LF to the logical form for the sentence (as in Section 4.1), and instantiating `Type` to `query` or `assertion` depending on whether the sentence was interrogative or declarative.

```
parse(Sentence, LF, assertion) :-
    s(finite, LF, nogap, Sentence, []).
parse(Sentence, LF, query) :-
    q(LF, Sentence, []).
```

The grammar used in the `talk` program is based on that developed in previous chapters, in particular Program 4.5, but modified to allow questions and declarative sentences with the copular verb "be". The analysis of the copula which we use here is sorely inadequate. It serves merely as an expedient to allow certain sentences needed for nontrivial dialogues. More sophisticated analyses of auxiliaries that mesh more nicely with the copula could be inserted. Semantically, the verb "be" requires a complement noun phrase which is existentially quantified, i.e., of the form `(X^Q)^exists(X,P&Q)`. The logical form of a sentence containing "be" is constructed by applying the subject LF to the property P, ignoring Q altogether.

As in Program 4.3, the terms that give the meanings of content words such as *book* are now marked with the prefix operator " ' ", as in `'book(X)`. This makes the translation from logical form to Prolog easier, because it clearly distinguishes logical connectives from subject domain operators.

The logical forms for questions are implications C => `answer`(a), meaning that a is an answer for the question if condition C representing the text of the question holds. For yes-no questions, the answer is `yes` if the text of the question holds. For WH-questions, the answers are the instantiations of a that satisfy the goal. Note that this differs from the semantics given by Program 4.5.

5.2.3   LF Conversion

Logical forms are converted to Horn clauses by the predicate `clausify`. A literal `clausify(Formula, Clause, Vars)` holds if `Clause` is the clausal form of the FOL formula `Formula` and `Vars` is a list of the variables free in the antecedent of the clause. (The need for `Vars` will be explained later.)

The main point to note about `clausify` is that it is a partial function. Although all logical forms generated by the grammar are closed first-order formulas, some of them are not Horn clauses. For example, the question "Who wrote every book?" has the logical form

```
all(B,book(B) => wrote(X,B)) => answer(X).     ,
```

which is not a Horn clause. We leave as an exercise for the reader to determine what sentence types may or may not be represented by Horn clauses. As we have seen, Horn clauses must obey several restrictions. Outermost quantifiers must be universally quantified. Thus, to clausify a universally quantified expression, we merely strip off the quantifier and clausify the rest.

```
clausify(all(X,F0),F,[X|V]) :- clausify(F0,F,V).
```

If a clause has an implication symbol, the consequent must be a single literal, and the antecedent must have variables existentially quantified with no other implication symbols.

```
clausify(A0=>C0,(C:-A),V) :-
    clausify_literal(C0,C),
    clausify_antecedent(A0,A,V).
```

Otherwise, if the clause has no implication symbol it must be a unit clause, a single literal.

```
clausify(C0,C,[]) :-
    clausify_literal(C0,C).
```

As mentioned above, antecedents must have variables quantified existentially, but may consist of several literals, not just the one allowed in the consequent.

```
clausify_antecedent(L0,L,[]) :-
    clausify_literal(L0,L).
clausify_antecedent(E0&F0,(E,F),V) :-
    clausify_antecedent(E0,E,V0),
    clausify_antecedent(F0,F,V1),
    conc(V0,V1,V).
clausify_antecedent(exists(X,F0),F,[X|V]) :-
    clausify_antecedent(F0,F,V).
```

Finally, literals are clausified merely by removing the backquote marker.

```
clausify_literal('L,L).
```

Note that each clause for `clausify` and `clausify_antecedent` includes a third argument that keeps track of the variables free in the antecedent of the clause.

In the translation from logical form to Prolog we can also see how Prolog clauses are represented as Prolog terms with the binary functors ":-" and "," used for implication and conjunction, respectively. On the second clause of `clausify` we have the term `(C:-A)`[3] used to construct a clause representation, and in the second clause of `clausify_antecedent` we have the term `(E,F)` being used to build a conjunction in the antecedent of a clause.

---

[3]The parentheses are required as usual for reasons of operator precedence.

Here also we see another instance of the previously discussed "confusion" between object level and metalevel. In the clauses for `clausify` and `clausify_antecedent`, variables are used to stand for fragments of logical forms and Prolog clauses. At the same time, quantified variables in the logical form are also represented by Prolog variables, and end up as the variables of the resulting Prolog clause.

5.2.4 Constructing A Reply

Finally, once the sentence has been parsed and its logical form converted to a clause, a reply is constructed. If the sentence is declarative, the clause is merely asserted into the Prolog database so that future queries will use it.

```
reply(assertion, _FreeVars, Assertion,
      asserted(Assertion)) :-
   assert(Assertion), !.
```

Clauses associated with queries are always of the form `answer(Answer) :-` `Condition`, by virtue of the semantics given to questions in the grammar. The `Answer`s associated with all solutions of `Condition` are generated using `setof` and this set forms the reply. If no answers are generated, the simple reply "no" is used.

```
reply(query, FreeVars,
      (answer(Answer):-Condition), Reply) :-
   (setof(Answer, FreeVars^Condition, Answers)
      -> Reply = Answers
      ; Reply = [no]), !.
```

For example, the question "Who wrote a book?" would be translated into the Prolog clause

```
answer(X) :- book(B), wrote(X,B).
```

This is then evaluated by the goal

```
setof(X,[B]^(book(B),wrote(X,B)),S)     ;
```

that is, S is the set of Xs such that there is a book B that X wrote. Note the use of the set of free clause variables that we took pains to recover in the LF conversion predicates. By existentially quantifying them inside the `setof` predicate, we guarantee that all solutions for any assignment to the free variables are recovered, not just for one assignment to them.

Finally, any other type of sentence generates an error message. The cuts in previous clauses prevent backtracking into this clause once another clause has matched.

```
reply(_Type, _FreeVars, _Clause,
      error('unknown type')).
```

5.3   User Interaction

The mode of interaction of the `talk` program as it stands requires putting to the Prolog interpreter goals encoding the sentence as a list. For instance, we might have the following dialog.

```
?- talk([principia, is, a, book], Reply).
Reply = asserted(book(principia))
yes

?- talk([bertrand, wrote, every, book], Reply).
Reply = asserted((wrote(bertrand,B):-book(B)))
yes

?- talk([what, did, bertrand, write], Reply).
Reply = answer([principia])
yes
```

A more natural mode of interaction would enable the user to type sentences directly, and receive replies from the system not as variable assignments, but as an appropriate response to the input. To enable such interfaces to be written, Prolog systems include built-in commands for performing input to and output from a terminal or other device.

Input/output specification is typically the most idiosyncratic and variable part of any programming language, and Prolog is no exception. We will therefore present just a few very primitive commands—sufficient to write a user interface for `talk`—which tend to be supported by most Prolog systems. Readers will undoubtedly want to refer to the manuals for their own systems to determine the range of input/output commands that are available.

Note that all of these commands work through side effects such as changing the state of the terminal screen or input buffer. Since side effects have no place in the declarative semantics of Prolog, these are all members of the strictly extralogical part of Prolog. Retrying such commands or backtracking through them does not cause their side effects to be undone, and they work only in certain modes.

5.3.1   Simple Input/Output Commands

The unary **write** command prints its term argument to the standard output (usually the terminal). Its inverse, **read**, reads a term delimited by a period and newline from the standard input (usually the terminal as well) and unifies its argument with the term that is read. Typically, it is called in mode **read(-)**, so that its argument is a variable that is bound to the term read.

Input/output behavior at the character rather than term level is possible with commands **get** and **put**. The **get** command reads a single printing character from the input stream, unifying its argument with the integer that is the ASCII code for the character read. Nonprinting characters (like spaces, tabs, newlines and control characters) are skipped. Its companion command **get0** works the same, except that nonprinting characters are not skipped. To print a character to the standard output, the **put** command is called with the integer corresponding to the character to be printed as its argument. The zero-ary predicate **nl** puts a newline character to the standard output.

5.3.2   A Simple User Interface

Using these commands, we can develop a simple user interface for the **talk** program. First, we need a program to read sentences from the terminal. The predicate **read_sent** will return a list of words which were typed separated by spaces and ended by a newline character.

```
read_sent(Words) :-
    get0(Char),
    read_sent(Char, Words).
```

It gets the next character from the input stream as a lookahead and, depending on the lookahead character, either continues reading or stops. If the lookahead is a newline, input is ended.

```
read_sent(C, []) :- newline(C), !.
```

If the lookahead is a space, it is ignored, as spaces are not part of the next word.

```
read_sent(C, Words) :- space(C), !,
    get0(Char),
    read_sent(Char, Words).
```

Any other character is assumed to start a word. The auxiliary predicate read_word is called to retrieve the characters that constitute the next word from the input. Then the built-in predicate name packs this list of characters into an atom. Finally, more words are read from the input.

```
read_sent(Char, Words) :-
    read_word(Char, Chars, Next),
    name(Word, Chars),
    read_sent(Next, Words).
```

Reading a word from the input stream proceeds similarly. The predicate read_word takes the lookahead character and builds a list of characters starting with the lookahead that comprise the word. The new lookahead, the delimiter following the word, is matched with the third argument to read_word. Newlines and spaces delimit the words.

```
read_word(C, [], C) :- space(C), !.
read_word(C, [], C) :- newline(C), !.
```

All other characters are added to the list of characters to be formed into a word.

```
read_word(Char, [Char|Chars], New) :-
    get0(Next),
    read_word(Next, Chars, New).
```

Using read_sent, we can write a top-level loop that reads sentences, computes the appropriate reply with talk, and prints that reply.

```
main_loop :-
    write('>> '),
    read_sent(Words),
    talk(Words, Reply),
    print_reply(Reply),
    main_loop.
```

The final recursive call of main_loop starts the read-compute-print loop over again.

Finally, a program to print the replies in a more satisfactory fashion was assumed in the definition of main_loop. This predicate, print_reply, is listed in the Appendix A code. As it presents no interesting problems, its definition is not repeated here.

Interacting with the `talk` program through this interface, although not ideal, is considerably more natural as evidenced by the dialogue presented at the beginning of Section 5.2. The full commented listing for the `talk` program is given in Appendix A.

5.4   Bibliographic Notes

Most of the extralogical facilities of Prolog discussed in this chapter go back to the original Marseille Prolog (Roussel, 1975). In that system, `!`, `assert` and `=..` were called respectively `/` (the *slash*, suggesting the cutting of alternative branches of the search space), `AJOUT`, and `UNIV`.

The general question of extralogical facilities has led to much discussion in the logic programming community. At their best, those facilities can be seen as operators on axiom sets and derivations, for which a reasonable semantics might be forthcoming (Bowen and Kowalski, 1981; Bowen and Weinberg, 1985). At their worst, extralogical facilites are just means of simulating imperative language features within Prolog. Often, these simulations not only detract from the logical semantics of Prolog but also incur considerable performance penalties, since the most efficient aspects of Prolog are generally those with a clean semantics (Warren, 1977).

Of all extralogical operations in Prolog, the cut seems to be the most often used and the source of most controversy. The primitive storage management techniques of early Prolog systems meant that nondeterminate computations used very large amounts of space. Since the cut operator makes a subcomputation determinate, "green" cuts were used in early Prolog programs as the main method of storage conservation. More recently, improved storage management techniques and better determinacy detection in Prolog compilers (Warren, 1977; Tick and Warren, 1984; Pittomvils et al., 1985; Bowen et al., 1986) have made that use of cut less important, at least for those with access to state-of-the-art Prolog systems.

The use of cut to implement a limited form of negation as nonprovability also goes back to Marseille, although it is difficult to give a precise reference to the first appearance of the technique. The overall question of the meaning of negation-as-nonprovability has been extensively researched. Lloyd's book (1984) presents some of the main theoretical concepts and results on the subject, originally discovered by Clark (1978), Apt and van Emden (1982) and Jaffar, Lassez, and Lloyd (1983). These results include denotational characterizations of the meaning of different possible notions of negation, and proofs of the soundness and completeness of negation-as-failure with respect to the *completions* of definite-clause programs. A more recent survey of results and open problems was given by Jaffar, Lassez and

Maher (1986). These theoretical developments proceeded in parallel with the discovery of computational mechanisms allowing sound implementations of negation-as-failure, embodied in Colmerauer's Prolog-II (1986) and Naish's MU-Prolog (1986). These mechanisms involve delaying negations (or, as a special case, inequalities) until variables become "sufficiently" bound.

The set construction operator `setof` we use here is due to D. H. D. Warren (1982) and was first implemented in DEC-10 Prolog (Bowen, 1982). From a practical point of view, the requirement that all narrow-scope existentially quantified variables be explicitly marked with the ^ operator is sometimes burdensome. Other proposed set operators (Morris et al., 1986) adopt the opposite convention.

Our `talk` program is a rather simplistic example of a natural-language interface to a knowledge base. A comparable example program was given as an example of application of Colmerauer's metamorphosis grammars (1978). The program's structure and operation are closely modeled on those of more comprehensive Prolog natural-language database interfaces such as those by Dahl (1981), F. C. N. Pereira (1982), Pereira and Warren (1982), and McCord (1982), even though those systems dealt only with questions and not with assertions. The limitation of allowable assertions to those whose meaning can be expressed by definite clauses circumvents the difficult question of what to do with assertions that contradict existing system knowledge (Haas and Hendrix, 1981). More generally, natural-language interface systems should be able to deal with unmet presuppositions in questions and commands as well as with assertions that contradict existing information (Winograd, 1972).

As we pointed out, our example program cannot acquire new words not in its initial vocabulary. In general, this is a difficult question. Besides the determination of syntactic category and features, word acquisition should be able to determine use and meaning constraints for the word, either from other information supplied in natural language (Haas and Hendrix, 1981) or from specialized acquisition-dialogue mechanisms (Grosz et al., 1987; Ballard and Stumberger, 1986).

6

Interpreters

In previous chapters we have seen that a very powerful grammar formalism, definite-clause grammars, can be used to describe a variety of NL-related phenomena and can be directly embedded in Prolog. In so doing, the grammar engenders a top-down, recursive-descent, backtrack parser for the language of the grammar. For applications where such a parser is sufficient, this technique can be quite useful. We have, however, already seen evidence of frailties of Prolog and DCGs. For instance,

- Since Prolog programs with left-recursion have termination problems, so will direct Prolog execution of DCGs with left-recursive rules.

- Arguments in DCG rules having a regular, predictable structure— e.g., those which enforce filler-gap dependencies, build parse trees building, or construct logical forms—tend to proliferate and complicate grammars.

These and similar problems have been addressed in logic-programming research. Some of the tools for solving them—by extending or modifying Prolog or the grammar formalism—exist within Prolog itself, but rely on using the language in different ways. Rather than embedding programs or grammars directly in Prolog, we can define an *interpreter* for the extended language in Prolog itself. An interpreter is a *meta-program* in that it uses other programs as data.[1] By writing specialized interpreters, it is possible not only to cover new language constructs, but also to try out new evaluation strategies for a language.

---

[1] For this reason, what we call interpreters are sometimes referred to somewhat confusingly as *meta-interpreters*, even though they do not in general interpret interpreters.

6.1   Prolog in Prolog

We will begin our discussion of interpreters with the basis for extensions to Prolog, namely, an interpreter for pure Prolog, written in pure Prolog itself. Such interpreters written in their own object language are often called *meta-circular interpreters*. In fact, we have seen one meta-circular Prolog interpreter already, the predicate `prove` in Program 5.1. In this less trivial example, we assume that the object-level Prolog program to be interpreted is encoded with the unary predicate `clause`. For instance, the conc predicate, defined as Program 3.3, would be encoded *as data for the interpreter* by the clauses[2]

```
clause((   conc([], L, L) :- true      )).
clause((   conc([E|R], L, [E|RL]) :-
               conc(R, L, RL)          )).
```

Notice that the clauses are encoded by Prolog terms and the object-level variables by meta-level variables. We have seen this kind of "level-shifting" between object- and meta-level before, for instance, in the use of Prolog (meta-level) variables to encode lambda-calculus (object-level) variables (see Section 4.1.3). In the writing of interpreters, such level-crossing is ubiquitous.

The interpreter is implemented by the predicate `prove`, which takes an object level goal (encoded as a term) and follows the Prolog proof procedure using the program axiomatized by `clause` clauses. The intention is that the goal `prove(Goal)` be provable by Prolog if the goal `Goal` is as well. Clearly, the trivial goal `true` is always provable.

```
prove(true).
```

Any other goal is provable only if there is some clause which matches it and whose body is provable.

```
prove(Goal) :-
    clause((Goal :- Body)),
    prove(Body).
```

Finally, if the body consists of the conjunction of two subgoals, they must be proved independently.

---

[2]The extra parentheses around each clause are required by Edinburgh Prolog syntax to inhibit Prolog from interpreting the :- with its normal precedence, which would cause it to be taken as binding weaker than the `clause` predicate itself. The parentheses force it to be interpreted in the natural way as taking just the material inside the parentheses as arguments. The same trick was used in Section 2.8.1.

```
prove((Body1, Body2)) :-
    prove(Body1),
    prove(Body2).
```

These three clauses, summarized as Program 6.1, constitute a full interpreter for pure Prolog written in Prolog.

Program 6.1
```
prove(true).
prove(Goal) :-
    clause((Goal :- Body)),
    prove(Body).
prove((Body1, Body2)) :-
    prove(Body1),
    prove(Body2).
```

By tracing the execution of the program proving a goal and comparing it to the trace of Prolog executing the same goal directly, as in Figure 6.1, we can see the parallelism between the interpreter's axiomatization of the object-level Prolog interpreter and the object-level interpreter itself.

6.1.1   Absorption

The difference between the three-clause interpreter and the trivial one-clause interpreter using `call` (Program 5.1) resides in the amount of work of the interpreter that is done by the Prolog execution mechanism the interpreter is being executed by. In the case of the trivial interpreter, all of the interpretation process is *absorbed* by the Prolog that is executing the interpreter. In the three-clause interpreter, much, but not all, of the work is being absorbed. For example, the unification of goal literals and clause heads is absorbed into the unification of terms in the executing Prolog. The order of clause choice is also absorbed. In fact, the only part that is not absorbed is the selection of literals in a conjunctive goal.

Interpreters are written so that portions of the interpretation process can be manipulated, changed, and otherwise investigated. The part of the interpretation process absorbed by the program executing the interpreter is not subject to such manipulation. Thus, if we are interested in experimenting with alternate literal selection rules, the one-clause interpreter will be insufficient for our purposes (since it absorbs literal selection), whereas the three-clause interpreter does allow changes in that area (since it makes literal selection explicit). However, if we wish to experiment with alternate unification methods (as is commonly done), neither of these interpreters suffices; they both absorb unification into the underlying execution. Note

```
?- conc([a,b],[c,d],A).

(1) 0 Call : conc([a,b],[c,d],L_1)

(2) 1 Call : conc([b],[c,d],RL_2)

(3) 2 Call : conc([],[c,d],RL_3)

(3) 2 Exit : conc([],[c,d],[c,d])

(2) 1 Exit : conc([b],[c,d],[b,c,d])

(1) 0 Exit : conc([a,b],[c,d],[a,b,c,d])

A = [a,b,c,d]

yes
```

```
?- prove( conc([a,b],[c,d],A) ).

(1) 0 Call : prove(conc([a,b],[c,d],L_1))
(2) 1 Call : clause((conc([a,b],[c,d],L_1):-Body_2))
(2) 1 Exit : clause((conc([a,b],[c,d],[a|RL_2]):-
                conc([b],[c,d],RL_2)))

(3) 1 Call : prove(conc([b],[c,d],RL_2))
(4) 2 Call : clause((conc([b],[c,d],RL_2):-Body_4))
(4) 2 Exit : clause((conc([b],[c,d],[b|RL_3]):-
                conc([],[c,d],RL_3)))

(5) 2 Call : prove(conc([],[c,d],RL_3))
(6) 3 Call : clause((conc([],[c,d],RL_3):-Body_6))
(6) 3 Exit : clause((conc([],[c,d],[c,d]):-true))
(7) 3 Call : prove(true)
(7) 3 Exit : prove(true)

(5) 2 Exit : prove(conc([],[c,d],[c,d]))

(3) 1 Exit : prove(conc([b],[c,d],[b,c,d]))

(1) 0 Exit : prove(conc([a,b],[c,d],[a,b,c,d]))

A = [a,b,c,d]

yes
```

Figure 6.1. Comparison of Direct Execution and Indirect Interpretation.

that the interpreters presented so far all absorb the various facets of the control structure of Prolog by implementing them with the *same* facets in the underlying execution. This circularity is not necessary, but is often the simplest method of absorption.

6.1.2 Keeping Proof Trees

As an example of one sort of extension to the language that interpreters make possible, we consider a version of Prolog that automatically generates proof trees for goals that it proves. An extra argument in the interpreter keeps track of the proof tree of the goal being proved. The proof tree encoding is as follows: If a literal L is proved by virtue of subproofs $P_1, \ldots, P_n$, then the proof tree for L

is encoded as the Prolog term

```
L :- P1, ..., Pn    .
```

The following interpreter accomplishes this task:

Program 6.2
```
prove(true, true).
prove(Goal, (Goal :- BodyProof)) :-
    clause((Goal :- Body)),
    prove(Body, BodyProof).
prove((Body1, Body2), (Body1Proof, Body2Proof)) :-
    prove(Body1, Body1Proof),
    prove(Body2, Body2Proof).
```

As an example, the interpreter generates the following proofs (manually indented for readability) for queries concerning the `shuffle` predicate defined as Program 3.4.

```
?- prove(shuffle([a,b],[1,2],S), Proof).

S = [1,2,a,b],
Proof = shuffle([a,b],[1,2],[1,2,a,b]):-
          (conc([],[a,b],[a,b]):-
            true),
          (shuffle([a,b],[2],[2,a,b]):-
            (conc([],[a,b],[a,b]):-
```

```
            true),
        (shuffle([a,b],[],[a,b]):-
            true),
        (conc([],[2,a,b],[2,a,b]):-
            true)),
    (conc([],[1,2,a,b],[1,2,a,b]):-
        true) ;

S = [1,a,2,b],
Proof = shuffle([a,b],[1,2],[1,a,2,b]):-
        (conc([],[a,b],[a,b]):-
            true),
        (shuffle([a,b],[2],[a,2,b]):-
            (conc([a],[b],[a,b]):-
                (conc([],[b],[b]):-
                    true)),
            (shuffle([b],[],[b]):-
                true),
            (conc([a],[2,b],[a,2,b]):-
                (conc([],[2,b],[2,b]):-
                    true))),
        (conc([],[1,a,2,b],[1,a,2,b]):-
            true)

yes
```

Using techniques of this sort, one can imagine writing interpreters that trace the execution of a program, detect looping in a program's execution, or allow interactive single-stepping of a program.

6.1.3 Unit Clauses

The three-clause Prolog interpreter does not allow unit clauses, e.g.,

```
conc([], L, L).
```

to be stated directly, say as

```
clause(conc([], L, L)).
```

Instead, they are encoded as

```
clause((conc([], L, L) :- true)).
```

Extending the interpreter to handle unit clauses correctly has one subtlety, in that the straightforward "solution" of adding a new clause to the
interpreter

```
prove(Goal) :-
    clause(Goal).
```

does not accurately reflect the top-to-bottom clause ordering that Prolog
uses. Instead, we could introduce a new predicate `aclause`, which picks up
clauses from the database and in the case of unit clauses, instantiates the
body of the clause as `true`.

Program 6.3
```
aclause((Head :- Body)) :-
    clause(Clause),
    (Clause = (Head :- Body)
        -> true
        ;  (Clause = Head, Body = true)).
```

Because the `clause` goal does not distinguish unit from nonunit clauses,
the top-to-bottom clause ordering will be respected in backtracking through
`aclause`.

6.2   Problem Section: Prolog Interpreters

6.2.1   Consecutively Bounded Depth-First Search

Because of its depth-first control regime, Prolog may fail to find a solution
to a query even when one exists. One solution to this problem is to sub-
stitute for depth-first execution an alternative regime called *consecutively
bounded depth-first* execution, which we will define in terms of a simpler,
but highly incomplete, control regime called *depth-bounded* execution.

In depth-bounded execution of a goal, the goal is proved in a depth-first
manner until a given depth of recursion is reached. At that point, if no
solution has been found, that branch of computation is considered to have
failed, and the system backtracks. For a given depth bound n, we will refer
to n-depth-bounded execution.

A depth-bounded Prolog interpreter will never loop infinitely. However, it will fail to find solutions that involve proofs that are deeper than the
depth bound. A compromise control regime that, unlike depth-bounded execution, can find arbitrarily complex proofs, yet that will not loop infinitely
in a depth-first manner, is consecutively bounded depth-first execution. In
this regime, a goal is executed by executing it under a 1-depth-bounded

regime. If no solutions are found, the system uses 2-depth-bounded execution, then 3-depth-bounded, and so on. If a proof exists, the system will eventually attempt to execute the goal with a large enough depth bound, and the proof will be found. Since each depth-bounded execution terminates, the consecutively bounded regime has the benefit that if a proof exists, it will eventually be found—a property that Prolog's depth-first regime does not share.

Of course, consecutively bounded execution involves a redundancy in computation, since later depth-bounded executions reiterate all the computation of earlier ones. The cost may not be as much as it appears at first blush, however, as the cost of executing the first $n - 1$ levels is only a constant factor of the cost of executing level n. Further analysis of the cost of this method is well beyond the scope of this problem.

Problem 6.1 *Write an interpreter for Prolog that uses a consecutively bounded depth-first control regime. Try it on a left-recursive program like Program 2.3 to demonstrate that it finds proofs where Prolog's control regime would not.*

6.2.2   An Interpreter For Cut

The interpreters devised so far have been concerned only with pure Prolog. In this section we consider the problem of writing an interpreter for pure Prolog augmented with the impure cut operator. For the purposes of this problem, we will assume that clauses have at most one cut in them. There are two cases we must consider. If there is no cut in the clause, we can interpret it as before. If there is a cut in the clause, we must interpret the part before the cut, then cut away further choices of `clause` clauses, and then interpret the part after the cut. (Notice the nice symmetry here: The pure Prolog meta-circular interpreter was written in pure Prolog. Augmenting the object language with cut requires the same augmentation to the meta-language. In essence, we will absorb the execution of cut using the cut of the underlying execution.) We will need a predicate, call it `cut_split(Body, Before, After)` which takes a `Body` of a clause and finds the part `Before` and `After` the cut (if there is one). The predicate fails if there is no cut.

Problem 6.2 *Write* `cut_split` *and use it to augment the interpreter to handle clauses with at most one cut per clause. Make sure the top-to-bottom clause ordering is respected.*

Problem 6.3 *(More difficult.) Write an interpreter that can correctly interpret Prolog programs with more than one cut per clause.*

6.3   Interpreters for DCGs

Extensions to the DCG formalism can be implemented just as extensions to Prolog, by extending an interpreter for DCGs. The DCG interpreter will use definite-clause grammars encoded in Prolog using the same encoding as in Section 3.7, except that the main functor will be ---> rather than -->, as declared by the following operator declaration:

```
:- op(1200,xfx,--->).
```

We use a different arrow for the same reason we used the clause predicate in the Prolog interpreters—to prevent the DCG from being automatically interpreted by the normal Prolog mechanism, since it is merely data for the interpreter.

6.3.1   DCG in Prolog

We turn now to the design of a DCG interpreter in Prolog. The structure of the interpreter—its use of pairs of string positions to keep track of the portion of string parsed—should by now be familiar.

The interpreter is implemented by the predicate parse corresponding to the predicate prove in the Prolog interpreter. The literal parse(NT, P0, P) holds if the string between positions P0 and P can be parsed as (i.e., is covered by) the nonterminal NT according to the definite-clause grammar. A nonterminal covers a string between two positions if the body of a matching rule does also.

```
parse(NT, P_0, P) :-
    (NT ---> Body),
    parse(Body, P_0, P).
```

If the body has several parts, all must be matched, in order.

```
parse((Body1, Body2), P_0, P) :-
    parse(Body1, P_0, P_1),
    parse(Body2, P_1, P).
```

The empty string, encoded with [], covers no string.

```
parse([], P, P).
```

A list of terms is treated as a list of terminal symbols to be found directly connecting the positions in the string.

```
parse([Word|Rest], P_0, P) :-
    connects(Word, P_0, P_1),
    parse(Rest, P_1, P).
```

Finally, recall that the Prolog/DCG brace notation allows a kind of level-crossing between DCGs and Prolog—an "escape" to Prolog. To implement this level-crossing, we need a way of interpreting terms as literals and executing them. The `call` predicate serves this purpose; its use in implementing the DCG escape to Prolog is as follows:

```
parse({Goals}, P, P) :- call(Goals).
```

For completeness, we repeat the definition of the `connects` predicate, originally defined by Program 3.8 in Section 3.4.2.

```
connects(Word, [Word|Rest], Rest).
```

Exercise 6.4 *Test the DCG interpreter just defined with a small DCG on a few sentences to convince yourself that it actually implements the DCG correctly.*

6.3.2   DCG in DCG

The astute reader may have noticed that the DCG interpreter presented above is in just the form of a DCG translated into Prolog. Thus, the interpreter could have been more succinctly stated by writing it as a DCG itself! In particular, the following DCG implements a meta-circular DCG interpreter.

Program 6.4

```
:- op(1200,xfx,--->).

parse(NT) -->
    {NT ---> Body},
    parse(Body).

parse((Body1,Body2)) -->
    parse(Body1),
    parse(Body2).

parse([]) --> [].
parse([Word|Rest]) -->
```

```
[Word],
parse(Rest).

parse({Goals}) --> {call(Goals)}.
```

Exercise 6.5 *Extend the DCG interpreter in Program 6.4 so that it auto-matically builds a parse tree representation of the parsed expression. This corresponds exactly to the problem of automatically generating a proof tree in the Prolog interpreter. You may want to refer to the discussion preceding Problem 3.7 for an applicable tree encoding method or use the =.. operator of Section 5.1.6 to build more standard tree encodings.*

6.3.3   An Interpreter for Filler-Gap DCGs

Filler-gap dependencies constitute a set of linguistic phenomena with a quite cumbersome encoding in DCGs, as we have seen in Sections 4.2.3 and 4.2.7. This problem has been noted by many people working on the design of logic grammars, and has been the inspiration for a large number of the logic grammar formalisms extending DCGs. As noted in Section 4.2.7, the gap-threading encoding of filler-gap dependencies lends itself to use in implementing an extension of DCGs to handle filler-gap dependencies because of the simple, regular structure of the extra filler-list argument it requires.

In this section we will develop a formalism, FG-DCG, that allows a simpler statement of filler-gap constraints and construct an interpreter for it. FG-DCG rules appear, for the most part, identical to DCG rules (except using the operator ---> as usual for interpretation). However, to directly state filler-gap constraints we must add to DCGs the ability to declare which constituents are fillers, which are islands, and what nonterminals can be realized as gaps. Various extensions to DCGs to handle filler-gap phenomena have taken different approaches to this notational problem. We will use the following notations.

- o A filler of type ϕ requiring a gap of type γ will be notated as a term of the form ϕ `fills` γ, where `fills` is an infix Prolog operator.

- o An island of type ϕ will be notated as a term of the form ϕ `island`, where `island` is a postfix Prolog operator.

- o The fact that a gap of type γ can be realized as α (usually, the empty string), is notated by the FG-DCG rule:

  `gap`(γ) `--->` α.

The interpretation of the special filler and island specifications in an FG-DCG rule is as follows: A term ϕ `fills` γ matches a constituent of type ϕ, but requires that a gap of type γ be found *within some sibling to the right of ϕ*. A phrase covered by the term ϕ `island` can never have a gap within it that is filled outside it. A use of a rule of the form `gap`(γ) `--->` α. must always fill a gap.

As a simple example of an FG-DCG grammar, we rewrite the grammar of Program 4.4 in the new notation. For brevity, we leave out the lexicon, which is unchanged from the earlier grammar. We also add a new rule for ditransitive verb phrases to highlight the fact that this grammar does not fall prey to the difficulties mentioned in Section 4.2.7.

Program 6.5

```
s ---> np island, vp.

np ---> det, n, optrel.
np ---> pn.

vp ---> dv, np, np.
vp ---> tv, np.
vp ---> iv.

optrel ---> [].
optrel ---> [that] fills np, s.
optrel ---> [that], vp.

gap(np) ---> [].
```

Note that the grammar encodes the filler-gap dependencies that were implicit in the earlier grammar far more simply and directly.

An interpreter for FG-DCGs is a straightforward extension to the DCG meta-circular interpreter of Program 6.4. First, we declare the necessary operators.

```
:- op(1200,xfx,--->).
:- op(300, xfx, fills).
:- op(300, xf, island).
```

Next, we augment the `parse` predicate with an argument for the filler list. Thus the clauses of the interpreter become

```
parse(NT, F0-F) -->
    {NT ---> Body},
    parse(Body, F0-F).
```

```
parse((Body1,Body2),F0-F) -->
    parse(Body1,F0-F1),
    parse(Body2,F1-F).

parse([], F0-F0) --> [].
parse([Word|Rest], F0-F) -->
    [Word],
    parse(Rest, F0-F).

parse({Goals}, F0-F0) --> {call(Goals)}.
```

Finally, we require special rules for islands, fillers, and gaps. An island is parsed as a constituent with empty filler list.

```
parse(NT island, F0-F0) -->
    parse(NT, F0-F0).
```

A list of nonterminals the first of which is a filler is parsed by parsing the filler, then parsing the rest of the list but with an additional element on the filler list—the type of gap that this filler corresponds to.

```
parse((NT fills GapType,Body2), F0-F) -->
    parse(NT,F0-F0),
    parse(Body2,[GapType|F0]-F).
```

Finally, a nonterminal NT can be realized as a gap corresponding to a filler in the filler list if there is a rule

```
gap(NT) ---> Body.
```

and the Body can itself be parsed. Of course, in most cases, Body will encode the empty string, but this additional ability to specify nonempty bodies of "gap" constituents allows us to use FG-DCGs for other long-distance dependencies such as resumptive pronouns in which the filler is associated with a pronoun embedded in the sentence.

```
parse(GapType, [GapType|F0]-F0) -->
    {gap(GapType) ---> Body},
    parse(Body, F0-F0).
```

Exercise 6.6 *Modify the grammar of Program 4.5 to use the FG-DCG notation.*

6.4 Partial Execution and Compilers

Using an interpreter to interpret a Prolog program is in general much less efficient than executing the program directly. Thus interpreters are of little use unless the language they interpret is an *extension* of Prolog; otherwise, using Prolog itself is an equivalent and more efficient method. We can recoup some of the efficiency lost in using an interpreter by *translating* or *compiling* the extended language into Prolog rather than *interpreting* it with an interpreter. For just this reason, DCGs are compiled into equivalent Prolog programs upon their being read into the Prolog system.

From an intuitive standpoint, the difference between a compilation and subsequent execution of a program and interpretation of the program is that the former moves some of the predictable proof steps to an earlier phase of processing. The idea of performing proof steps at an earlier stage is reminiscent of the notion of *partial execution* introduced in Section 4.1.4. In this section, we ground this intuition by developing a program to partially execute clauses and using it to build a compiler for definite-clause grammars.

6.4.1 Partial Execution Revisited

Recall the basic Prolog proof step of SLD resolution (Section 3.5.3). Resolution proceeds by picking a literal in a clause and replacing it with the body of a matching clause under the unifying substitution of the literal and the head of the clause. Partial execution of a clause merely performs certain of these resolution steps at an earlier stage of computation, called *compile time*. Since the order of resolutions is thereby changed, partial execution is only sound in the subset of Prolog in which the order of selection of literals is not critical to the correctness of execution of the program, that is, in pure Prolog. A clause (which we will call the *program clause*) is thus partially executed with respect to a set of predicates (called *auxiliary predicates*) by resolving the clause on literals containing these predicates and recursively partially executing the resolvent, until no more such resolutions can be performed.

Executing a goal involving the *program predicate* (the predicate defined by the program clause or clauses) using all possible partial executions of the program clauses is equivalent to executing it using the original program clauses plus all the auxiliary clauses as well. Consequently, we can replace the program and auxiliary clauses by the clauses resulting from partial execution. It is not necessary to resolve literals in the program clauses against the program clauses themselves, as their equivalents will be available at run time anyway. Furthermore, it is fortunate that such recursive resolutions are not needed, as they might lead to nontermination of the partial execution facility.

Partial execution thus requires a recursive traversal of a clause and its literals just as an interpreter does. But instead of proving each subgoal, we replace it with its definition. Thus the definition of a predicate to compute the relation between a program clause and its partial executions follows the form of an interpreter relatively closely. To partially execute a clause, we merely partially execute its body.

```
partially_execute((Head:-Body),
                  (Head:-ExpandedBody)) :- !,
    partially_execute(Body, ExpandedBody).
```

To partially execute a conjunction of goals, we partially execute the first literal and the rest of the literals and conjoin their expansions.

```
partially_execute((Literal, Rest), Expansion) :- !,
    partially_execute(Literal, ExpandedLiteral),
    partially_execute(Rest, ExpandedRest),
    conjoin(ExpandedLiteral, ExpandedRest,
            Expansion).
```

We will replace literals with their definitions only if they are specified as auxiliary literals. The predicate aux_literal specifies which literals are subject to partial execution. Furthermore, we require that there exist at least one clause matching the literal. Otherwise, the literal is left unchanged.

```
partially_execute(Literal, Expansion) :-
    ( aux_literal(Literal),
      match_exists(Literal) )
    -> ( clause((Literal :- Body)),
         partially_execute(Body, Expansion) )
    ;  Expansion = Literal.
```

Testing Existence and Double Negation

To determine whether a match exists, we can check that the set of clauses with the literal as head contains at least one element.

```
match_exists(Literal) :-
    setof(Body, Literal^clause((Literal:-Body)),
          [_Clause|_Others]).
```

This definition, though correct, is quite inefficient. A naive implementation of `match_exists` merely looks for a matching clause.

```
match_exists(Literal) :-
    clause((Literal :- Body)).
```

However, this definition has the unwanted side effect of actually binding variables in `Literal` depending on what clause was found. Furthermore, if there are several matching clauses, this definition will allow backtracking.

A common trick for solving problems of unwanted bindings is the double use of the negation-as-failure operator `\+`. In the case at hand, we can change the definition as follows:

Program 6.6
```
match_exists(Literal) :-
    \+ \+ clause((Literal :- Body)).
```

Looking just at the logic, p and $\neg\neg p$ are equivalent. However, the implementation of negation as failure makes sure that in executing a goal `\+` G all bindings to G will be undone; thus `match_exists` will leave `Literal` unchanged.

This double use of negation is a very common device in Prolog metaprogramming. It must be stressed that nothing in the device has a direct logical interpretation. In particular, `\+` is being used to undo bindings of variables, but as we have seen `\+` cannot be interpreted as "failure to prove" if called with a nonground argument!

A Sample Partial Execution

Using this definition of partial execution we can check the earlier claims made about it in Chapter 4. For instance, we can partially execute the clause at the end of Section 4.1.5

```
vp(Z^S) -->
    tv(TV), np(NP),
    {reduce(TV,Z,IV),
     reduce(NP,IV,S)}.
```

with respect to `reduce` literals

```
aux_literal( reduce(_,_,_) ).
```

under the definition of reduce given in Program 4.1

```
clause(( reduce(Arg^Expr, Arg, Expr) :- true )).
```

with the query

```
?- partially_execute( (vp(Z^S, P0, P) :-
                            tv(TV, P0, P1),
                            np(NP, P1, P),
                            reduce(TV,Z,IV),
                            reduce(NP,IV,S) ),
                       Expansion ).
Expansion = vp(Z^S, P0, P) :-
                tv(Z^IV, P0, P1),
                np(IV^S, P1, P)
yes
```

Notice that this is just the Prolog encoding of the partial execution result given in Section 4.1.5.

6.4.2 Compiling by Partial Execution

A simple compiler for an object language can be written using partial execution of its interpreter. We divide the clauses of the interpreter (*metaclauses*) into program and auxiliary clauses; the clauses that actually interpret the *object clauses* of the object language are the program clauses, the rest auxiliary. We will distinguish the two clauses by using the predicate clause for the auxiliary clauses (as above) and program_clause for program clauses.

The compiler generates all possible partial executions of the program clauses with respect to predicates defined in the auxiliary clauses and asserts the resolvents generated. The driver for the compiler is, then, quite simple.

```
compile :-
    program_clause(Clause),
    partially_execute(Clause, CompiledClause),
    assert(CompiledClause),
    fail.
```

This clause backtracks repeatedly (because of the fail) until no more partial executions of program clauses are possible. This method for cycling through solutions is known as a *failure-driven loop*. As a side effect, it asserts all of the partial executions into the Prolog database. The Prolog interpreter, processing queries using these asserted clauses, is executing a compiled form of the object language.

As an example, we build a compiler for DCGs. We merely separate the DCG interpreter into a single program clause

```
program_clause(( parse(NT, P_0, P) :-
                 (NT ---> Body),
                 parse(Body, P_0, P)   )).
```

and several auxiliary clauses, treating `parse` and `--->` as auxiliary predicates.

Suppose the DCG of Program 3.11 is compiled using this compiler, that is, the compiler and the DCG (encoded using the operator `--->`) are loaded into Prolog, and the `compile` predicate is invoked. One possible partial execution of the program clause involves resolving the literal `NT ---> Body` against the first rule of the grammar. This resolution requires the unifying substitution $NT = s(s(NP,VP))$, $Body = (np(NP),vp(VP))$. The body of the unit clause is just `true`. The partial execution of `parse((np(NP), vp(VP)), P0, P)` results in the conjunction `parse(np(NP), P0, P1)`, `parse(vp(VP), P1, P)`. Conjoining this with the body of the unit clause expanding the first literal leaves the former unchanged. Thus the full partial execution of the program clause is, in this instance,

```
parse(s(s(NP,VP)), P0, P) :-
    parse(np(NP), P0, P1),
    parse(vp(VP), P1, P).
```

Clearly, this is a compilation of the DCG rule into Prolog, albeit slightly more complex than the standard compilation, namely

```
s(s(NP,VP), P0, P) :-
    np(NP, P0, P1),
    vp(VP, P1, P).
```

The full text of the compiler, including the program for partial execution and the encoding of the interpreter is given in Appendix A. This version adds a rewriting step to convert literals of the form

```
parse(nt(...), Pi, Pj)
```

to literals of the more familiar form

```
nt(..., Pi, Pj)     .
```

A sample run of the compiler using the grammar of Program 3.11 is as follows:

```
?- compile.
Asserting "s(s(NP,VP),P0,P):-
            np(NP,P0,P1),vp(VP,P1,P)."
Asserting "np(np(Det,N,Rel),P0,P):-
            det(Det,P0,P1),
            n(N,P1,P2),
            optrel(Rel,P2,P)."
Asserting "np(np(PN),P0,P):-pn(PN,P0,P)."
Asserting "vp(vp(TV,NP),P0,P):-
            tv(TV,P0,P1),np(NP,P1,P)."
Asserting "vp(vp(IV),P0,P):-iv(IV,P0,P)."
Asserting "optrel(rel(epsilon),P0,P):-true."
Asserting "optrel(rel(that,VP),P0,P):-
            connects(that,P0,P1),
            vp(VP,P1,P)."
Asserting "pn(pn(terry),P0,P):-
            connects(terry,P0,P)."
Asserting "pn(pn(shrdlu),P0,P):-
            connects(shrdlu,P0,P)."
Asserting "iv(iv(halts),P0,P):-
            connects(halts,P0,P)."
Asserting "det(det(a),P0,P):-
            connects(a,P0,P)."
Asserting "n(n(program),P0,P):-
            connects(program,P0,P)."
Asserting "tv(tv(writes),P0,P):-
            connects(writes,P0,P)."
Asserting "connects(Word,[Word|Rest],Rest):-true."
no

?- s(Tree, [terry,writes,a,program,that,halts], []).
Tree = s(np(pn(terry)),
          vp(tv(writes),
             np(det(a),
                n(program),
                rel(that,
                    vp(iv(halts))))))
yes
```

Compare this behavior with that of the original DCG as described in Section 3.7.1.

6.4.3 Generality of the Method

The technique used here to build the DCG compiler is quite general. The `compile` and `partially_execute` predicates can be thought of together as a metacompiler, in that they will convert *any* interpreter for a language written in pure Prolog into a compiler for the same language. Since the only operations performed on the interpreter are resolutions, the compiler thereby derived is guaranteed to be sound with respect to the interpreter. And since all possible resolutions are done, the compiler is complete as well. Thus partial execution provides a way of generating correct compilers for a language given an interpreter for the language.

Furthermore, by adjusting which clauses are program clauses whose partial executions will remain in the compiled version and which are auxiliary clauses that are to be "compiled away", the degree of compilation can be tuned. By increasing the number of auxiliary clauses, more of the work is done at compile time and faster compiled grammars are derived. However, there are limits to this process. If too much work is attempted at compile time, the compile-time step may not terminate, or the compiled grammar may grow explosively in size. The generality of this method allows solutions to such trade-offs to be developed experimentally.

Another method for even more finely tuning the partial executor, beyond the ability to make clauses program or auxiliary clauses, is to predicate partial execution on various conditions specified in the antecedent of `auxiliary` literals. For instance, we could require that literals of a given auxiliary predicate be partially executed only when the literal is of a certain mode or its arguments are of a certain form. An especially interesting condition on partial execution is that the literal match exactly one clause in the database. Under this requirement, partial execution will only remove literals that can be resolved deterministically. Many other possibilities for controlling the partial executor could be easily implemented in this way.

Exercise 6.7 *Write a compiler which compiles DCGs into Prolog programs that parse sentences while building parse trees for them simultaneously and automatically. You may want to use the solution to Exercise 6.5.*

Exercise 6.8 *Suppose we compile the pure Prolog program for* conc *given in Program 3.3 into Prolog using a compiler generated from the Prolog interpreter of Program 6.1. What does Program 3.3 compile to?*

6.5 Bottom-Up Parsing

Prolog supplies by default a top-down, left-to-right, backtrack parsing algorithm for DCGs. It is well known that top-down parsing algorithms of this kind will loop on left-recursive rules (cf. the example of Program 2.3). Although techniques are available to remove left recursion from context-free grammars, these techniques are not readily generalizable to DCGs, and furthermore they can increase grammar size by large factors.

As an alternative, we may consider implementing a bottom-up parsing method directly in Prolog. Of the various possibilities, we will consider here the *left-corner* method in one of its adaptations to DCGs.

For programming convenience, the input grammar for the left-corner DCG interpreter is represented in a slight variation of the DCG notation. The right-hand sides of rules are given as lists rather than conjunctions of literals. Thus rules are unit clauses of the form, e.g.,

```
s ---> [np, vp].
```

or

```
optrel ---> [].
```

Terminals are introduced by dictionary unit clauses of the form

```
word(w,PT).
```

in which PT is the preterminal category of terminal w. As an example, the grammar of Program 3.11 would be encoded in this format as

```
s(s(NP,VP)) ---> [np(NP), vp(VP)].
np(np(Det,N,Rel)) --->
    [det(Det), n(N), optrel(Rel)].
np(np(PN)) ---> [pn(PN)].
vp(vp(TV,NP)) ---> [tv(TV), np(NP)].
vp(vp(IV)) ---> [iv(IV)].
optrel(rel(epsilon)) ---> [].
optrel(rel(that,VP)) ---> [relpro, vp(VP)].

word(that, relpro).
word(terry, pn(pn(terry))).
word(shrdlu, pn(pn(shrdlu))).
word(halts, iv(iv(halts))).
word(a, det(det(a))).
word(program, n(n(program))).
word(writes, tv(tv(writes))).
```

Before we discuss left-corner parsing, we need to introduce some terminology. The *left-corner of a phrase* is the leftmost subconstituent of that phrase. Similarly, the *left corner of a rule* is the first element on the right-hand-side of the rule. Often we will refer to the transitive closure of the left-corner relation using the term *left corner* as well, letting context determine the particular sense we mean. Thus, in the parse tree of Figure 2.4, *NP* is *the* left corner of *S*, but *Det* and *S* are left corners of *S* as well.

The basic idea of left-corner parsing is to key each rule off of its left corner. When a phrase is found, rules that have that phrase type as their left corner are tried in turn by looking for phrases that span the rest of the right-hand-side of the rule. If the rest of a rule is satisfied, the left-hand side is used to iterate the process by picking rules with that phrase type as left corner. Parsing thus proceeds *bottom-up* by looking for phrases whose left-most subphrase has already been found. The entire process begins with a subphrase that is guaranteed to be a left corner of the whole expression, namely, the leftmost leaf of the parse tree. To parse an expression as being of type `Phrase`, we take the next potential leaf in the expression and prove that it is a left corner of the phrase.

```
parse(Phrase) -->
    leaf(SubPhrase),
    lc(SubPhrase, Phrase).
```

Terminal symbols are obviously candidate leaves of the parse tree. We use the binary predicate `word(Word, Cat)` to encode the lexicon.

```
leaf(Cat) --> [Word], {word(Word,Cat)}.
```

In addition, a category can be considered a leaf if there is a rule admitting it with an empty right-hand side.

```
leaf(Phrase) --> {Phrase ---> []}.
```

The proof that some subconstituent of type `SubPhrase` is a left corner of a `SuperPhrase` involves parsing the part of `SuperPhrase` to the right of the left corner. The `lc(SubPhrase, SuperPhrase)` literal thus covers all of the `SuperPhrase` *except* for its left corner `SubPhrase`. The base case for proving the left corner relationship follows from any phrase being a left corner of itself.

```
lc(Phrase, Phrase) --> [].
```

Otherwise, we can infer that `SubPhrase` is a left corner of `SuperPhrase` if we can find a rule that `SubPhrase` is a left corner of and parse the remainder of the rule, finally proving that the left-hand side of the rule is itself a left corner of `SuperPhrase`.

```
lc(SubPhrase, SuperPhrase) -->
   {Phrase ---> [SubPhrase|Rest]},
   parse_rest(Rest),
   lc(Phrase, SuperPhrase).
```

Parsing the rest of the right-hand side involves a standard list recursion.

```
parse_rest([]) --> [].
parse_rest([Phrase|Phrases]) -->
   parse(Phrase),
   parse_rest(Phrases).
```

As an example of the operation of the left-corner parser interpreting a grammar, we will consider the sentence "a program halts" parsed with the grammar above. The initial query is

```
?- parse(s(Tree), [a, program, halts], []).
```

To prove this is a grammatical S, we find a leaf and prove it is the left-corner of the S. There are two possible leaves at the beginning of the string, namely, the leaf(det(det(a))) derived from the lexical entry for the word a, and the leaf(optrel(rel(epsilon))) derived from the rule for empty relative clauses. Choosing the former, we must prove lc(det(det(a)), s(Tree)). Since the two arguments are not unifiable, the first lc rule is not appropriate. Instead, the second rule is invoked. We must find a rule with a determiner as its left corner, namely

```
np(np(Det,N,Rel)) --->
   [det(Det), n(N), optrel(Rel)].
```

Using this rule, we must parse the rest of the right-hand side to prove that the *Det* is the immediate left corner of an *NP*. We will omit details of this subproof, which proceeds by left-corner parsing itself. The proof does succeed, covering the string "program" and instantiating N to n(program) and Rel to rel(epsilon). Finally, we must prove that the np(np(det(a), n(program), rel(epsilon)) is the left corner of the entire S. Notice that we have made some progress. We started out attempting to prove that the *Det* is the left corner of the S and have generated the smaller task of proving that the *NP* is.

The *NP* is the left corner of S by virtue of the rule

```
s(s(NP,VP)) ---> [np(NP), vp(VP)].
```

But two subgoals are required to be proved. First, we must parse the rest of the right-hand side, the *VP*. Again, we will omit details, but note that the goal succeeds binding VP to vp(iv(halts)). Then we must prove that s(...) is a left corner of s(s(Tree)). This succeeds by the first lc clause, binding Tree to the parse tree for the entire sentence, namely

```
s(np(det(a),
     n(program),
     rel(epsilon))
  vp(iv(halts)))
```

This completes the proofs of the various pending lc goals and the original query itself.

6.5.1   Linking

In the previous discussion, we glossed over a problem in the directedness of the left-corner parser. The parser, in choosing among possible grammar rules or leaves makes no use of information concerning what type of expression it is attempting to parse. For instance, in the discussion of the choice between leaf(det(det(a))) and leaf(optrel(rel(epsilon))) at the start of the parse, we merely noted that the former was correct. Of course, if the parser had chosen to pursue the latter, it would eventually discover that it had followed a blind alley and backtrack to the correct choice. But a considerably more efficient way of eliminating the latter possibility is to notice (by inspection of the grammar) that an optrel of *any* sort can never be a left corner of an s.

Suppose we tabulate some very general constraints of this sort concerning possible left corners, using (for historical reasons) the predicate link.

```
link( np(_),   s(_)        ).
link( det(_),  np(_)       ).
link( det(_),  s(_)        ).
link( pn(_),   np(_)       ).
link( pn(_),   s(_)        ).
link( tv(_),   vp(_)       ).
link( iv(_),   vp(_)       ).
link( relpro,  optrel(_)   ).
link( NT,      NT          ).
```

(The last clause says that any nonterminal is a left corner of itself.) We can use the information as an inexpensive test of whether a branch in the parsing search space can at least potentially yield a solution. For example, the `parse` clause could be changed to make use of the `link` table as follows:

```
parse(Phrase) -->
    leaf(SubPhrase),
    {link(SubPhrase, Phrase)},
    lc(SubPhrase, Phrase).
```

With this modified definition, the `leaf(optrel(rel(epsilon)))` would fail the linking test; consequently no further computation would be expended on that possibility.

Similarly the second rule for `lc` could be changed to

```
lc(SubPhrase,SuperPhrase) -->
    {Phrase ---> [SubPhrase|Rest],
     link(Phrase, SuperPhrase)},
    right(Rest),
    lc(Phrase, SuperPhrase).
```

to limit rule choice to those which could at least potentially be left corners of the `SuperPhrase` being looked for.

The modification of the left-corner parser using linking information provides an element of *top-down filtering* into the parsing process. Such a parser does not follow a purely bottom-up or a purely top-down regimen, but uses both kinds of information in finding a parse.

We will not pursue further here the question of finding good `link` definitions. Clearly, however, we would want to use automatic methods for developing the link tables, rather than the hand coding used in this section.

6.5.2   Compiling DCGs into Left-Corner Parsers

Using the techniques of Section 6.4.2, we can write a DCG compiler that converts DCG grammars encoded as for the left-corner interpreter into left-corner Prolog parsers. The program clauses are those that actually interpret the parts of the encoded grammar: the two `leaf` clauses and the two `lc` clauses. In addition, the single clauses defining `connects` and `parse` are added as program clauses so that they will be passed through unchanged into the compiled state, just as the `connects` clause was in the previous compiler.

The rest of the clauses (including those embodying the DCG itself) are auxiliary clauses defining the auxiliary predicates `--->`, `word`, and `parse_rest`.

Exercise 6.9 *Modify the DCG compiler given in Appendix A as described* *above so that it constitutes a program to compile DCGs into left-corner parsers. The final rewriting step should be removed.*

Executing the compiler on the encoded grammar of Program 3.11 yields the following behavior.

```
?- compile.
Asserting "connect(Word,[Word|Rest],Rest) :- true."
Asserting "parse(Phrase,P0,P) :-
            leaf(SubPhrase,P0,P1),
            lc(SubPhrase,Phrase,P1,P)."
Asserting "leaf(pn(pn(terry)),P0,P) :-
            connect(terry,P0,P)."
Asserting "leaf(pn(pn(shrdlu)),P0,P) :-
            connect(shrdlu,P0,P)."
Asserting "leaf(iv(iv(halts)),P0,P) :-
            connect(halts,P0,P)."
Asserting "leaf(det(det(a)),P0,P) :-
            connect(a,P0,P)."
Asserting "leaf(n(n(program)),P0,P) :-
            connect(program,P0,P)."
Asserting "leaf(tv(tv(writes)),P0,P) :-
            connect(writes,P0,P)."
Asserting "leaf(relpro,P0,P) :-
            connect(that,P0,P)."
Asserting "leaf(optrel(rel(epsilon)),P0,P0):-true."
Asserting "lc(Phrase,Phrase,P0,P0) :- true."
Asserting "lc(np(NP),SuperPhrase,P0,P) :-
            parse(vp(VP),P0,P1),
            lc(s(s(NP,VP)),SuperPhrase,P1,P)."
Asserting "lc(det(Det),SuperPhrase,P0,P) :-
            parse(n(N),P0,P1),
            parse(optrel(Rel),P1,P2),
            lc(np(np(Det,N,Rel)),
               SuperPhrase,P2,P)."
Asserting "lc(pn(PN),SuperPhrase,P0,P) :-
            lc(np(np(PN)),SuperPhrase,P0,P)."
Asserting "lc(tv(TV),SuperPhrase,P0,P) :-
            parse(np(NP),P0,P1),
            lc(vp(vp(TV,NP)),SuperPhrase,P1,P)."
Asserting "lc(iv(IV),SuperPhrase,P0,P) :-
            lc(vp(vp(IV)),SuperPhrase,P0,P)."
Asserting "lc(relpro,SuperPhrase,P0,P) :-
```

```
        parse(vp(VP),P0,P1),
        lc(optrel(rel(that,VP)),
            SuperPhrase,P1,P)."
no

?- parse(s(Tree),
        [terry, writes, a, program, that, halts],
        []).
Tree = s(np(pn(terry)),
        vp(tv(writes),
            np(det(a),
                n(program),
                rel(that,
                    vp(iv(halts)))))))
yes
```

The first two rules are copies of the definitions for parse and connects. The next six are the compiled version of the lexicon; these are followed by the single compiled epsilon rule. Finally, the compiled versions of the other grammar rules are generated. Again, the compiled grammar computes the same language and trees as if directly interpreted by Prolog. However, Prolog's top-down control strategy in executing the compiled grammar produces the same behavior as that of the left-corner control strategy in executing the original DCG. Furthermore, because the general left-corner interpreter has been replaced by specialized rules, the resulting program will run much faster than the interpreter operating over the original grammar.

6.6   Tabular Parsing

6.6.1   Inefficiencies of Backtracking

As we have seen, Prolog uses strict chronological backtracking to search for a proof of a goal. If a particular subgoal cannot be resolved, all the work since the most recent resolved goal for which there are still alternative clauses will be undone. Intuitively, this is the reason for the worst-case exponential cost of backtrack search (Aho and Ullman, 1972). In practical applications this theoretical worst case may not matter, because there may be practical bounds on input length (e.g., typical English sentences are short) and the efficiency of Prolog may offset the potential gains of more sophisticated search procedures for practically occurring inputs. Nevertheless, it is worthwhile to look at the issue in more detail to get a good understanding of the tradeoffs involved.

We will start with a very simple example. A ditransitive verb like *give* can be used in two ways.

Alfred gave a book to every student
Alfred gave every student a book

An obvious way of covering these two constructions is to use the two rules

```
vp --> dv, np, pp(to).
vp --> dv, np, np.
```

Now suppose that we are using these DCG rules to analyze the verb phrase in the second sentence above, and that we have appropriate rules for the noun phrase, prepositional phrase, and ditransitive verb. Prolog will first try the earlier vp rule. The word *gave* will be assigned to the category dv and the phrase *every student* to the category np. The parser will look next for a prepositional phrase beginning with the preposition *to*. However, the next word is *a*, so Prolog backtracks. Assuming no more choices in the analysis of "every student" as a noun phrase or in the assignment of the ditransitive verb category to *gave*, Prolog will have to undo these intermediate analyses and try the next alternative rule for verb phrase, the second rule above. This rule will immediately go on to reassign the category dv to *gave* and reanalyze "every student" as np, even though this analysis had already been done when attempting the first rule.

The redundancy just described is not restricted to top-down parsing methods. The same argument would show similar redundancies in using the left-corner algorithm discussed earlier. In fact, the situation here is even worse because the left-corner algorithm has less top-down guidance.

6.6.2   Tabular Parsing in the Abstract

In *tabular* parsers for context-free grammars, the redundancy just described is avoided by storing phrases just recognized in a *phrase table* (also called a *chart* or *well-formed-substring table*) indexed by the start and end positions of the phrases in the input string.

In general, at any point in its execution a parser will be looking for phrases of some type N starting in a certain range of positions S and finishing in a certain range of positions E in the input string. In the discussion that follows, we will represent these constraints on what the parser is looking for by the expression $N(S, E)$. The connection of this notation with the mapping from nonterminals to predicates in a DCG is no coincidence, as we shall see. For the moment, we will take a phrase type as representing some set of acceptable nonterminals and a position range as denoting some set of string positions.

Thus, when looking for some type of phrase $N(S, E)$, the phrase table is consulted for phrases $p(i, j)$ *satisfying* $N(S, E)$, that is, with $p \in N$, $i \in S$ and $j \in E$. There is a crucial subtlety here. If the table does not already contain *all* possible phrases satisfying $N(S, E)$, the parser will not know whether to use some phrase from the table or to try and recognize alternative phrases satisfying $N(S, E)$ using the rules in the grammar. But the latter option is just as costly as looking for phrases afresh without the phrase table. Thus the phrase table is usable only if all phrases of a given type are stored in the table before any attempt is made to use the table to look for phrases of that type. Consequently, there must be a way of recognizing whether the table is *complete* for a certain type. We call this constraint on table entries the *completeness condition*.[3] In tabular context-free parsers, completeness is achieved by looking only for certain specific phrase types and building the table in a certain order that guarantees a phrase type will be consulted only after it is completed.

For instance, the generalized Cocke-Kasami-Younger (CKY) bottom-up context-free parser can be thought of in this way. In the CKY algorithm, smaller phrases are always added to the table before larger phrases. The phrase types under consideration by the algorithm are of the form $V(i, j)$ where V stands for the set of all grammar symbols (terminals and nonterminals) and i and j are specific string positions. Since the table is complete for all substrings of the string between i and j, we merely need to check each rule, say, $A \rightarrow B_1 \cdots B_n$ in G, and look for $n + 1$ positions k_0 through k_n such that $i = k_0$ and $k_n = j$ and each k_i is greater than k_{i-1}, and such that the B_m are in the table under $V(k_{m-1}, k_m)$. If such a set of positions exists, then A can be added to the table under $V(i, j)$. By performing the search for rules and positions in all possible ways, we can complete the table for $V(i, j)$, in which case larger strings can then be analyzed.

Thus the CKY parsing algorithm builds the table by looking for phrases of type $V(i, j)$ for larger and larger $j - i$.

6.6.3   Top-Down Tabular Parsing

In top-down parsing, on the other hand, the algorithm will in general be looking for phrases of a given type t starting at a given position i but with unknown end position (symbolically $t(i, \{j | j \geq i\})$). Thus the algorithm will have to produce and store in the table all possible t phrases starting at i before moving on. If the analysis later fails and the same phrase type is looked for at the same position, there will be no need to use the grammar,

---

[3]Not to be confused with the logical notion of completeness.

all possible relevant phrases will already be in the table. In terms of the previous example, all noun phrases starting with the word *every* will have been stored when the first verb phrase rule looks for a noun phrase after the verb, so when the second rule looks for a noun phrase at the same position the analyzed np will be immediately found.

With the definite-clause encoding of grammars, a phrase table is just a store of *lemmas*, that is, consequences of the grammar axioms that have been recorded for future use. The existence of a noun phrase between positions 2 and 4 of an input string can be represented by the lemma expressed as a unit clause

```
np(2, 4).
```

Actually, for ease of access by an interpreter, we will use the ternary predicate known_phrase.

```
known_phrase(np, 2, 4).
```

Thus, in general a phrase table may be built by asserting appropriate facts as they are proved. We can change the Prolog top-down parser to keep such a table by modifying the DCG interpreter of Program 6.4. We will assume at first that grammars are context-free, that is, that all nonterminals are atomic, and also that the initial string position for the analysis is given. As the analysis proceeds from left to right, the initial position of any phrase being sought will thus be known. These restrictions will be lifted later.

The interpreter uses the predicate known_phrase(Type, P0, P) to store previously proved lemmas that a phrase of type Type exists between positions P0 and P and the predicate complete(Type, P0) to indicate that the known_phrase table is complete for the phrase type Type starting at the string position P0. The predicate nonterminal identifies the nonterminals in the specific grammar being interpreted.[4]

Much of the interpreter is identical to the meta-circular DCG interpreter it is modeled on. In fact, the interpreter differs only on the first clause for parse. This clause checks that its argument NT is a nonterminal and then calls find_phrase to find phrases of type NT.

```
parse(NT, P0, P) :-
    nonterminal(NT),
    find_phrase(NT, P0, P).
```

The remaining clauses for the `parse` predicate are repeated here merely for completeness.

```
parse((Body1, Body2), P0, P) :-
    parse(Body1, P0, P1),
    parse(Body2, P1, P).

parse([], P, P).
parse([Word|Rest], P0, P) :-
    connects(Word, P0, P1),
    parse(Rest, P1, P).

parse({Goals}, P, P) :- call(Goals).
```

The predicate `find_phrase` first checks to see if the table is complete for phrases of type `NT` starting at `P0`, and if so, uses it to pick up appropriate phrases that have been previously computed and stored in the `known_phrase` table. The cut guarantees that only the table is used and no recomputation of phrases is performed if the table is complete.

```
find_phrase(NT, P0, P) :-
    complete(NT, P0), !,
    known_phrase(NT, P0, P).
```

Otherwise, if the table has not been completed for that phrase type, grammar rules are used to find remaining phrases of type `NT`, and each such phrase is asserted as a known phrase. As we are trying to construct the table of all phrases of type `NT` starting at `P0`, we do not restrict rule expansion to phrases terminating with `P`, but rather leave the check for a phrase's final position until after asserting that a phrase has been found.

```
find_phrase(NT, P0, P) :-
    (NT ---> Body),
    parse(Body, P0, P1),
    assert(known_phrase(NT, P0, P1)),
    P1 = P.
```

Finally, when no remaining alternative ways of finding a phrase of type `NT` starting at `P0` exist, the table is marked as complete for that phrase type at that starting position, and the branch of computation that required more alternatives is failed. If some other branch of the computation later requires that same type of constituent starting at the same position, only the first clause of `find_phrase` will be used.

```
find_phrase(NT, P0, _) :-
   assert(complete(NT, P0)),
   fail.
```

We have used here the nullary predicate `fail`, which is always false, that is, always fails.

It is clear that `find_phrase` above has been designed for its side-effects rather than its logical content. This is common practice in building interpreters: To achieve the appropriate behavior in an interpreter for a declarative language, one has to deal with procedural issues such as the sequencing of operations.

Checking Nonterminal Status

The definition of the `nonterminal` predicate can proceed in several ways. First of all, extensional definition is possible by merely listing all the possible nonterminal terms, e.g.,

```
nonterminal(s(_)).
nonterminal(np(_)).
nonterminal(det(_)).
   ...
```

Alternatively, the definition can be made intensionally. We can define nonterminals as those terms which occur on the left-hand side of some rule.

```
nonterminal(LHS) :-
    \+ \+ (LHS ---> _Body).
```

The double negation is used as usual to prevent bindings from the particular rule that licenses the terminal from affecting the term. This definition thus works in the same way as the `match_exists` predicate of Program 6.6.

Henceforth, we will assume the former method.

6.6.4   Subsumption

The interpreter in the previous section works correctly only for atomic nonterminals and an instantiated initial string position for any phrase being sought. These restrictions were needed to ensure that the completeness constraint is obeyed. To see why this is so, consider the following trivial grammar:

```
s ---> t.
```

```
t ---> x(a, X).
t ---> x(Y, b).

x(W, W) ---> [W].

nonterminal(s).
nonterminal(t).
nonterminal(x(_, _)).
```

as used to parse (as an s) the input *b* encoded as

```
connects(b, 0, 1).
```

(From a practical point of view, when building tabular parsers it is more convenient to have input strings represented by facts and string positions by constants. In this way, the new facts asserted by the parser will not have to include the possibly long lists that encode string positions in the list representation of input strings.)

At some point in executing the query parse(s, 0, 1), find_phrase will be called to find phrases x(a, X) starting at 0. Clearly there are no such phrases, so a single clause will be added to the database.

```
complete(x(a, X), 0).
```

Later in the execution, find_phrase will be called for phrases of type x(Y, b) starting at 0. As this matches the complete fact in the database, find_phrase will go on to call known_phrase(x(a, b), 0, P) which will immediately fail. Thus, the overall analysis will fail, even though the given string is in the language accepted by the grammar.

The problem here is that the interpreter is not careful enough in implementing the notion of "being complete for a given phrase type". With atomic nonterminals and ground first argument, there is no problem because unification in the first clause of find_phrase is just doing an identity check. But in the general case, unification is the wrong operation to use. The presence of the fact complete(x(a, X), 0) indicates that the parser has found all phrases x(a, *t*) starting at position 0 for some term *t*. The phrases that can satisfy x(Y, b) at position 0 may include *some* that satisfy x(a, X), namely any phrases that satisfy the unification x(a, b) of the two phrase types, but will in general also contain *others*, such as the solution x(b, b), that do not satisfy x(a, X).

The correct check for completeness of a phrase type is thus not unification, which corresponds to intersection of the corresponding solution sets, but subsumption or instantiation (Section 3.5.1), which corresponds to containment of solution sets. More specifically, we can consider the phrase table complete for a certain phrase type t only if it contains all phrases satisfying t or any other type t' that subsumes t. Thus we should modify the first clause of `find_phrases` to be

```
find_phrase(NT, PO, P) :-
    complete(GeneralNT, GeneralPO),
    subsumes((GeneralNT,GeneralPO), (NT, PO)), !,
    known_phrase(NT, PO, P).
```

The subsumption test `subsumes((GeneralNT, GeneralPO), (NT, PO))` checks whether the nonterminal-position pair `(NT, PO)` is a special case of an already completed phrase type `(GeneralNT, GeneralPO)`.

In general, the subsumption check $\text{subsumes}(t, t')$ should test whether there is a substitution σ for variables in t such that $[t]\sigma = t'$. This is clearly a meta-level facility, as it is sensitive to the particular state of instantiation of terms. Thus the implementation of `subsumes` in Prolog requires the use of other meta-level facilities. One of the easiest methods of implementation is based on the observation that t subsumes t' if and only if t is unifiable with t'', where t'' is obtained from t' by replacing each distinct variable in t' with a distinct constant term not occurring in t. Equivalently, t subsumes t' if and only if the most general unifier of t and t' does not bind any variable in t'.

Exercise 6.10 *Prove the above assertions.*

Suppose we have an extralogical predicate `make_ground` which instantiates all the variables in its argument to distinct new constants. It would then seem that the following is a reasonable implementation of `subsumes`:

```
subsumes(General, Specific) :-
    make_ground(Specific),
    General = Specific.
```

However, this program has the unwanted side-effect of binding the variables in `Specific` to constants and also possibly instantiating `General`. This observation leads to a revision of the implementation of the subsumption test making use of the properties of double negation discussed in Section 6.4.1.[5]

---

[5] However, this version of `subsumes` is only correct if the variables in `General` and `Specific` are disjoint. Otherwise, the execution of `make_ground` will inappropriately bind variables in `General`.

```
subsumes(General, Specific) :-
   \+ \+ ( make_ground(Specific),
           General = Specific ).
```

Finally, it remains to see how the predicate make_ground is implemented. The predicate numbervars(t, m, n), available in many Prolog systems, instantiates each of the $n - m$ distinct variables of term t to a distinct term of the form $f(i)$ where $m \leq i < n$. (The functor f is implementation-dependent chosen so as not normally to occur in user programs.) We could thus implement make_ground as follows:

```
make_ground(Term) :-
   numbervars(Term, 0, _).
```

Alternatively, we could implement the variable numbering scheme directly.

```
make_ground(Term) :-
  make_ground(Term,0, _).

make_ground(Term, M, N) :- var(Term), !,
   Term = 'A-Var'(M), N is M + 1.
make_ground(Term, M, M) :- atomic(Term), !.
make_ground('A-Var'(_), M, M) :- !.
make_ground(Term, M, N) :-
   Term =.. [_Functor|Args],
   make_ground_list(Args, M, N).

make_ground_list([], M, M).
make_ground_list([Term|Terms], M, N) :-
   make_ground(Term, M, K),
   make_ground_list(Terms, K, N).
```

Here, we assume that no term of the form 'A-Var'(i) appears in the rest of the program. (See Section 5.1.6 for descriptions of the various built-in predicates used in make_ground.)

6.6.5   The Top-Down Tabular Parser in Action

We now show how the top-down tabular parser avoids the redundancies of backtracking in the example of Section 6.6.1. To avoid cluttering the example, we will use the following simple grammar fragment:

```
vp ---> dv, np, pp(to).
vp ---> dv, np, np.
```

```
np ---> det, n.
pp(P) ---> p(P), np.

dv ---> [gave].
det ---> [every].
det ---> [a].
n ---> [student].
n ---> [book].
p(P) ---> [P], {p(P)}.
p(to).
```

The example verb phrase is

$_0$ gave $_1$ every $_2$ student $_3$ a $_4$ book $_5$

We will examine a trace of the execution of the goal

```
?- parse(vp, 0, 5).
```

which asks whether the given string is a verb phrase.

The main predicates of interest in understanding the parser's execution are find_phrase, complete and known_phrase. The first attempt to prove the goal above involves the first vp rule. This leads to the following sequence of calls to find_phrase and assertions,[6] where the assertions are indicated by messages of the form "Asserted *f*" for some fact *f*:

```
?- parse(vp, 0, 5).
    (6) 1 Call: find_phrase(vp,0,5)
   (20) 4 Call: find_phrase(dv,0,P_1)
            Asserted known_phrase(dv,0,1)
   (20) 4 Exit: find_phrase(dv,0,1)
   (49) 5 Call: find_phrase(np,1,P_2)
   (63) 8 Call: find_phrase(det,1,P_3)
            Asserted known_phrase(det,1,2)
   (63) 8 Exit: find_phrase(det,1,2)
   (87) 8 Call: find_phrase(n,2,P_4)
            Asserted known_phrase(n,2,3)
   (87) 8 Exit: find_phrase(n,2,3)
            Asserted known_phrase(np,1,3)
   (49) 5 Exit: find_phrase(np,1,3)
  (115) 5 Call: find_phrase(pp(to),3,P_5)
```

---

[6]The invocation numbers are not consecutive because we are omitting the trace messages for other calls. Also, *Redo* ports (Section 2.4.1) are not shown.

```
(129) 8 Call: find_phrase(p(to),3,P_6)
        Asserted complete(p(to),3)
(129) 8 Fail: find_phrase(p(to),3,P_6)
        Asserted complete(pp(to),3)
(115) 5 Fail: find_phrase(pp(to),3,_5)
```

At this point, the parser has recognized the verb and the noun phrase that follows it, and has just failed to find a prepositional phrase as the second complement of the verb. The recognized verb, determiner, noun and noun phrase have been asserted as known_phrase lemmas. The failed search for a prepositional phrase at position 3 led to the assertion of complete facts for the prepositional phrase and its starting preposition, meaning that no phrases of those types are available at position 3. Notice that no complete facts have been asserted yet for the phrases recognized so far, since the parser has not yet tried other alternatives for those phrases.

The execution continues by failing back into the already recognized phrases and trying to find them in alternative ways. When these attempts fail, complete assertions are made for the failed phrases.

```
        Asserted complete(n,2)
(87) 8 Fail: find_phrase(n,2,P_4)
        Asserted complete(det,1)
(63) 8 Fail: find_phrase(det,1,P_3)
        Asserted complete(np,1)
(49) 5 Fail: find_phrase(np,1,P_2)
        Asserted complete(dv,0)
(20) 4 Fail: find_phrase(dv,0,P_1)
```

Now the first vp rule has failed and we have complete information for all the phrases the parser attempted to find during that rule's execution. The execution now moves to the second vp rule.

```
(184) 4 Call: find_phrase(dv,0,P_1)
(223) 5 Call: known_phrase(dv,0,P_1)
(223) 5 Exit: known_phrase(dv,0,1)
(184) 4 Exit: find_phrase(dv,0,1)
```

The table for phrases of type dv is complete at position 0, so the lemmas stored in known_phrase can be used instead of the rules for dv. The situation is similar for the first np complement of the vp, thereby *saving a reparse of that noun phrase.*

```
(234) 5 Call: find_phrase(np,1,P_2)
```

```
(267)  6 Call: known_phrase(np,1,P_2)
(267)  6 Exit: known_phrase(np,1,3)
(234)  5 Exit: find_phrase(np,1,3)
```

The analysis then proceeds as normal until the original goal is proved.

```
(273)  5 Call: find_phrase(np,3,P_3)
(323)  8 Call: find_phrase(det,3,P_4)
          Assert known_phrase(det,3,4)
(323)  8 Exit: find_phrase(det,3,4)
(389)  8 Call: find_phrase(n,4,P_5)
          Assert known_phrase(n,4,5)
(389)  8 Exit: find_phrase(n,4,5)
          Assert known_phrase(np,3,5)
(273)  5 Exit: find_phrase(np,3,5)
          Assert known_phrase(vp,0,5)
  (6)  1 Exit: find_phrase(vp,0,5)
```

6.6.6   General Tabular Parsing

The phrase table for top-down parsing that we have just discussed improves the performance of top-down parsing by stopping redundant reanalyses, but it does not do anything to alleviate a much more serious redundancy, the redundancy of top-down computation that leads to nontermination in grammars with left-recursive rules.

As we have seen, a top-down parser may fail to terminate when given left-recursive rules because it works by guessing (or *predicting*) that a phrase of some type X occurs and then trying all ways of building an X. If one of those ways involves looking for an X to start with, the procedure gets into a *prediction loop* and never terminates. One way of dealing with this problem is to avoid it totally by using a bottom-up algorithm, as described in Section 6.5. Unfortunately, this is achieved by losing the accurate top-down predictions available in a top-down parser. Techniques such as the use of linking information discussed in Section 6.5.1 can alleviate this problem, but in the worst case even a left-corner parser with linking information will generate many unextensible partial analyses that a top-down parser would never attempt.

At first sight, it might appear as if the left-recursion problem for top-down parsers has a solution analogous to that for the redundancy problem which we have just discussed. What would be needed is to record the fact that the parser has predicted a phrase of type X starting at some position i so that the parser can recognize when it is about to get into a prediction loop. However, it is not immediately clear what should occur when a prediction loop is recognized. Clearly, for the prediction to be fulfilled there should be some phrase of type X at i, so we cannot just give up looking for an X at i. Furthermore, we cannot decide in advance how many X phrases start at i, as can be seen by considering the rules

$$X \rightarrow X \, a$$
$$X \rightarrow b$$

applied to strings ba^n for different values of n. Finally, a prediction loop may occur with rules with apparently non-left-recursive rules such as

$$X \rightarrow Y \, X \, b$$
$$Y \rightarrow \epsilon$$

because a prefix of the body of a rule may cover the empty string, as with Y in the rules above. Thus, in general loop detection is needed when forming predictions on the basis of any symbol in a rule body.

The above problems can be solved by splitting the operation of the parser into two alternating phases, *prediction* and *resolution*, dealing respectively with top-down predictions and bottom-up rule applications.[7]

To explain the process in more detail, we will not work in terms of DCG rules but rather in terms of the corresponding definite clauses. From a deductive point of view, prediction selects instances of rules that may apply to resolve against a particular literal (nonterminal). For instance, suppose we are parsing an expression according to the DCG encoded in Program 2.4 and repeated here for reference.

```
s(P0, P) :- np(P0, P1), vp(P1, P).
np(P0, P) :- det(P0, P1), n(P1, P2), optrel(P2, P).
np(P0, P) :- pn(P0, P).
vp(P0, P) :- tv(P0, P1), np(P1, P).
vp(P0, P) :- iv(P0, P).
optrel(P, P).
optrel(P0, P) :- connects(that, P0, P1), vp(P1, P).

pn(P0, P) :- connects(terry, P0, P).
pn(P0, P) :- connects(shrdlu, P0, P).
iv(P0, P) :- connects(halts, P0, P).
det(P0, P) :- connects(a, P0, P).
n(P0, P) :- connects(program, P0, P).
tv(P0, P) :- connects(writes, P0, P).
```

---

[7]Earley used the term *completion* for what we call *resolution*.

Starting with a query of the form

```
:- s(0, 2)
```

the Prolog proof procedure will predict that the first rule in the grammar is applicable. Unifying the goal literal with the prediction, we have the new clause

```
s(0, 2) :- np(0, P1), vp(P1, 2).
```

This clause is an instance of the first rule and a consequence of the grammar together with the initial goal. Selecting the first literal in this new rule, we might then predict the second or third rule, in the latter case yielding

```
np(0, P) :- pn(0, P).      ,
```

from which can be predicted

```
pn(0, P) :- connects(bertrand, 0, P).
```

This clause can be *resolved* by matching a literal in its right-hand-side against a unit clause in the program, say,

```
connects(bertrand, 0, 1).
```

The resolvent is formed by removing the matched literal.

```
pn(0, 1).
```

Now this clause can be used to resolve against another clause forming the resolvent

```
np(0, 1).      ,
```

which resolves against the original prediction.

```
s(0,2) :- vp(1,2).
```

Now the process can start over, this time predicting the rules for verb phrases. Eventually, if a verb phrase is found between positions 1 and 2, the clause

```
vp(1,2).
```

will be generated, which can resolve the previous clause to

```
s(0, 2).
```

The existence of this clause formed by alternately predicting and resolving demonstrates that the initial goal has been proved.

Thus the normal Prolog proof procedure can be seen as operating by prediction and resolution, and the results of prediction and resolution (the *derived clauses*) are lemmas, logical consequences of the program. The insight of methods of parsing and deduction based on Earley's algorithm is that this general flow of control can be made into a tabular parsing method by storing each lemma in a table, and only forming a new predicted or resolved clause if the table does not already contain it (or one which is more general).

We now describe the extended algorithm more precisely.

The *predictor* operates on clauses with nonempty antecedents, what we have in the past called *rules*, but will call *active clauses* by analogy with the use of the term *active edge* in the parsing literature. A literal is selected from the antecedent of the active clause and a matching program clause is found. The clause instance formed by unifying the selected literal and the matching clause is then added as a lemma. In general, this new clause will be active.

The *resolver* operates on clauses with empty antecedents, what we have in the past called *unit clauses* or *facts*, but will call *passive clauses* within the discussion of Earley deduction. An active clause is chosen whose selected (leftmost) literal matches the passive clause[8] and the resolvent of the two, which may be either active or passive, is added as a lemma. Newly derived clauses have one less literal in their bodies than the active clause from which they were formed so that repeated resolution will eventually create new derived passive clauses.

In each case, addition of the lemma occurs only if no subsuming clause exists in the table.

The predictor and the resolver interact as follows. The proof process is set off by calling the predictor on the goal to be proved—in the case at hand,

---

[8]This leftmost-literal selection rule is the same one that Prolog uses. Other selection rules are possible, leading to different parsing algorithms. For example, one could have a notion of *head* for rules and always start by resolving head literals. It is a common mistake to assume that it is necessary to try resolutions with all body literals, rather than just with the one given by the selection function. However, resolution only against the selected literal is sufficient, because if a resolution step with some other body literal is required in a proof, any selection function will sooner or later (maybe infinitely many steps later) come to select that literal. This is because resolution removes a literal from the body, so that the selection function has fewer and fewer literals from which to select.

the grammar start symbol with appropriate string arguments for DCGs. Each time an active clause is added to the table, the predictor is called on the selected literal of the active clause to create new rule instances. Each time a passive clause is added to the table, the resolver is called to resolve the passive clause against appropriate active clauses.

We can see now how the loop check on predictions is implemented. Top-down prediction from a literal X creates rule instances that may be used to conclude an X. The predictor is recursively applied on the selected literals of the newly added rule instances. If this prediction process leads to another attempt to predict from X because of left recursion, the potential derived rule instances for X will have already been added to the lemma table for the earlier instance of X, and the prediction will stop.

The family of proof procedures based on the method just described has been given the collective name of *Earley deduction* because of its close connection to Earley's parsing algorithm for CFGs. However, the more specific constraints of CF parsing allow a simplification that we cannot take advantage of here, and that we glossed over in the above description. In Earley's algorithm, derived clause creation proceeds strictly from left to right. Therefore, any passive clause needed to resolve against some active clause is guaranteed to be constructed after the active clause is created. Thus, to perform all the pertinent resolutions, the algorithm need only look for active clauses at the time when a passive clause is created. A general Earley deduction proof procedure cannot guarantee this, so in general it is necessary to run the resolver not only when passive clauses are added, but also when active clauses are added as well.

We will now present a definite clause interpreter that operates according to the Earley deduction method. Turning the method into a specific procedure requires specifying a literal selection function (we will assume the Prolog one) and a particular interleaving of prediction and resolution steps. There is also room for ingenuity in choosing a representation for the table of derived clauses that will speed up the search for resolving derived clauses. The implementation below does not use such methods, however, since it is intended to illustrate the basic algorithm as cleanly as possible.

In this implementation, user-supplied clauses (i.e., the program to be interpreted) and derived clauses (the results of prediction and resolution) are represented as P <= $[P_1, \ldots, P_n]$ and P <*= $[P_1, \ldots, P_n]$ respectively, where <= and <*= are appropriately declared infix operators.

The table of lemmas will be implemented by asserting <*= clauses into the Prolog database. However, we will need a temporary storage for clauses that the predictor and resolver produce. This will store clauses that have been added to the table but have not yet been processed to see what further clauses they engender (by prediction or resolution). For this purpose, we

add an *agenda* of derived clauses that remain to be processed, which we will
encode as a Prolog list. The main predicate of the program takes the initial
goal, uses the predictor to find all the predicted clauses thereby forming
the initial agenda, and processes each derived clause. If the passive clause
encoding the goal can be proved by this process, the goal itself has been
proved.

```
prove(Goal) :-
    predict(Goal, Agenda),
    process(Agenda),
    Goal <*= [].
```

The agenda of derived clauses is processed one by one by the predicate
`process_one`. If the list is empty, all consequences of the axioms relevant
to proving the initial goal have been already derived. Otherwise, the first
clause in the agenda is considered, leading to some set `SubAgenda` of new
derived clauses to consider, which is combined with the rest of the main
agenda and given to `process`. Here we are actually adding the new derived
clauses to the front of the main agenda; that is, we have a stack rather than
a queue discipline and consequently a kind of depth-first search. If the new
clauses were appended to the back of the agenda instead (as in a queue),
the search would be breadth-first.

```
process([]).
process([Head <*= Body | OldAgenda]) :-
    process_one(Head, Body, SubAgenda),
    conc(SubAgenda, OldAgenda, Agenda),
    process(Agenda).
```

Each new derived clause is processed according to its form. If the
derived clause body is empty, we have a passive clause that should be
given to the resolver.

```
process_one(Head, [], Agenda) :-
    resolve_passive(Head, Agenda).
```

If the derived clause is active, the predictor has to be called with the
clause's selected literal, the first body literal in this implementation. Furthermore, as we observed earlier it may be that some passive clauses were
added before active clauses they should resolve with, so there is a supple-
mentary call to `resolve` to deal with those belated resolutions. The clause
sets resulting from prediction and resolution are combined to give the set
of clauses newly derived from the clause being considered.

```
process_one(Head, [First|Body], Agenda) :-
   predict(First, Front),
   resolve_active(Head <*= [First|Body], Back),
   conc(Front, Back, Agenda).
```

The predictor, the passive clause resolver, and the active clause resolver are all very similar. They use the meta-predicate all_solutions(x, g, l) to find the list l of all instantiations of x such that g holds. This is defined to be just like the metapredicate bagof (Section 5.1.4), except that it returns the empty list when g has no solutions and does not backtrack for alternative instantiations of free variables. As can be seen in the clause below, in all calls of all_solutions all variables are either bound in x or in an existential quantifier, so there will be no free variables to instantiate in alternative ways in any case.

A prediction is simply the instantiation of a derived clause by the goal. A prediction is actually made and stored only if the call to store succeeds.

```
predict(Goal, Agenda) :-
   all_solutions(Clause,
                 Goal^prediction(Goal, Clause),
                 Agenda).

prediction(Goal, Goal <*= Body) :-
   Goal <= Body,
   store(Goal <*= Body).
```

The resolver for passive clauses takes a derived passive clause Fact and finds active derived clauses whose selected literal unifies with Fact, returning the results of the corresponding resolutions.

```
resolve_passive(Fact, Agenda) :-
   all_solutions(Clause,
                 Fact^p_resolution(Fact, Clause),
                 Agenda).

p_resolution(Fact, Goal <*= Body) :-
   Goal <*= [Fact|Body],
   store(Goal <*= Body).
```

The resolver for active clauses works the opposite way to the one for passive clauses: it takes an active clause Clause and finds passive clauses whose head unifies with the selected literal of Clause.

```
resolve_active(Clause, Agenda) :-
   all_solutions(NewClause,
                 Clause^a_resolution(Clause,
                                     NewClause),
                 Agenda).

a_resolution(Head <*= [First|Body], Head <*= Body) :-
   First <*= [],
   store(Head <*= Body).
```

Newly derived clauses are stored only if they are not subsumed by an existing derived clause.

```
store(Clause) :-
   \+subsumed(Clause),
   assert(Clause).

subsumed(Clause) :-
   GenHead <*= GenBody,
   subsumes(GenHead <*= GenBody, Clause).
```

Finally, the implementation of `all_solutions` is simply:

```
all_solutions(Var, Goal, Solutions) :-
   bagof(Var, Goal, Solutions) -> true ; Solutions = [].
```

As we saw in Section 3.8.2, the Prolog proof procedure loops on left-recursive rules such as those for the English possessive construction.

$$NP \rightarrow Det\ N$$
$$DET \rightarrow NP\ 's$$

However, our new proof procedure will cope with rules like the above. The clauses below encode an extension of Program 3.11 to cover the possessive construction in the format required by the Earley deduction interpreter.

```
s(s(NP,VP), P0, P) <=
   [np(NP, P0, P1), vp(VP, P1, P)].
np(np(Det,N,Rel), P0, P) <=
   [det(Det, P0, P1),
    n(N, P1, P2),
    optrel(Rel, P2, P)].
```

```
np(np(PN), P0, P) <= [pn(PN, P0, P)].
det(gen(NP), P0, P) <=
    [np(NP, P0, P1), connects('''s', P1, P)].
det(Det, P0, P) <= [art(Det, P0, P)].
vp(vp(TV,NP), P0, P) <=
    [tv(TV, P0, P1), np(NP, P1, P)].
vp(vp(IV), P0, P) <= [iv(IV, P0, P)].
optrel(rel(epsilon), P, P) <= [].
optrel(rel(that,VP), P0, P) <=
    [connects(that, P0, P1), vp(VP, P1, P)].

pn(pn(terry), P0, P) <= [connects(terry, P0, P)].
pn(pn(shrdlu), P0, P) <= [connects(shrdlu, P0, P)].
iv(iv(halts), P0, P) <= [connects(halts, P0, P)].
art(art(a), P0, P) <= [connects(a, P0, P)].
n(n(program), P0, P) <= [connects(program, P0, P)].
tv(tv(writes), P0, P) <= [connects(writes, P0, P)].
```

To show the operation of the algorithm, we use the input sentence

Terry's program halts.

encoded as

```
connects(terry, p0, p1) <= [].
connects('''s', p1, p2) <= [].
connects(program, p2, p3) <= [].
connects(halts, p3, p4) <= [].
```

The listing below shows the derived clauses generated by the algorithm in order of derivation. To unclutter the listing, we have replaced by ellipses the derived clauses used in recognizing preterminal symbols (art, pn, n, iv and tv).

```
(1)  s(s(B,C),p0,p4) <*= [np(B,p0,D),vp(C,D,p4)].
(2)  np(np(B,C,D),p0,E) <*=
           [det(B,p0,F),n(C,F,G),optrel(D,G,E)].
(3)  np(np(B),p0,C) <*= [pn(B,p0,C)].
(4)  det(gen(B),p0,C) <*=
           [np(B,p0,D),connects('s,D,C)].
(5)  det(B,p0,C) <*= [art(B,p0,C)].
         . . .
(10) pn(pn(terry),p0,p1) <*= [].
(11) np(np(pn(terry)),p0,p1) <*= [].
```

```
(12) s(s(np(pn(terry)),B),p0,p4) <*= [vp(B,p1,p4)].
(13) det(gen(np(pn(terry))),p0,B) <*=
         [connects('s,p1,B)].
(14) vp(vp(B,C),p1,p4) <*= [tv(B,p1,D),np(C,D,p4)].
(15) vp(vp(B),p1,p4) <*= [iv(B,p1,p4)].
     ...
(19) det(gen(np(pn(terry))),p0,p2) <*= [].
(20) np(np(gen(np(pn(terry))),B,C),p0,D) <*=
         [n(B,p2,E),optrel(C,E,D)].
     ...
(23) n(n(program),p2,p3) <*= [].
(24) np(np(gen(np(pn(terry))),
          n(program),
          B),
        p0,C) <*= [optrel(B,p3,C)].
(25) optrel(rel(epsilon),p3,p3) <*= [].
(26) optrel(rel(that,B),p3,C) <*=
         [connects(that,p3,D),vp(B,D,C)].
(27) np(np(gen(np(pn(terry))),
          n(program),
          rel(epsilon)),
        p0,p3) <*= [].
(28) s(s(np(gen(np(pn(terry))),
          n(program),
          rel(epsilon)),
        B),
        p0,p4) <*= [vp(B,p3,p4)].
(29) det(gen(np(gen(np(pn(terry))),
              n(program),
              rel(epsilon))),
        p0,B) <*= [connects('s,p3,B)].
(30) vp(vp(B,C),p3,p4) <*= [tv(B,p3,D),np(C,D,p4)].
(31) vp(vp(B),p3,p4) <*= [iv(B,p3,p4)].
     ...
(35) iv(iv(halts),p3,p4) <*= [].
(36) vp(vp(iv(halts)),p3,p4) <*= [].
(37) s(s(np(gen(np(pn(terry))),
          n(program),
          rel(epsilon)),
        vp(iv(halts))),
      p0,p4) <*= [].
```

Derived clause (4) is the instantiation of the left-recursive determiner rule that the Prolog proof procedure cannot handle. It is easy to see that the predictions from the first literal in that clause are instances of derived clauses (2) and (3), so the subsumption check will avoid the loop.

6.6.7   Earley Deduction and Earley's CF Parsing Algorithm

We have already informally indicated the connection between Earley deduction and Earley's context-free parsing algorithm. For readers who are familiar with Earley's algorithm, it may be useful to describe the relationship more specifically. We will make the connection a bit more precise here by considering the application of Earley deduction to the definite-clause representation of a context-free grammar. In Earley's parsing algorithm, the state of the parser at input position j is represented by a collection of *dotted items* $I = [X \rightarrow \alpha \cdot \beta, i]$, where $X \rightarrow \gamma$ is some grammar rule, $\gamma = \alpha\beta$, and i is an input position with $i \leq j$. It is very easy to interpret these items in terms of our definite-clause representation. If β is empty, the item I above is called a *completed item* and represents the unit derived clause $X(i, j)$. If $\gamma = Y_1 \cdots Y_m$ and $\beta = Y_k \cdots Y_m$, item I represents the derived clause

$$X(i, p) \Leftarrow Y_k(j, p_k) \wedge \cdots \wedge Y_m(p_{m-1}, p) \quad .$$

6.6.8   Limitations of Tabular Parsers

We have just seen how loops and redundant analyses are avoided by using a tabular parser rather than a depth-first backtracking one. However, these advantages are bought at the cost of having to store dotted items to represent intermediate states of the analysis explicitly. For context-free grammars, tabular parsers have an overwhelming advantage because dotted items can be efficiently encoded as triples of a rule number, position of the dot within the rule, and item start position. In contrast, storing a lemma (derived clauses) requires storing the bindings for the variables in the clause or clauses from which the lemma was derived. The Prolog proof procedure avoids these costs by considering only one alternative analysis at a time, but the whole point of tabular parsing and tabular proof procedures is to be able to use lemmas from one alternative proof path in other proof paths. In our example interpreters above, we use the implicit copying provided by **assert** to store lemmas with their corresponding bindings. More sophisticated schemes are available that may reduce the overhead, but in the worst case tabular parsing for DCGs is asymptotically as bad as top-down backtrack parsing, and substantially worse if one considers constant factors. On the whole, the decision between tabular algorithms and Prolog for DCG parsing can only be done empirically with particular classes of grammar in mind.

Similar observations apply to the question of termination. Even though Earley deduction terminates for a larger class of programs than Prolog, it is easy to construct programs for which Earley deduction loops, such as the following DCG:

$$P(succ(x)) \rightarrow P(x) \; a$$
$$P(0) \quad\quad \rightarrow b$$

Our Earley deduction procedure applied to the definite-clause representation of this grammar will loop in the predictor for any start symbol matching $p(succ^n(0))$ for infinitely many values of n. This is because the subsumption test on derived clauses stops loops in which the clause or a more general one already exists in the table, but this grammar predicts ever more specific instances of the first rule.

Exercise 6.11 *Check that Earley deduction loops on this grammar.*

6.7   Problem Section: DCG Interpreters and Compilers

Problem 6.12 *Extend the DCG interpreter of Section 6.3.1 to handle the intersection operator as defined in Problem 2.13.*

Problem 6.13 *Write a compiler for the extended language of the previous problem.*

Problem 6.14 *The DCG compiler given by the combination of* compile, partially_execute, *and* parse *(the DCG interpreter) compiles a grammar by using the partial executor to interpret the DCG interpreter. This process could be made more efficient by partially executing the partial executor with respect to the* parse *predicate, akin to compiling the DCG interpreter. Perform this compilation to yield a more efficient DCG compiler. What is lost in this process?*

FG-DCG Analyses

Topicalization is a construction in English in which a filler constituent is prefixed to a sentence with a gap of the appropriate type. For the purposes of this problem, we will assume that the filler is always an NP. The following sentences exemplify the topicalization construction:

This book, Bertrand gave to Gottlob.
The professor that wrote this book, Alfred met.

The English *left dislocation* construction is a similar construction, except that instead of the empty string in the position associated with the filler, there is a pronoun (called a *resumptive pronoun*) filling that position, e.g.,

This book, Bertrand gave it to Gottlob.
The professor that wrote this book, Alfred met her.

Problem 6.15 *Add FG-DCG rules to Program 6.5 to handle the English topicalization and left dislocation construction. Be careful to avoid the ungrammatical*

*Bill read the book that Alfred wrote it.

Extending Earley Deduction with Restriction

In Section 6.6.8, we mentioned that even with the advantages of tabular parsing in being able to parse left-recursive and other grammars not parsable by other means, there are still problematic grammars for the methods outlined. The subsumption test for stopping prediction loops requires that eventually a new entry will be no more specific than an existing one. But the sample grammar given in that section predicts rules with ever larger terms. One method for solving this problem is to limit the amount of structure that can be passed in the prediction process, using a technique called *restriction*. When a literal G is to be predicted, we look for rules that might be useful in resolving against G. But instead of performing this test by unifying G itself with the head of the rule, we first *restrict G to G'* by eliminating all but a finite amount of structure from G. The restricted version G' is then matched against possible rules. Since the amount of information in G' can be bounded, the nontermination problem disappears for the problematic cases discussed in Section 6.6.8.

There are many possible ways of restricting a term to only a finite amount of structure. We might replace all subterms below a given depth (say 2) by variables. Then the term `f(g(h(a), s(b)), c)` would be restricted to `f(g(X, Y), c)`. Another alternative is to define restriction templates that eliminate certain information. For instance, the unit clause

```
restrict(f(g(A,B),c), f(g(X,Y),c)).
```

can be used to state the relationship between the sample term (and terms like it) and the restricted form.

Problem 6.16 *Modify the Earley deduction program to perform restriction before predicting using either of the methods of restricting terms. Test it on the problematic grammar of Section 6.6.8 to demonstrate that the algorithm now terminates.*

6.8   Bibliographic Notes

Interpreters for Prolog-like languages in Prolog have been used since the early days of Prolog as a means to explore different execution regimes for definite clauses and for trying out extensions to the language (Gallaire and Lasserre, 1982; Porto, 1982; L. M. Pereira, 1982; Mukai, 1985). One of the advantages of this approach is that it is not necessary to construct an interpreter for all the features of the new language because the aspects not being investigated are just absorbed by the underlying Prolog implementation.

The technique we suggest for a Prolog-in-Prolog with cut (Section 6.2.2) seems to have been first used in a version of the interpreter in the DEC-10 Prolog system due to David H. D. Warren, although it might have been in the folklore before then. A version is given by O'Keefe (1985).

Consecutively bounded depth-first search (Section 6.2.1) has been described and analysed by Stickel and Tyson (1985) and, under the name "depth-first iterative deepening" by Korf (1985).

Compilation by partial execution (Section 6.4) has been discussed in a logic programming context by Kahn (1982) and by Takeuchi and Furukawa (1985). However, much of what is done in this area by logic programming researchers is still unpublished, so our particular approach to the problem is to a great extent independently derived.

Left-corner parsers for context-free languages were discussed in a form close to the one used here (Section 6.5) by Rosenkrantz and Lewis (1970), although the basic idea seems to be earlier. The subject is also extensively covered in the exercise sections of Aho and Ullman's textbook (1972). Rosenkrantz and Lewis introduce an algorithm that transforms a context-free grammar to an equivalent one in which nonterminals are pairs of nonterminals of the original grammar. Left-corner derivations for the initial grammar correspond to top-down derivations for the new grammar. The BUP parser for definite-clause grammars (Matsumoto, et al., 1983) uses a similar technique, except that the nonterminal pairs are instantiated at run time rather than at grammar compilation time. The link relation (Section 6.5.1) gives a finite approximation of the in general infinite set of DCG nonterminals that would be the result of applying the Rosenkrantz and Lewis process to a DCG. Pratt (1985) developed a tabular parser based on similar notions.

Tabular parsers for context-free languages are the result of the application of "divide-and-conquer", dynamic-programming methods to the context-free parsing problem to avoid the exponential costs of backtracking (Aho and Ullman, 1972). The Cocke-Kasami-Younger (CKY) algorithm is the first of these, but it does not use any top-down predictions so it will generate many useless subphrases. Earley's algorithm (1970; Aho and Ullman, 1972) uses left-context to its full extent so that any recognized subphrase is guaranteed to fit into an analysis of a sentence having as a prefix all the input symbols seen so far. The algorithm of Graham, Harrison, and Ruzzo (1980; Harrison, 1978) combines a generalization of the CKY algorithm with preconstructed top-down prediction tables to achieve the best practical performance known so far for a general context-free parsing algorithm.

The Earley deduction proof procedure is due to D. H. D. Warren (1975), but the first published discussion of the procedure and its application in natural-language parsing is given by Pereira and Warren (1983). The trade-offs between termination and detail of top-down prediction are discussed by Shieber (1985c) for a class of formalisms with similar properties to definite-clause grammars. A further difficulty with the extended Earley's algorithm is the cost of maintaining rule instantiations, which does not occur in the original algorithm because grammar symbols are atomic. Boyer and Moore invented an instantiation-sharing method for clausal theorem provers (1972). The special constraints of parsing allow some further optimizations for their method (Pereira, 1985).

The idea of parsing from the heads of phrases outwards has often attracted attention, even though its computational merits are still to be proven. Instances of this idea are McCord's slot grammars (1980) and head-driven phrase-structure grammar (Sag and Pollard, 1986), and the use of a head-selection rule for DCGs (Pereira and Warren, 1983).

Topicalization and left dislocation are discussed by Ross (1967).

A

Listing of Sample Programs

This appendix includes commented listings of the `talk` program developed in Chapter 5 and the DCG compiler of Chapter 6. Besides combining all of the bits of code that were distributed throughout that and other chapters, this listing provides an example of one commenting style for Prolog.

A.1   A Note on Programming Style

We have adopted the following stylistic conventions in the programs in this appendix and elsewhere in the book. Although these particular conventions are not sacrosanct, adherence to some set of uniform conventions in Prolog programming (and, indeed, for programming in any language) is desirable.

We attempted to use variable names that are long enough to provide some mnemonic power. Predicate names were chosen to be as "declarative" in tone as possible (without sacrificing appropriateness). Thus, we used the name `conc` (for "concatenation") rather than the more common, procedural term `append`. Of course, certain predicates which rely on side-effects are more appropriately named with procedural terms such as `read_word` or `print_reply`.

Conventionally, the words in multi-word variable names are demarcated by capitalization of the first letter, e.g., `VariableName`. Multiple words in functor symbols, on the other hand, are separated with underbar, e.g., `multiple_word`. These conventions are relatively widespread in Prolog culture.

As mentioned in Section 3.4, we use the Prolog notational convention of giving a name beginning with an underbar to variables whose role is not to pass a value but merely to be a place holder. Anonymous variables (notated with a single underbar) are used for place-holder variables for those rare occasions in which naming the variable would detract from program readability. Such occasions occurred only in two areas: in specifying the tables for lexical entries and in listing generic forms for auxiliary literals.

Despite statements to the contrary, no programming language is self-documenting. Since the sample programs presented in the text have been surrounded by a discussion of their operation, no comments were interspersed. However, the commenting of programs is an important part of programming.

The commenting style used here includes an introductory description of each predicate defined, including a description of its arguments. The normal mode of execution of the predicate is conveyed by the direction of arrows (==> or <==) for each argument. In addition, the individual clauses are commented when appropriate.

It is usually preferable to place comments pertaining to a particular literal on the same line as the literal as is done, for instance, in the commented version of `main_loop` below. Unfortunately, page width limitations necessitated interleaving these comments in many cases.

In general, cuts, asserts, and similar metalogical operations are suspect in Prolog code. In the programs that follow, cuts are used only to encode conditionals. The conditional construct, though typically preferred, was not used in several cases because it was deemed less readable than the version using the cut. Asserts in these programs are not used as part of the program's control strategy, but rather, as the output of meta-programs.

A.2 The TALK Program

```
/******************************************************

                    TALK Program

******************************************************/


/*=====================================================
                    Operators
=====================================================*/

:- op(500,xfy,&).
:- op(510,xfy,=>).
:- op(100,fx,').
```

```
/*=======================================================
                   Dialogue Manager
=====================================================*/

%%% main_loop
%%% =========

main_loop :-
    write('>> '),        % prompt the user
    read_sent(Words),    % read a sentence
    talk(Words, Reply),  % process it with TALK
    print_reply(Reply),  % generate a printed reply
    main_loop.           % pocess more sentences


%%% talk(Sentence, Reply)
%%% =====================
%%%
%%%     Sentence ==> sentence to form a reply to
%%%     Reply    <== appropriate reply to the sentence

talk(Sentence, Reply) :-
    % parse the sentence
    parse(Sentence, LF, Type),
    % convert the FOL logical form into a Horn
    % clause, if possible
    clausify(LF, Clause, FreeVars), !,
    % concoct a reply, based on the clause and
    % whether sentence was a query or assertion
    reply(Type, FreeVars, Clause, Reply).

% No parse was found, sentence is too difficult.
talk(_Sentence, error('too difficult')).


%%% reply(Type, FreeVars, Clause, Reply)
%%% ====================================
%%%
%%%     Type     ==> the constant "query" or "assertion"
%%%                  depending on whether clause should
%%%                  be interpreted as a query or
%%%                  assertion
%%%     FreeVars ==> the free variables (to be
%%%                  interpreted existentially) in the
%%%                  clause
```

```
%%%     Clause   ==> the clause being replied to
%%%     Reply    <== the reply
%%%
%%%     If the clause is interpreted as an assertion,
%%%     the predicate has a side effect of asserting
%%%     the clause to the database.

% Replying to a query.
reply(query, FreeVars,
      (answer(Answer):-Condition), Reply) :-
    % find all the answers that satisfy the query,
    % replying with that set if it exists, or "no"
    % or "none" if it doesn't.
    (setof(Answer, FreeVars^Condition, Answers)
        -> Reply = answer(Answers)
     ;  (Answer = yes
            -> Reply = answer([no])
         ; Reply = answer([none]))), !.

% Replying to an assertion.
reply(assertion, _FreeVars,
      Assertion, asserted(Assertion)) :-
    % assert the assertion and tell user what we asserted
    assert(Assertion), !.

% Replying to some other type of sentence.
reply(_Type, _FreeVars, _Clause, error('unknown type')).


%%% print_reply(Reply)
%%% ==================
%%%
%%%     Reply ==> reply generated by reply predicate
%%%               that is to be printed to the
%%%               standard output.

print_reply(error(ErrorType)) :-
    write('Error: "'), write(ErrorType), write('."'), nl.

print_reply(asserted(Assertion)) :-
    write('Asserted "'), write(Assertion), write('."'), nl.

print_reply(answer(Answers)) :-
    print_answers(Answers).
```

```
%%% print_answer(Answers)
%%% =====================
%%%
%%%     Answers ==> nonempty list of answers to be printed
%%%                 to the standard output separated
%%%                 by commas.

print_answers([Answer]) :- !,
   write(Answer), write('.'), nl.

print_answers([Answer|Rest]) :-
   write(Answer), write(', '),
   print_reply(answer(Rest)).


%%% parse(Sentence, LF, Type)
%%% =========================
%%%
%%%     Sentence ==> sentence to parse
%%%     LF       <== logical form (in FOL) of sentence
%%%     Type     <== type of sentence
%%%                  (query or assertion)

% Parsing an assertion: a finite sentence without gaps.
parse(Sentence, LF, assertion) :-
   s(LF, nogap, Sentence, []).

% Parsing a query: a question.
parse(Sentence, LF, query) :-
   q(LF, Sentence, []).



/*=========================================================
                      Clausifier
=======================================================*/

%%% clausify(FOL, Clause, FreeVars)
%%% ===============================
%%%
%%%     FOL      ==> FOL expression to be converted
%%%                  to clause form
%%%     Clause   <== clause form of FOL expression
%%%     FreeVars <== free variables in clause
```

```
% Universals: variable is left implicitly scoped.
clausify(all(X,F0),F,[X|V]) :- clausify(F0,F,V).

% Implications: consequent must be a literal,
%               antecedent is clausified specially.
clausify(A0=>C0,(C:-A),V) :-
   clausify_literal(C0,C),
   clausify_antecedent(A0,A,V).

% Literals: left unchanged (except literal
%           marker is removed).
clausify(C0,C,[]) :- clausify_literal(C0,C).

% Note that conjunctions and existentials are
% disallowed, since they can't form Horn clauses.


%%% clausify_antecedent(FOL, Clause, FreeVars)
%%% ==========================================
%%%
%%%     FOL       ==> FOL expression to be converted
%%%                   to clause form
%%%     Clause    <== clause form of FOL expression
%%%     FreeVars  ==> list of free variables in clause

% Literals: left unchanged (except literal
%           marker is removed).
clausify_antecedent(L0,L,[]) :- clausify_literal(L0,L).

% Conjunctions: each conjunct is clausified separately.
clausify_antecedent(E0&F0,(E,F),V) :-
   clausify_antecedent(E0,E,V0),
   clausify_antecedent(F0,F,V1),
   conc(V0,V1,V).

% Existentials: variable is left implicitly scoped.
clausify_antecedent(exists(X,F0),F,[X|V]) :-
   clausify_antecedent(F0,F,V).

%%% clausify_literal(Literal, Clause)
%%% =================================
%%%
%%%     Literal   ==> FOL literal to be converted
%%%                   to clause form
%%%     Clause    <== clause form of FOL expression
```

```
% Literal is left unchanged (except literal
% marker is removed).
clausify_literal('L,L).


/*=========================================================
                         Grammar

Nonterminal names:

        q          Question
        sinv       INVerted Sentence
        s          noninverted Sentence
        np         Noun Phrase
        vp         Verb Phrase
        iv         Intransitive Verb
        tv         Transitive Verb
        aux        AUXiliary verb
        rov        subject-Object Raising Verb
        optrel     OPTional RELative clause
        relpron    RELative PRONoun
        whpron     WH PRONoun
        det        DETerminer
        n          Noun
        pn         Proper Noun

Typical order of and values for arguments:

  1. verb form:

     (main verbs)  finite, nonfinite, etc.
     (auxiliaries and raising verbs)  Form1-Form2
         where Form1 is form of embedded VP
               Form2 is form of verb itself)

  2. FOL logical form

  3. gap information:

     nogap or gap(Nonterm, Var)
         where Nonterm is nonterminal for gap
                   Var is the LF variable that
                          the filler will bind
=========================================================*/
```

```
%%%                     Questions

q(S => 'answer(X)) -->
   whpron, vp(finite, X^S, nogap).
q(S => 'answer(X)) -->
   whpron, sinv(S, gap(np, X)).
q(S => 'answer(yes)) -->
   sinv(S, nogap).
q(S => 'answer(yes)) -->
   [is],
   np((X^S0)^S, nogap),
   np((X^true)^exists(X,S0&true), nogap).

%%%              Declarative Sentences

s(S, GapInfo) -->
   np(VP^S, nogap),
   vp(finite, VP, GapInfo).

%%%               Inverted Sentences

sinv(S, GapInfo) -->
   aux(finite/Form, VP1^VP2),
   np(VP2^S, nogap),
   vp(Form, VP1, GapInfo).

%%%                  Noun Phrases

np(NP, nogap) -->
   det(N2^NP), n(N1), optrel(N1^N2).
np(NP, nogap) --> pn(NP).
np((X^S)^S, gap(np, X)) --> [].

%%%                  Verb Phrases

vp(Form, X^S, GapInfo) -->
   tv(Form, X^VP),
   np(VP^S, GapInfo).
vp(Form, VP, nogap) -->
   iv(Form, VP).
vp(Form1, VP2, GapInfo) -->
   aux(Form1/Form2, VP1^VP2),
   vp(Form2, VP1, GapInfo).
```

```
vp(Form1, VP2, GapInfo) -->
   rov(Form1/Form2, NP^VP1^VP2),
   np(NP, GapInfo),
   vp(Form2, VP1, nogap).
vp(Form2, VP2, GapInfo) -->
   rov(Form1/Form2, NP^VP1^VP2),
   np(NP, nogap),
   vp(Form1, VP1, GapInfo).
vp(finite, X^S, GapInfo) -->
   [is],
   np((X^P)^exists(X,S&P), GapInfo).
```

%%%   Relative Clauses

```
optrel((X^S1)^(X^(S1&S2))) -->
   relpron, vp(finite,X^S2, nogap).
optrel((X^S1)^(X^(S1&S2))) -->
   relpron, s(S2, gap(np, X)).
optrel(N^N) --> [].
```

```
/*========================================================
                        Dictionary
========================================================*/
```

```
/*--------------------------------------------------------
                        Preterminals
-------------------------------------------------------*/
```

```
det(LF) --> [D], {det(D, LF)}.
n(LF)   --> [N], {n(N, LF)}.
pn((E^S)^S) --> [PN], {pn(PN, E)}.
```

```
aux(Form, LF) --> [Aux], {aux(Aux, Form, LF)}.
relpron --> [RP], {relpron(RP)}.
whpron --> [WH], {whpron(WH)}.
```

```
% Verb entry arguments:
%   1. nonfinite form of the verb
%   2. third person singular present tense form of the verb
%   3. past tense form of the verb
%   4. past participle form of the verb
%   5. pres participle form of the verb
%   6. logical form of the verb
```

```
iv(nonfinite,      LF) --> [IV], {iv(IV, _, _, _, _, LF)}.
iv(finite,         LF) --> [IV], {iv(_, IV, _, _, _, LF)}.
iv(finite,         LF) --> [IV], {iv(_, _, IV, _, _, LF)}.
iv(past_participle, LF) --> [IV], {iv(_, _, _, IV, _, LF)}.
iv(pres_participle, LF) --> [IV], {iv(_, _, _, _, IV, LF)}.

tv(nonfinite,      LF) --> [TV], {tv(TV, _, _, _, _, LF)}.
tv(finite,         LF) --> [TV], {tv(_, TV, _, _, _, LF)}.
tv(finite,         LF) --> [TV], {tv(_, _, TV, _, _, LF)}.
tv(past_participle, LF) --> [TV], {tv(_, _, _, TV, _, LF)}.
tv(pres_participle, LF) --> [TV], {tv(_, _, _, _, TV, LF)}.

rov(nonfinite     /Requires, LF)
          --> [ROV], {rov(ROV, _, _, _, _, LF, Requires)}.
rov(finite        /Requires, LF)
          --> [ROV], {rov(_, ROV, _, _, _, LF, Requires)}.
rov(finite        /Requires, LF)
          --> [ROV], {rov(_, _, ROV, _, _, LF, Requires)}.
rov(past_participle/Requires, LF)
          --> [ROV], {rov(_, _, _, ROV, _, LF, Requires)}.
rov(pres_participle/Requires, LF)
          --> [ROV], {rov(_, _, _, _, ROV, LF, Requires)}.


/*-------------------------------------------------------
                    Lexical Items
----------------------------------------------------*/

relpron( that ).
relpron( who  ).
relpron( whom ).

whpron( who  ).
whpron( whom ).
whpron( what ).

det( every, (X^S1)^(X^S2)^   all(X,S1=>S2) ).
det( a,     (X^S1)^(X^S2)^exists(X,S1&S2)  ).
det( some,  (X^S1)^(X^S2)^exists(X,S1&S2)  ).

n( author,    X^ 'author(X)     ).
n( book,      X^ 'book(X)       ).
n( professor, X^ 'professor(X)  ).
n( program,   X^ 'program(X)    ).
n( programmer, X^ 'programmer(X) ).
n( student,   X^ 'student(X)    ).
```

```
pn( begriffsschrift, begriffsschrift ).
pn( bertrand,        bertrand        ).
pn( bill,            bill            ).
pn( gottlob,         gottlob         ).
pn( lunar,           lunar           ).
pn( principia,       principia       ).
pn( shrdlu,          shrdlu          ).
pn( terry,           terry           ).

iv( halt,       halts,      halted,
    halted,     halting,    X^ 'halt(X)          ).

tv( write,      writes,     wrote,
    written,    writing,    X^Y^ 'writes(X,Y)  ).
tv( meet,       meets,      met,
    met,        meeting,    X^Y^ 'meets(X,Y)   ).
tv( concern,    concerns,   concerned,
    concerned,  concerning, X^Y^ 'concerns(X,Y) ).
tv( run,        runs,       ran,
    run,        running,    X^Y^ 'runs(X,Y)    ).

rov( want,      wants,      wanted,
     wanted,    wanting,
     % semantics is partial execution of
     % NP ^ VP ^ Y ^ NP( X^want(Y,X,VP(X)) )
     ((X^ 'want(Y,X,Comp))^S) ^ (X^Comp) ^ Y ^ S,
     % form of VP required:
     infinitival).

aux( to,   infinitival/nonfinite, VP^ VP        ).
aux( does, finite/nonfinite,      VP^ VP        ).
aux( did,  finite/nonfinite,      VP^ VP        ).


/*=========================================================
                 Auxiliary Predicates
=========================================================*/


%%% conc(List1, List2, List)
%%% =========================
%%%
%%%     List1 ==> a list
%%%     List2 ==> a list
%%%     List  <== the concatenation of the two lists
```

```
conc([], List, List).

conc([Element|Rest], List, [Element|LongRest]) :-
    conc(Rest, List, LongRest).



%%% read_sent(Words)
%%% ================
%%%
%%%      Words ==> set of words read from the
%%%                standard input
%%%
%%%      Words are delimited by spaces and the
%%%      line is ended by a newline.  Case is not
%%%      folded; punctuation is not stripped.

read_sent(Words) :-
    get0(Char),                  % prime the lookahead
    read_sent(Char, Words).      % get the words

% Newlines end the input.
read_sent(C, []) :- newline(C), !.

% Spaces are ignored.
read_sent(C, Words) :- space(C), !,
    get0(Char),
    read_sent(Char, Words).

% Everything else starts a word.
read_sent(Char, [Word|Words]) :-
    read_word(Char, Chars, Next),  % get the word
    name(Word, Chars),             % pack the characters
                                   % into an atom
    read_sent(Next, Words).        % get some more words



%%% read_word(Chars)
%%% ================
%%%
%%%      Chars ==> list of characters read from standard
%%%                input and delimited by spaces or
%%%                newlines
```

```
% Space and newline end a word.
read_word(C, [], C) :- space(C), !.
read_word(C, [], C) :- newline(C), !.

% All other chars are added to the list.
read_word(Char, [Char|Chars], Last) :-
    get0(Next),
    read_word(Next, Chars, Last).


%%% space(Char)
%%% ===========
%%%
%%%     Char === the ASCII code for the space
%%%               character

space(32).


%%% newline(Char)
%%% =============
%%%
%%%     Char === the ASCII code for the newline
%%%               character

newline(10).
```

A.3   The DCG Compiler

```
/*****************************************************

                    DCG Compiler

*****************************************************/


/*=================================================
                Operator Declarations
=================================================*/

:- op(1200,xfx,--->).

%%% These declarations are required by certain Prolog
%%% systems for predicates that are to be asserted
%%% at run-time.  Predicates are specified by terms
%%% of the form name/arity.
:- dynamic (--->)/2, parse/3, connect/3.



/*=================================================
                  Compiler Driver
=================================================*/

%%% compile
%%% =======
%%%
%%%         Generates compiled clauses by partial
%%%         execution of the DCG metainterpreter below,
%%%         and adds them to the Prolog database.

compile :-
    program_clause(Clause),
    partially_execute(Clause, CompiledClause),
    add_rule(CompiledClause),
    fail.
```

```
%%% add_rule(Clause)
%%% =================
%%%
%%%         Clause   ==>   clause to be added to database
%%%                        after rewriting into a normal
%%%                        form that changes calls to parse
%%%                        into calls on particular
%%%                        nonterminals

add_rule((Head :- Body)) :-
    rewrite(Head, NewHead),
    rewrite(Body, NewBody),
    write('Asserting "'),
    write((NewHead :- NewBody)),
    write('."'), nl,
    assert((NewHead :- NewBody)).


%%% rewrite(Term, NewTerm)
%%% ======================
%%%
%%%         Term     ==>   a term encoding a literal or
%%%                        sequence of literals
%%%         NewTerm  <==   the term rewritten so literals
%%%                        of the form
%%%                            parse(s(...),...)
%%%                        are rewritten into the form
%%%                            s(...,...)

rewrite((A,B), (C,D)) :- !,
    rewrite(A, C), rewrite(B, D).
rewrite(parse(Term, P1, P2), NewLiteral) :- !,
    Term =.. [Function|Args],
    conc(Args, [P1, P2], AllArgs),
    NewLiteral =.. [Function|AllArgs].
rewrite(Term,Term).
```

```
/*=======================================================
            Partial Execution of Prolog Programs
=======================================================*/

%%% partially_execute(Term, NewTerm)
%%% ================================
%%%
%%%       Term    ==> term encoding Prolog clause,
%%%                       literal list or literal to be
%%%             partially executed with respect to the
%%%             program clauses and auxiliary clauses
%%%             given by program_clause and clause
%%%             predicates respectively.
%%%
%%%       NewTerm <== the partially executed term.

% Partially executing a clause involves
% expanding the body.
partially_execute((Head:-Body),
                    (Head:-ExpandedBody)) :- !,
    partially_execute(Body, ExpandedBody).

% Partially expanding a literal list involves
% conjoining the respective expansions.
partially_execute((Literal, Rest), Expansion) :- !,
    % expand the first literal
    partially_execute(Literal, ExpandedLiteral),
    % and the rest of them
    partially_execute(Rest, ExpandedRest),
    % and conjoin the results
    conjoin(ExpandedLiteral, ExpandedRest, Expansion).

% Partially executing an auxiliary literal involves
% replacing it with the body of a matching clause (if
% there are any).  Nonauxiliary literals, or those
% not matching any clauses, are left unchanged.
partially_execute(Literal, Expansion) :-
    ( aux_literal(Literal),
      setof(Body, Literal^aclause((Literal :- Body)),
            [_Clause|_Others]) )
    -> ( aclause((Literal :- Body)),
         partially_execute(Body, Expansion) )
    ;  Expansion = Literal.
```

```
/*-------------------------------------------------------
                      Utilities
----------------------------------------------------*/

%%% conc(List1, List2, List)
%%% ========================
%%%
%%%         List1 ==> a list
%%%         List2 ==> a list
%%%         List  <== the concatenation of the two lists

conc([], List, List).

conc([Element|Rest], List, [Element|LongRest]) :-
    conc(Rest, List, LongRest).


%%% conjoin(Conjunct1, Conjunct2, Conjunction)
%%% ==========================================
%%%
%%%         Conjunct1   ==>  two terms to be conjoined
%%%         Conjunct2   ==>
%%%         Conjunction <==  result of the conjunction

% Conjoining a conjunction works just like
% concatenation (conc).
conjoin((A,B), C, ABC) :- !,
    conjoin(B, C, BC),
    conjoin(A, BC, ABC).

% Conjoining true and anything leaves the other
% conjunct unchanged.
conjoin(true, A, A) :- !.
conjoin(A, true, A) :- !.

% Otherwise, use the normal comma conjunction
% operator.
conjoin(A, C, (A,C)).
```

```
%%% aclause(Clause)
%%% ===================
%%%
%%%         Clause <== the head and body of a clause
%%%                    encoded with the unary 'clause';
%%%                    unit clauses can be encoded directly
%%%                    with clause and the Body returned will
%%%                    be 'true'. Furthermore, the top-to-
%%%                    bottom clause ordering is preserved.

aclause((Head :- Body)) :-
    clause(Clause),
    (Clause = (Head :- Body)
        -> true
        ;  (Clause = Head, Body = true)).



/*=========================================================
               Program to Partially Execute
=========================================================*/



/*-------------------------------------------------------
          Control Information for Partial Executor
-----------------------------------------------------*/

aux_literal( (_ ---> _)      ).
aux_literal( parse(_, _, _) ).


/*-------------------------------------------------------
          DCG Metainterpreter to be Partially Executed
          Encoded form of program in Section 6.3.1
-----------------------------------------------------*/


program_clause(( parse(NT, P_0, P) :-
                 (NT ---> Body),
                 parse(Body, P_0, P)            )).

program_clause(( connect(Word, [Word|Rest], Rest) :-
                 true                          )).
```

```
clause((          parse((Body1, Body2), P_0, P) :-
                      parse(Body1, P_0, P_1),
                      parse(Body2, P_1, P)                )).

clause((          parse([], P, P)                         )).

clause((          parse([Word|Rest], P_0, P) :-
                      connect(Word, P_0, P_1),
                      parse(Rest, P_1, P)                 )).

clause((          parse({Goals}, P, P) :- call(Goals))).
```

```
/*=======================================================
                   Operators
=====================================================*/


/*--------------------------------------------------
    Sample Data for Program to Partially Execute:
    The parse-tree building DCG of Program 3.11
--------------------------------------------------*/
```

```
clause((   s(s(NP,VP)) ---> np(NP), vp(VP)               )).
clause((   np(np(Det,N,Rel)) --->
               det(Det),
               n(N),
               optrel(Rel)                               )).
clause((   np(np(PN)) ---> pn(PN)                        )).
clause((   vp(vp(TV,NP)) ---> tv(TV), np(NP)             )).
clause((   vp(vp(IV)) ---> iv(IV)                        )).
clause((   optrel(rel(epsilon)) ---> []                  )).
clause((   optrel(rel(that,VP)) ---> [that], vp(VP)      )).

clause((   pn(pn(terry)) ---> [terry]                    )).
clause((   pn(pn(shrdlu)) ---> [shrdlu]                  )).
clause((   iv(iv(halts)) ---> [halts]                    )).
clause((   det(det(a)) ---> [a]                          )).
clause((   n(n(program)) ---> [program]                  )).
clause((   tv(tv(writes)) ---> [writes]                  )).
```

Bibliography

Abelson, Harold and Gerald Jay Sussman with Julie Sussman. 1985. *Structure and Interpretation of Computer Programs*. Cambridge, Massachusetts: MIT Press.

Abramson, Harvey. 1984. Definite clause translation grammars. In *Proceedings of the 1984 International Symposium on Logic Programming*, 233–240. Silver Springs, Maryland: IEEE Computer Society Press.

Ades, Anthony E. and Mark J. Steedman. 1982. On the order of words. *Linguistics and Philosophy*, 4(4):517–558.

Aho, Alfred V. 1968. Indexed grammars—an extension of context-free grammars. *Journal of the ACM*, 15(4):647–671.

Aho, Alfred V. and Jeffrey D. Ullman. 1972. *The Theory of Parsing, Translation and Compiling*. Volume 1. Englewood Cliffs, New Jersey: Prentice-Hall.

———. 1977. *Principles of Compiler Design*. Reading, Massachusetts: Addison-Wesley.

Andreka, H. and I. Nemeti. 1976. *The Generalized Completeness of Horn Predicate Logic as a Programming Language*. DAI Report 21, Department of Artificial Intelligence, University of Edinburgh, Edinburgh, Scotland.

Andrews, Peter B. 1986. *An Introduction to Mathematical Logic and Type Theory: to Truth Through Proof*. Computer Science and Applied Mathematics Series. Orlando, Florida: Academic Press.

Apt, Kristoff R. and Maarten H. van Emden. 1982. Contributions to the theory of logic programming. *Journal of the ACM*, 29(3):841–862.

Backus, John. 1978. Can programming be liberated from the von Neumann style? *Communications of the ACM*, 21(8):613–641.

Baker, Carl L. 1978. *Introduction to Generative-Transformational Syntax*. Englewood Cliffs, New Jersey: Prentice-Hall.

Balbin, Isaac and Koenraad Lecot. 1985. *Logic Programming: A Classified Bibliography*. Victoria, Australia: Wildgrass Books.

Ballard, Bruce W. and Douglas E. Stumberger. 1986. Semantic acquisition in TELI: a transportable, user-customized natural language processor. In *Proceedings of the 24th Annual Meeting of the Association for Computational Linguistics*, 20–29. Columbia University, New York, New York.

Bar-Hillel, Yehoshua. 1964. *Language and Information*. Reading, Massachusetts: Addison-Wesley.

Bates, Madeleine. 1978. The theory and practice of augmented transition network grammars. In *Natural Language Communication with Computers*. New York, New York: Springer-Verlag.

Boolos, George S. and Richard C. Jeffrey. 1980. *Computability and Logic*. Second edition. Cambridge, England: Cambridge University Press.

Bowen, David L., Lawrence Byrd, Fernando C. N. Pereira, Luís M. Pereira, and David H. D. Warren. 1982. *DECsystem-10 Prolog User's Manual*. Occasional Paper 27, Department of Artificial Intelligence, University of Edinburgh, Edinburgh, Scotland.

Bowen, Kenneth A., Kevin A. Buettner, Ilyas Cicekli, and Andrew K. Turk. 1986. The design and implementation of a high-speed incremental portable Prolog compiler. In Ehud Shapiro, ed., *Proceedings of the Third International Conference on Logic Programming*, 650–655. Berlin, Germany: Springer-Verlag.

Bowen, Kenneth A. and Robert A. Kowalski. 1981. *Amalgamating Language and Metalanguage in Logic Programming*. Technical Report, School of Computer and Information Science, Syracuse University, Syracuse, New York.

Bowen, Kenneth A. and Tobias Weinberg. 1985. A meta-level extension of Prolog. In *Proceedings of the 1985 Symposium on Logic Programming*, 48–53. Washington, D.C.: IEEE Computer Society Press.

Boyer, Robert S. and J. Strother Moore. 1972. The sharing of structure in theorem-proving programs. In Bernard Meltzer and Donald Michie, eds., *Machine Intelligence 7*, 101–116. New York, New York: John Wiley and Sons.

Brachman, Ronald J. and Hector J. Levesque, eds. 1985. *Readings in Knowledge Representation*. Los Altos, California: Morgan Kaufmann.

Buchberger, Bruno. 1985. Basic features and development of the critical-pair/completion procedure. In Jean-Pierre Jouannaud, ed., *Rewriting Techniques and Applications*, 1–45. Berlin, Germany: Springer-Verlag.

Burstall, Rod M. and John Darlington. 1977. A transformation system for developing recursive programs. *Journal of the ACM*, 24(1):44–67.

Byrd, Lawrence. 1980. Understanding the control flow of Prolog programs. In Sten-Åke Tärnlund, ed., *Proceedings of the Logic Programming Workshop*, 127–138. Debrecen, Hungary.

Chomsky, Noam. 1956. Three models for the description of language. In *IRE Trans. Information Theory IT-2*, 113–124.

Church, Kenneth A. 1980. *On Memory Limitations in Natural Language Processing*. Master's thesis, Massachusetts Institute of Technology. Published as Report MIT/LCS/TR-245.

Church, Kenneth A. and Ramesh Patil. 1982. Coping with syntactic ambiguity or how to put the block in the box on the table. *Computational Linguistics*, 8(3-4):139–149.

Clark, Keith L. 1978. Negation as failure. In H. Gallaire and J. Minker, eds., *Logic and Data Bases*. New York, New York: Plenum Press.

Clark, Keith L. and Frank McCabe. 1981. The control facilities of IC-PROLOG. In Donald Michie, ed., *Expert Systems in the Micro Electronic Age*, 122–149. Edinburgh, Scotland: Edinburgh University Press.

Clark, Keith L. and Sharon Sickel. 1977. Predicate logic: a calculus for deriving programs. In *Proceedings of the 5th International Joint Conference on Artificial Intelligence*, 419–420. Department of Computer Science, Carnegie-Mellon University, Pittsburgh, Pennsylvania.

Clark, Keith L. and Sten-Åke Tärnlund. 1977. A first order theory of data and programs. In *Proceedings of the IFIP-77 Congress*. Amsterdam, Netherlands: North-Holland.

Clocksin, William F. and Christopher S. Mellish. 1981. *Programming in Prolog*. Berlin, Germany: Springer-Verlag.

Colmerauer, Alain. 1970. *Les Systèmes-Q ou un Formalisme pour Analyser et Synthétiser des Phrases sur Ordinateur*. Internal Publication 43, Département d'Informatique, Université de Montreal, Canada.

———. 1978. Metamorphosis grammars. In Leonard Bolc, ed., *Natural Language Communication with Computers*. Berlin, Germany: Springer-Verlag. First appeared as "Les Grammaires de Metamorphose", Groupe d'Intelligence Artificielle, Université de Marseille II, November 1975.

———. 1982. An interesting subset of natural language. In Keith L. Clark and Sten-Åke Tärnlund, eds., *Logic Programming*, 45–66. New York, New York: Academic Press.

———. 1986. Theoretical model of Prolog II. In Michel van Caneghem and David H. D. Warren, eds., *Logic Programming and Its Applications*, chapter 1, 3–31. Norwood, New Jersey: Ablex.

Colmerauer, Alain, Henri Kanoui, Robert Pasero, and Phillipe Roussel. 1973. *Un Système de Communication Homme-Machine en Français*. Rapport, Groupe d'Intelligence Artificielle, Université d'Aix-Marseille II.

Cooper, Robin. 1983. *Quantification and Syntactic Theory*. Synthese Language Library, volume 21. Dordrecht, Netherlands: D. Reidel.

Cresswell, M. J. 1973. *Logics and Languages*. London, England: Methuen and Co. Ltd.

Dahl, Veronica. 1981. Translating Spanish into logic through logic. *Computational Linguistics*, 7(3):149–164.

Dahl, Veronica and Harvey Abramson. 1984. On gapping grammars. In *Proceedings of the Second International Logic Programming Conference*, 77–88. Uppsala University, Uppsala, Sweden.

Dahl, Veronica and Michael McCord. 1983. Treating coordination in logic grammars. *Computational Linguistics*, 9(2):69–91.

DeGroot, Doug and Gary Lindstrom, eds. 1986. *Logic Programming— Functions, Relations, and Equations*. Englewood Cliffs, New Jersey: Prentice-Hall.

Deliyanni, A. and Robert A. Kowalski. 1979. Logic and semantic networks. *Communications of the ACM*, 22(3):184–192.

Dowty, David R., Robert E. Wall, and Stanley Peters. 1981. *Introduction to Montague Semantics*. Synthese Language Library, volume 11. Dordrecht, Netherlands: D. Reidel.

Earley, Jay. 1970. An efficient context-free parsing algorithm. *Communications of the ACM*, 13(2):94–102. Reprinted in (Grosz et al., 1986).

Eisinger, Norbert. 1986. What you always wanted to know about clause graph resolution. In Jörg H. Siekmann, ed., *8th International Conference on Automated Deduction*, 316–336. Berlin, Germany: Springer-Verlag.

Gallaire, Hervé and Claudine Lasserre. 1982. Metalevel control for logic programs. In Keith L. Clark and Sten-Åke Tärnlund, eds., *Logic Programming*, 173–185. New York, New York: Academic Press.

Gallier, Jean H. 1986. *Logic for Computer Science*. New York, New York: Harper & Row.

Gazdar, Gerald. 1981. Unbounded dependencies and coordinate structure. *Linguistic Inquiry*, 12:155–184.

Gazdar, Gerald, Ewan Klein, Geoffrey K. Pullum, and Ivan A. Sag. 1985. *Generalized Phrase Structure Grammar*. Cambridge, Massachusetts: Harvard University Press.

Gazdar, Gerald, Geoffrey K. Pullum, and Ivan A. Sag. 1982. Auxiliaries and related phenomena in a restrictive theory of grammar. *Language*, 58:591–638.

Ginsburg, Seymour. 1966. *The Mathematical Theory of Context-Free Languages*. New York, New York: McGraw-Hill.

Graham, Susan L., Michael A. Harrison, and William L. Ruzzo. 1980. An improved context-free recognizer. *ACM Transactions on Programming Languages and Systems*, 2(3):415–462.

Green, Cordell. 1968. Theorem-proving by resolution as a basis for question-answering systems. In Bernard Meltzer and Donald Michie, eds., *Machine Intelligence 4*, 183–205. Edinburgh, Scotland: Edinburgh University Press.

Greibach, Sheila A. 1981. Formal languages: origins and directions. *Annals of the History of Computing*, 3(1):14–41.

Gross, Maurice. 1975. *Méthodes en Syntaxe*. Paris, France: Hermann.

Grosz, Barbara, Douglas E. Appelt, Paul Martin, and Fernando Pereira. 1987. TEAM: an experiment in the design of transportable natural language interfaces. *Artificial Intelligence*, to appear.

Grosz, Barbara J., Karen Sparck Jones, and Bonnie Lynn Webber, eds. 1986. *Readings in Natural Language Processing.* Los Altos, California: Morgan Kaufmann.

Haas, Norman and Gary G. Hendrix. 1981. *Machine Learning for Information Management.* Technical Note 252, Artificial Intelligence Center, SRI International, Menlo Park, California.

Harrison, Michael A. 1978. *Introduction to Formal Language Theory.* Reading, Massachussets: Addison-Wesley.

Hendrix, Gary G. 1979. Encoding knowledge in partitioned networks. In Nicholas V. Findler, ed., *Associative Networks—The Representation and Use of Knowledge in Computers.* New York, New York: Academic Press.

Hindley, J. Roger and Jonathan P. Seldin. 1986. *Introduction to Combinators and λ-Calculus.* London Mathematical Society Student Texts, volume 1. Cambridge, England: Cambridge University Press.

Hobbs, Jerry R. and Stuart M. Shieber. 1987. An algorithm for generating quantifier scopings. *Computational Linguistics*, to appear.

Hogger, Christopher J. 1981. Derivation of logic programs. *Journal of the ACM*, 28(2):372–392.

Hopcroft, John E. and Jeffrey D. Ullman. 1979. *Introduction to Automata Theory, Languages, and Computation.* Reading, Massachussets: Addison Wesley.

Huet, Gerard and Derek Oppen. 1980. Equations and rewrite rules, a survey. In Ron V. Book, ed., *Formal Languages: Perspectives and Open Problems.* New York, New York: Academic Press.

Jaffar, Joxan, Jean-Louis Lassez, and John W. Lloyd. 1983. Completeness of the negation as failure rule. In Alan Bundy, ed., *Proceedings of the Eighth International Joint Conference on Artificial Intelligence.* Los Altos, California: William Kaufmann Inc.

Jaffar, Joxan, Jean-Louis Lassez, and Michael J. Maher. 1986. Some issues and trends in the semantics of logic programming. In Ehud Shapiro, ed., *Proceedings of the Third International Conference on Logic Programming.* Berlin, Germany: Springer-Verlag.

Jaffar, Joxan, and Peter J. Stuckey. 1986. Semantics of infinite tree logic programming. *Theoretical Computer Science*, 46:141–158.

Jones, Neil and Harald Søndergaard. 1987. A semantics-based framework for the abstract interpretation of Prolog. In S. Abramsky and C. Henkin, eds., *Abstract Interpretation of Declarative Languages*. Chichester, West Sussex, England: Ellis Horwood.

Kahn, Kenneth M. 1982. A partial evaluator of Lisp programs written in Prolog. In Michel van Caneghem, ed., *First International Logic Programming Conference*, 19–25. ADDP-GIA, Faculté des Sciences de Luminy, Marseille, France.

Karttunen, Lauri. 1986. *The Relevance of Computational Linguistics*. Report 59, Center for the Study of Language and Information, Stanford, California.

Knuth, Donald E. 1973. *Searching and Sorting*. The Art of Computer Programming, volume 3. Reading, Massachusetts: Addison-Wesley.

Korf, Richard E. 1985. Depth-first iterative-deepening: an optimal admissible tree search. *Artificial Intelligence*, 27(1):97–109.

Kowalski, Robert A. 1974a. *Logic for Problem Solving*. DCL Memo 75, Department of Artificial Intelligence, University of Edinburgh, Scotland.

———. 1974b. Predicate logic as a programming language. In *Proceedings of the IFIP-74 Congress*, 569–574. Amsterdam, Netherlands: North-Holland.

———. 1975. A proof procedure using connection graphs. *Journal of the ACM*, 22(4):572–595.

———. 1980. *Logic for Problem Solving*. New York, New York: North-Holland.

Kowalski, Robert A. and David Kuehner. 1971. Linear resolution with selection function. *Artificial Intelligence*, 2:227–60.

Lambek, Joachim. 1961. On the calculus of syntactic types. In Roman Jakobson, ed., *Structure of Language and its Mathematical Aspects (Proceedings of the Symposia in Applied Mathematics, 12)*, 166–178. Providence, Rhode Island: American Mathematical Society. As cited in (Ades and Steedman, 1982).

Lewis, David. 1972. General semantics. In Donald Davidson and Gilbert Harman, eds., *Semantics of Natural Language.* Dordrecht, Netherlands: D. Reidel.

Lloyd, John W. 1984. *Foundations of Logic Programming.* Berlin, Germany: Springer-Verlag.

Maibaum, T. S. E. 1974. A generalized approach to formal languages. *Journal of Computer and System Sciences*, 8:409–439.

Matsumoto, Yuji, Hozumi Tanaka, Hideki Hirakawa, Hideo Miyoshi, and Hideki Yasukawa. 1983. BUP: a bottom-up parser embedded in Prolog. *New Generation Computing*, 1(2):145–158.

McCarthy, John, Paul W. Abrahams, Daniel J. Edwards, Timothy P. Hart, and Michael I. Levin. 1965. *LISP 1.5 Programmer's Manual.* Second ed. Cambridge, Massachusetts: MIT Press.

McCord, Michael C. 1980. Slot grammars. *Computational Linguistics*, 6(1):255–286.

———. 1982. Using slots and modifiers in logic grammars for natural language. *Artificial Intelligence*, 18(3):327–367.

Mellish, Christopher S. 1985. Some global optimizations for a Prolog compiler. *Logic Programming*, 2(1):43–66.

———. 1986. Abstract interpretation of logic programs. In Ehud Shapiro, ed., *Proceedings of the Third International Conference on Logic Programming*, 463–474. Berlin, Germany: Springer-Verlag.

Miller, Dale A. and Gopalan Nadathur. 1986. Some uses of higher-order logic in computational linguistics. In *Proceedings of the 24th Annual Meeting of the Association for Computational Linguistics*, 247–256. Columbia University, New York, New York.

Mishra, P. 1984. Towards a theory of types in Prolog. In *Proceedings of the 1984 International Symposium on Logic Programming*, 289–298. Silver Springs, Maryland: IEEE Computer Society Press.

Moore, Robert C. 1981. Problems in logical form. In *Proceedings of the 19th Annual Meeting of the Association for Computational Linguistics*, 117–124. Stanford University, Stanford, California. Reprinted in (Grosz et al., 1986).

Morris, Katherine, Jeffrey D. Ullman, and Allen Van Gelder. 1986. The design and implementation of a high-speed incremental portable Prolog compiler. In Ehud Shapiro, ed., *Proceedings of the Third International Conference on Logic Programming*, 554–568. Berlin, Germany: Springer-Verlag.

Mukai, K. 1985. *Unification over Complex Indeterminates in Prolog*. Technical Report TR-113, ICOT, Tokyo, Japan.

Mycroft, Alan and Richard A. O'Keefe. 1984. A polymorphic type system for Prolog. *Artificial Intelligence*, 23(3):295–307.

Naish, Lee. 1986. *Negation and Control in Prolog*. Lecture Notes in Computer Science, volume 238. Berlin, Germany: Springer-Verlag.

O'Donnell, Michael J. 1985. *Equational Logic as a Programming Language*. Foundations of Computing Series. Cambridge, Massachusetts: MIT Press.

O'Keefe, Richard A. 1985. On the treatment of cuts in Prolog source-level tools. In *Proceedings of the 1985 Symposium on Logic Programming*, 68–72. Washington, D.C.: IEEE Computer Society Press.

Partee, Barbara Hall, Alice ter Meulen, and Robert Wall. 1987. *Mathematical Methods for Linguistics*. Studies in Linguistics and Philosophy. Dordrecht, Netherlands: D. Reidel.

Pasero, Robert. 1973. *Representation du Français en Logique du Premier Ordre, en Vue de Dialoguer avec un Ordinateur*. Thèse de 3ème Cycle, Groupe d'Intelligence Artificielle, Université d'Aix-Marseille II.

Pereira, Fernando C. N. 1981. Extraposition grammars. *Computational Linguistics*, 7(4):243–256.

———. 1982. *Logic for Natural Language Analysis*. Ph.D. thesis, University of Edinburgh, Edinburgh, Scotland. Reprinted as Technical Note 275, January 1983, Artificial Intelligence Center, SRI International, Menlo Park, California.

———. 1985. A structure-sharing representation for unification-based grammar formalisms. In *Proceedings of the 23rd Annual Meeting of the Association for Computational Linguistics*, 137–144. University of Chicago, Chicago, Illinois.

Pereira, Fernando C. N. and David H. D. Warren. 1980. Definite clause grammars for language analysis—a survey of the formalism and a comparison with augmented transition networks. *Artificial Intelligence*, 13:231–278. Reprinted in (Grosz et al., 1986).

———. 1983. Parsing as deduction. In *Proceedings of the 21st Annual Meeting of the Association for Computational Linguistics*. Massachusetts Institute of Technology, Cambridge, Massachusetts.

Pereira, Luís M. 1982. Logic control with logic. In Michel van Caneghem, ed., *First International Logic Programming Conference*, 9–18. ADDP-GIA, Faculté des Sciences de Luminy, Marseille, France.

Pittomvils, Edwin, Maurice Bruynooghe, and Yves D. Willems. 1985. Towards a real time garbage collector for Prolog. In *Proceedings of the 1985 Symposium on Logic Programming*, 185–198. Washington, D.C.: IEEE Computer Society Press.

Porto, António. 1982. Epilog: a language for extended programming in logic. In Michel van Caneghem, ed., *First International Logic Programming Conference*, 31–37. ADDP-GIA, Faculté des Sciences de Luminy, Marseille, France.

Pratt, Vaughan R. 1975. LINGOL: a project report. In *Advance Papers of the Fourth International Joint Conference on Artificial Intelligence*, 422–428. Tbilisi, Georgia, USSR.

Quillian, M. Ross. 1967. Word concepts: a theory and simulation of some basic semantic capabilities. *Behavioral Science*, 12:410–430. Reprinted in (Brachman and Levesque, 1985).

Robinson, J. A. 1965. A machine-oriented logic based on the resolution principle. *Journal of the ACM*, 12:23–44.

———. 1979. *Logic: Form and Function*. Artificial Intelligence Series. New York, New York: North-Holland.

Rosenkrantz, Daniel J. and Philip M. Lewis II. 1970. Deterministic left corner parser. In *IEEE Conference Record of the 11th Annual Symposium on Switching and Automata Theory*, 139–152.

Rosenschein, Stanley J. and Stuart M. Shieber. 1982. Translating English into logical form. In *Proceedings of the 20th Annual Meeting of the Association for Computational Linguistics*, 1–8. University of Toronto, Toronto, Canada.

Ross, John R. 1967. *Constraints on Variables in Syntax.* Ph.D. thesis, Massachusetts Institute of Technology, Cambridge, Massachusetts. Excerpts reprinted in (Ross, 1974).

———. 1974. Excerpts from 'Constraints on Variables in Syntax'. In Gilbert Harman, ed., *On Noam Chomsky: Critical Essays.* Garden City, New York: Anchor Books.

Rounds, William C. 1969. Context-free grammars on trees. In *Proceedings of the ACM Symposium on the Theory of Computing.*

———. 1970. Tree-oriented proofs of some theorems on context-free and indexed languages. In *Proceedings of the ACM Symposium on the Theory of Computing.*

———. 1987. LFP: a logic for linguistic descriptions and an analysis of its complexity. *Computational Linguistics,* to appear.

Roussel, Phillipe. 1975. *Prolog: Manuel de Référence et Utilisation.* Technical Report, Groupe d'Intelligence Artificielle, Université d'Aix-Marseille II, Marseille, France.

Sag, Ivan A. and Carl Pollard. 1986. Head-driven phrase-structure grammar: an informal synopsis. Draft CSLI Report.

Schubert, Lenhart K. and Francis J. Pelletier. 1982. From English to logic: context-free computation of 'conventional' logical translation. *Computational Linguistics,* 8(1):26–44. Reprinted in (Grosz et al., 1986).

Shapiro, Ehud Y. 1982. Alternation and the computational complexity of logic programs. In Michel van Caneghem, ed., *First International Logic Programming Conference,* 154–163*bis.* ADDP-GIA, Faculté des Sciences de Luminy, Marseille, France.

———. 1983. *Algorithmic Program Debugging.* Cambridge, Massachusetts: MIT Press.

Shieber, Stuart M. 1985a. Criteria for designing computer facilities for linguistic analysis. *Linguistics,* 23:189–211.

———. 1985b. Evidence against the context-freeness of natural language. *Linguistics and Philosophy,* 8:333–343.

———. 1985c. Using restriction to extend parsing algorithms for complex-feature-based formalisms. In *Proceedings of the 23rd Annual Meeting of the Association for Computational Linguistics,* 145–152. University of Chicago, Chicago, Illinois.

Soames, Scott and David M. Perlmutter. 1979. *Syntactic Argumentation and the Structure of English.* Berkeley, California: University of California Press.

Sterling, Leon and Ehud Shapiro. 1986. *The Art of Prolog.* Cambridge, Massachusetts: MIT Press.

Stickel, Mark E. and W. M. Tyson. 1985. An analysis of consecutively bounded depth-first search with applications in automated deduction. In *Proceedings of the Ninth International Joint Conference on Artificial Intelligence*, 1073–1075. Los Angeles, California.

Tait, Katherine. 1975. *My Father Bertrand Russell.* New York, New York: Harcourt Brace Jovanovich.

Takeuchi, A. and K. Furukawa. 1985. *Partial Evaluation of Prolog Programs and its Application to Meta Programming.* Technical Report TR-126, ICOT, Tokyo, Japan.

Tamaki, Hisao and Taisuke Sato. 1984. Unfold/fold transformation of logic programs. In *Proceedings of the Second International Logic Programming Conference*, 127–138. Uppsala University, Uppsala, Sweden.

Tärnlund, Sten-Åke. 1977. Horn clause computability. *BIT*, 2:215–226.

Thomason, Richmond H., ed. 1974. *Formal Philosophy—Selected Papers of Richard Montague.* New Haven, Connecticut: Yale University Press.

Tick, Evan and David H. D. Warren. 1984. Towards a pipelined Prolog processor. In *Proceedings of the 1984 International Symposium on Logic Programming*, 29–40. Silver Springs, Maryland: IEEE Computer Society Press.

Uszkoreit, Hans J. 1986. *Categorial Unification Grammars.* Report 66, Center for the Study of Language and Information, Stanford, California.

Vanlehn, Kurt A. 1978. *Determining the Scope of English Quantifiers.* Master's thesis, Massachusetts Institute of Technology, Cambridge, Massachusetts. Published as Report AI-TR-483.

Warren, David H. D. 1975. Earley deduction. Unpublished note.

———. 1977. *Applied Logic—Its Use and Implementation as Programming Tool.* Ph.D. thesis, University of Edinburgh, Edinburgh, Scotland. Reprinted as Technical Note 290, Artificial Intelligence Center, SRI, International, Menlo Park, California.

———. 1979. Prolog on the DECsystem-10. In Donald Michie, ed., *Expert Systems in the Micro-Electronic Age*. Edinburgh, Scotland: Edinburgh University Press.

———. 1982. Higher-order extensions to Prolog—are they needed? In Hayes, Michie, and Pao, eds., *Machine Intelligence 10*. Chichester, West Sussex, England: Ellis Horwood.

———. 1983. *An Abstract Prolog Instruction Set*. Technical Note 309, Artificial Intelligence Center, SRI International, Menlo Park, California.

Warren, David H. D. and Fernando C. N. Pereira. 1982. An efficient easily adaptable system for interpreting natural language queries. *American Journal of Computational Linguistics*, 8(3-4):110–122.

Warren, David H. D., Luís M. Pereira, and Fernando C. N. Pereira. 1977. Prolog—the language and its implementation compared with Lisp. In *SIGPLAN/SIGART Newsletter*. ACM Symposium on Artificial Intelligence and Programming Languages.

Warren, David S. 1983. Using λ-calculus to represent meanings in logic grammars. In *Proceedings of the 21st Annual Meeting of the Association for Computational Linguistics*, 51–56. Massachusetts Institute of Technology, Cambridge, Massachusetts.

Warren, David S. and Joyce Friedman. 1982. Using semantics in non-context-free parsing of Montague grammar. *Computational Linguistics*, 8(3-4):123–138.

Winograd, Terry. 1972. *Understanding Natural Language*. New York, New York: Academic Press.

———. 1983. *Language as a Cognitive Process—Volume 1: Syntax*. Reading, Massachusetts: Addison-Wesley.

Woods, William A. 1970. Transition network grammars for natural language analysis. *Communications of the ACM*, 13:591–606.

———. 1975. What's in a link: foundations for semantic networks. In D. G. Bobrow and A. M. Collins, eds., *Representation and Understanding: Studies in Cognitive Science*, 35–82. New York, New York: Academic Press.

———. 1977. *Semantics and Quantification in Natural Language Question Answering*. Report 3687, Bolt Beranek and Newman Inc. Reprinted in (Grosz et al., 1986).

Wos, Larry, Ross Overbeek, Ewing Lusk, and Jim Boyle. 1984. *Automated Reasoning: Introduction and Applications.* Englewood Cliffs, New Jersey: Prentice-Hall.

van Benthem, Johan. 1986. *Essays in Logical Semantics.* Studies in Linguistics and Philosophy, volume 29. Dordrecht, Netherlands: D. Reidel.

van Caneghem, Michel and David H. D. Warren, eds. 1986. *Logic Programming and its Applications.* Ablex Series in Artificial Intelligence. Norwood, New Jersey: Ablex.

van Emden, Maarten H. and Robert A. Kowalski. 1976. The semantics of predicate logic as a programming language. *Journal of the ACM,* 23(4):733–742.

van Heijenoort, Jean, ed. 1967. *From Frege to Gödel—A Source Book in Mathematical Logic, 1879-1931.* Cambridge, Massachusetts: Harvard University Press.

Name Index

Subject Index

CSLI Reports

The following titles have been published in the CSLI Reports series. These reports may be obtained from CSLI Publications, Ventura Hall, Stanford University, Stanford, CA 94305.

Research Program on Situated Language. Rep. No. CSLI–84–1.
(Out of print)

The Situation in Logic–I. Jon Barwise. Rep. No. CSLI–84–2. *($2.00)*

Coordination and How to Distinguish Categories. Ivan Sag, Gerald Gazdar, Thomas Wasow, and Steven Weisler. Rep. No. CSLI–84–3. *($3.50)*

Belief and Incompleteness. Kurt Konolige. Rep. No. CSLI–84–4. *($4.50)*

Equality, Types, Modules and Generics for Logic Programming. Joseph Goguen and José Meseguer. Rep. No. CSLI–84–5. *($2.50)*

Lessons from Bolzano. Johan van Benthem. Rep. No. CSLI–84–6. *($1.50)*

Self-propagating Search: A Unified Theory of Memory. Pentti Kanerva. Rep. No. CSLI–84–7. *($9.00)*

Reflection and Semantics in LISP. Brian Cantwell Smith. Rep. No. CSLI–84–8. *($2.50)*

The Implementation of Procedurally Reflective Languages. Jim des Rivières and Brian Cantwell Smith. Rep. No. CSLI–84–9. *($3.00)*

Parameterized Programming. Joseph Goguen. Rep. No. CSLI–84–10.
($3.50)

Morphological Constraints on Scandinavian Tone Accent. Meg Withgott and Per-Kristian Halvorsen. Rep. No. CSLI–84–11. *($2.50)*

Partiality and Nonmonotonicity in Classical Logic. Johan van Benthem. Rep. No. CSLI–84–12. *($2.00)*

Shifting Situations and Shaken Attitudes. Jon Barwise and John Perry. Rep. No. CSLI–84–13. *($4.50)*

Aspectual Classes in Situation Semantics. Robin Cooper. Rep. No. CSLI–85–14–C. *($4.00)*

Completeness of Many-Sorted Equational Logic. Joseph Goguen and José Meseguer. Rep. No. CSLI–84–15. *($2.50)*

Moving the Semantic Fulcrum. Terry Winograd. Rep. No. CSLI–84–17.
($1.50)

On the Mathematical Properties of Linguistic Theories. C. Raymond Perrault. Rep. No. CSLI–84–18. *($3.00)*

A Simple and Efficient Implementation of Higher-order Functions in LISP. Michael P. Georgeff and Stephen F.Bodnar. Rep. No. CSLI–84–19.
($4.50)

263

A Complete Type-free, Second-order Logic and its Philosophical Foundations. Christopher Menzel. Rep. No. CSLI–86–40. ($4.50)

Possible-world Semantics for Autoepistemic Logic. Robert C. Moore. Rep. No. CSLI–85–41. ($2.00)

Deduction with Many-Sorted Rewrite. José Meseguer and Joseph A. Goguen. Rep. No. CSLI–85–42. ($1.50)

On Some Formal Properties of Metarules. Hans Uszkoreit and Stanley Peters. Rep. No. CSLI–85–43. ($1.50)

Language, Mind, and Information. John Perry. Rep. No. CSLI–85–44. ($2.00)

Constraints on Order. Hans Uszkoreit. Rep. No. CSLI–86–46. ($3.00)

Linear Precedence in Discontinuous Constituents: Complex Fronting in German. Hans Uszkoreit. Rep. No. CSLI–86–47. ($2.50)

A Compilation of Papers on Unification-Based Grammar Formalisms, Parts I and II. Stuart M. Shieber, Fernando C.N. Pereira, Lauri Karttunen, and Martin Kay. Rep. No. CSLI–86–48. ($4.00)

An Algorithm for Generating Quantifier Scopings. Jerry R. Hobbs and Stuart M. Shieber. Rep. No. CSLI–86–49. ($2.50)

Verbs of Change, Causation, and Time. Dorit Abusch. Rep. No. CSLI–86–50. ($2.00)

Noun-Phrase Interpretation. Mats Rooth. Rep. No. CSLI–86–51. ($2.50)

Noun Phrases, Generalized Quantifiers and Anaphora. Jon Barwise. Rep. No. CSLI–86–52. ($2.50)

Circumstantial Attitudes and Benevolent Cognition. John Perry. Rep. No. CSLI–86–53. ($1.50)

A Study in the Foundations of Programming Methodology: Specifications, Institutions, Charters and Parchments. Joseph A. Goguen and R. M. Burstall. Rep. No. CSLI–86–54. ($2.50)

Quantifiers in Formal and Natural Languages. Dag Westerståhl. Rep. No. CSLI–86–55. ($7.50)

Intentionality, Information, and Matter. Ivan Blair. Rep. No. CSLI–86–56. ($3.00)

Graphs and Grammars. William Marsh. Rep. No. CSLI–86–57. ($2.00)

Computer Aids for Comparative Dictionaries. Mark Johnson. Rep. No. CSLI–86–58. ($2.00)

The Relevance of Computational Linguistics. Lauri Karttunen. Rep. No. CSLI–86–59. ($2.50)

Grammatical Hierarchy and Linear Precedence. Ivan A. Sag. Rep. No. CSLI–86–60. ($3.50)

D-PATR: A Development Environment for Unification-Based Grammars. Lauri Karttunen. Rep. No. CSLI–86–61. ($*4.00*)

A Sheaf-Theoretic Model of Concurrency. Luís F. Monteiro and Fernando C. N. Pereira. Rep. No. CSLI–86–62. ($*3.00*)

Discourse, Anaphora and Parsing. Mark Johnson. Rep. No. CSLI–86–63. ($*2.00*)

Tarski on Truth and Logical Consequence. John Etchemendy. Rep. No. CSLI–86–64. ($*3.50*)

The LFG Treatment of Discontinuity and The Double Infinitive Construction in Dutch. Mark Johnson. Rep. No. CSLI–86–65. ($*2.50*)

Categorial Unification Grammars. Hans Uszkoreit. Rep. No. CSLI–86–66. ($*2.50*)

Generalized Quantifiers and Plurals. Godehard Link. Rep. No. CSLI–86–67. ($*2.00*)

Radical Lexicalism. Lauri Karttunen. Rep. No. CSLI–86–68. ($*2.50*)

What is Intention? Michael E. Bratman. Rep. No. CSLI–86–69. ($*2.00*)

Understanding Computers and Cognition: Four Reviews and a Response. Mark Stefik, Editor. Rep. No. CSLI–87–70. ($*3.50*)

The Corresponding Continuum. Brian Cantwell Smith. Rep. No. CSLI–87–71. ($*4.00*)

The Role of Propositional Objects of Belief in Action. David J. Israel. Rep. No. CSLI–87–72. ($*2.50*)

From Worlds to Situations. John Perry. Rep. No. CSLI–87–73. ($*2.00*)

Two Replies. Jon Barwise. Rep. No. CSLI–87–74. ($*3.00*)

Semantics of Clocks. Brian Cantwell Smith. Rep. No. CSLI–87–75. ($*3.50*)

Varieties of Self-Reference. Brian Cantwell Smith. Rep. No. CSLI–87–76. (*Forthcoming*)

The Parts of Perception. Alexander Pentland. Rep. No. CSLI–87–77. ($*4.00*)

Topic, Pronoun, and Agreement in Chicheŵa. Joan Bresnan and S. A. Mchombo. Rep. No. CSLI–87–78. ($*5.00*)

HPSG: An Informal Synopsis. Carl Pollard and Ivan A. Sag. Rep. No. CSLI–87–79. ($*2.50*)

The (Situated) Processing of (Situated) Languages. Susan Stucky. Rep. No. CSLI–87–80. ($*1.50*)

Muir: A Tool for Language Design. Terry Winograd. Rep. No. CSLI–87–81. ($*2.50*)

CSLI Lecture Notes

The titles in this series are distributed by the University of Chicago Press and may be purchased in academic or university bookstores or ordered directly from the distributor at 5801 Ellis Avenue, Chicago, Illinois 60637.

A Manual of Intensional Logic. Johan van Benthem. Lecture Notes No. 1.
(*Paper $8.95*)

Emotion and Focus. Helen Fay Nissenbaum. Lecture Notes No. 2. (*Paper $8.95*)

Lectures on Contemporary Syntactic Theories. Peter Sells with a Postscript by Thomas Wasow. Lecture Notes No. 3. (*Paper $11.95 Cloth $23.95*)

An Introduction to Unification-Based Approaches to Grammar. Stuart M. Shieber. Lecture Notes No. 4. (*Paper $8.95 Cloth $17.95*)

The Semantics of Destructive LISP. Ian A. Mason. Lecture Notes No. 5.
(*Paper $14.95 Cloth $29.95*)

An Essay on Facts. Kenneth Russell Olson. Lecture Notes No. 6.
(*Paper $11.95 Cloth $23.95*)

Logics of Time and Computation. Robert Goldblatt. Lecture Notes No. 7.
(*Paper $11.95 Cloth $23.95*)

Word Order and Constituent Structure in German. Hans Uszkoreit. Lecture Notes No. 8. (*Paper $12.95 Cloth $27.50*)

Color and Color Perception: A Study in Anthropocentric Realism. David Russel Hilbert. Lecture Notes No. 9. (*Forthcoming*)

Prolog and Natural-Language Analysis. Fernando C.N. Pereira and Stuart M. Shieber. Lecture Notes No. 10. ( )

Studies in Grammatical Theory and Discourse Structure: Interactions of Morphology, Syntax, and Discourse. Iida, M., Wechsler, S., and Zec, D. (Eds.) with an Introduction by Joan Bresnan.. Lecture Notes No. 11.
(*Forthcoming*)

Non-Well-Founded Sets. Peter Aczel. Lecture Notes No. 12. (*Forthcoming*)

An Information-Based Approach to Syntax and Semantics. Carl Pollard and Ivan Sag. Lecture Notes No. 13. (*Forthcoming*)

Probability and Induction. Richard Jeffrey. Lecture Notes No. 14. (*Forthcoming*)

An Introduction to Situated Automata. Stanley Rosenchein. Lecture Notes No. 15. (*Forthcoming*)